# McCOY'S MARINES

# MARINES

## DARKSIDE TO BAGHDAD

# McCOY'S MARINES

## DARKSIDE TO BAGHDAD

### JOHN KOOPMAN

ZENITH
PRESS

This edition published by Zenith Press, an imprint of MBI Publishing Company, Galtier Plaza, Suite 200, 380 Jackson Street, St. Paul, MN, 55101-3885 USA.

MBI Publishing Company Books are also available at discounts for in bulk quantities for industrial or sale-promotional use. For details write to Special Sales Manager at MBI Publishing Company, Galtier Plaza, Suite 200, 380 Jackson Street, St. Paul, MN, 55101-3885 USA

Cover and Layout by Tom Heffron

ISBN: 0-7603-2088-8

Front cover photograph: Lieutenant Colonel Bryan McCoy, Commander of 3rd Battalion, 4th Marines, during fighting in the town of Az Za' Faranea, the day before the seizing of the Diyala Bridge. "I was confident we had all but broken the back of any organized resistance and we definitely had our eye on the prize." *Gilles Bassignac/Gamma*

Spine and back cover photograph: *Brian Mangan*

Printed in the United States

*To Isabel. I love you more than you will ever know.*

*And Jordi. I'm proud to be your daddy.*

# CONTENTS

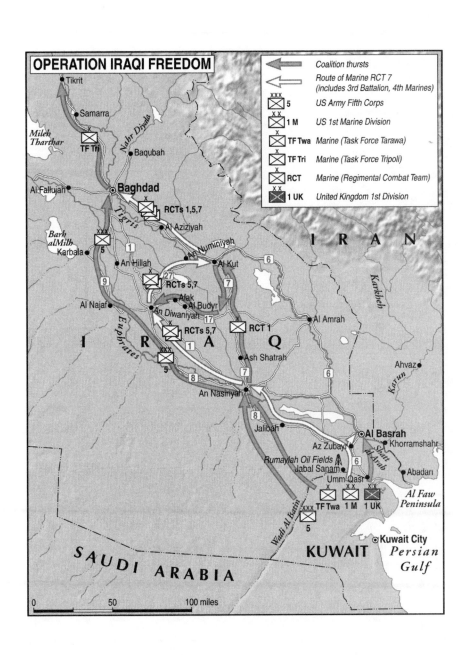

**OPERATION IRAQI FREEDOM**

Coalition thursts

Route of Marine RCT 7
(includes 3rd Battalion, 4th Marines)

5  US Army Fifth Corps

1 M  US 1st Marine Division

TF Twa  Marine (Task Force Tarawa)

TF Tri  Marine (Task Force Tripoli)

RCT  Marine (Regimental Combat Team)

1 UK  United Kingdom 1st Division

Tikrit

Samarra

*Mileb Tharthar*

TF Tri

Baqubah

*Nabr Diyala*

Al Fallujah

**Baghdad**

RCTs 1,5,7

*Tigris*

Al Aziziyah

*Barb alMilh*

5

Karbala

An Hillah

An Numiniyah

Al Kut

27  RCTs 5,7

*I R A N*

*Karkheh*

Al Najaf

Afak
Al Budyr

An Diwaniyah

17

RCTs 5,7

5

Al Amrah

RCT 1

Ash Shatrah

Ahvaz

*I  R  A  Q*

*Euphrates*

An Nasiriyah

Jalibah

*Karun*

**Al Basrah**

Khorramshahr

Az Zubayr

*Rumaylah Oil Fields*

Jabal Sanam

Abadan

Umm Qasr

*Al Faw Peninsula*

TF Twa  1 M  1 UK

5

*Wadi Al Batin*

**KUWAIT**

⊙ **Kuwait City**  *Persian Gulf*

*S A U D I   A R A B I A*

0        50        100 miles

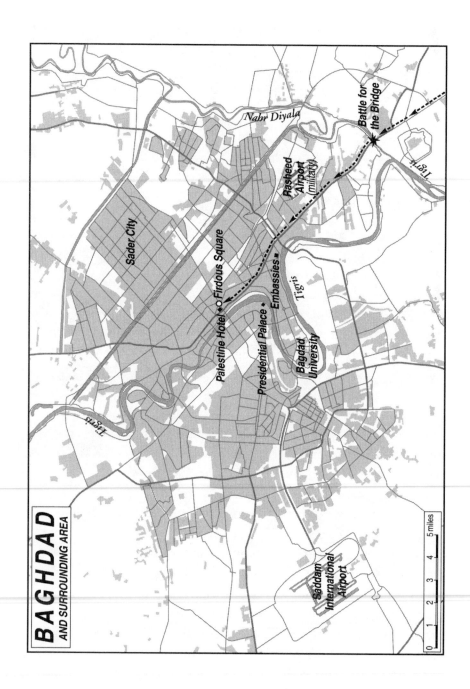

# BAGHDAD
## AND SURROUNDING AREA

Nahr Diyala

Battle for the Bridge

Tigris

Rasheed Airport (military)

Sader City

Palestine Hotel ○ Firdous Square

Embassies ■

Presidential Palace ◆

Tigris

Bagdad University

Tigris

Saddam International Airport

0  1  2  3  4  5 miles

# ACKNOWLEDGMENTS

I never intended to write a book. I'm a newspaperman. I went to cover the war for the *San Francisco Chronicle*, thinking only that I would file regular stories about the fighting and the troops and such. After the invasion, everyone started writing books about the war in Iraq. I never gave it much thought until Richard Kane from MBI Publishing called to see if I wanted to turn my stories into a book.

If I had it to do over again, I would have made arrangements to tell this story from a different perspective. From a Marine's point of view. But when it was all said and done, the only thing I had to write about was my own life, my own experience in the war. A lot of journalists have written books about the war, the planning and execution, and all the details. Soldiers and Marines have written personal tales.

All I had, and all I offer to you, is one man's experience. I tried to make the story about embedding, the good, the bad, and the filthy. It means you have to read a lot about me and my life. It's not very interesting, but it's my story and you're welcome to it.

I couldn't have done any of this without the help, friendship, and guidance of Lieutenant Colonel Bryan P. McCoy and Sergeant Major David Howell. It's important to note here that neither of these Marines assisted in this book. Not because they couldn't or wouldn't. I didn't ask them. Bryan and Dave are honest and selfless. They do not seek attention or publicity. One of the first things Dave Howell ever said to me was, "If I ever see my name in one of your stories, I'll pull your tongue out through your ass." He would do it, too.

When I started writing the book, I wondered if I should ask one or both to collaborate with me. But that would make them look like glory seekers, and they are anything but that. Plus, there are bound to be errors in this book. It is based on my notes, my stories, and my recollections. All of which are far from perfect. I felt that if the book were anything less than perfect, it would reflect badly on them as well as me. In any case, they did their jobs. Now it's time for me to do mine.

There were a lot of other Marines who helped me in one way or another. Eric Gentrup, Jack Coughlin, Jean-Paul Courville, Jon Kenney, Sean Barnes, Kevin Smith, Matt Baker, Dino Moreno, Martin Wetterauer, and all of McCoy's Marines, the 3rd Battalion, 4th Marine Regiment.

The Thundering Third.

Thanks to my bosses, executive editor Phil Bronstein and managing editor Robert Rosenthal, for putting together a war plan that included me. I want to thank them, and foreign editor Andrew S. Ross, for keeping my family informed and close during some very dark days.

Thanks to features editor Carolyn White, who worked with my copy after I got back and made it a hundred times better. Same goes for Richard Kane of MBI and Suzanne Herel of the *Chronicle*, who copy-edited the manuscript.

Thanks to my friend and attorney, Leo LaRocca, for his excellent legal advice.

Thanks to Amy and Marshall Senk for helping Jordi when he was missing his daddy.

Thanks to Takae Miller and Elizabeth Whipple for helping Isabel when she was missing her husband.

Thanks to mom and dad for trusting and believing.

Thanks to Bud Pagel and Dick Streckfuss for making me a reporter.

Thanks to the Marines' families for keeping me in their prayers.

# PROLOGUE

To the right of the road are buildings, houses, and shops. It's a crappy, cramped urban area. And it's swarming with Iraqi Fedayeen.

The Marines move about 100 yards down the road. . . .

Up ahead, we hear shots. Rifle shots, followed by machine gun fire. The column slows while the Marines engage in a slow-moving firefight.

I'm tired. So damn tired. I could sleep. The sun is warm. More shots. My head drops. More shots. I don't care. I nod off. Right in the middle of a firefight.

Boom! An RPG round explodes mid-air above us.

That'll wake you up.

I get out of the Humvee and move around to the back. Fire comes in from the buildings. Iraqi snipers firing from rooftops. RPGs rain down like the Fourth of July. . . .

"PPffffffffsssssssssssstttt! Boom!" An RPG round explodes 20 feet over our heads. There's a puff of black smoke. We hear bits of shrapnel hitting the pavement around us.

I get down and try to take cover.

PPffffffffsssssssssssstttt! Boom! Another RPG goes off overhead.

Boom! And another. Boom! A fourth RPG.

*"I think someone might be aiming at us," Moreno says.*

*"You think so?" I ask.*

*I hear that PPFFFFFFFSSSSSSSSSSSTTTT again and dive straight for the dirt. Boom! Another one directly overhead.*

*For the first time in the war, I think I might die. . . .*

*Someone told me once that the trick to keeping your wits in battle is to imagine that you're already dead. Or that you certainly will die. If you survive, all the better.*

*I try that now. It doesn't work.*

*But I am thinking I want to be one of those Marines on top of the vehicle. Give me a gun. Let me shoot back at those who are shooting at me. It's not that I want to kill anyone. I just want an equalizer. I feel completely exposed out there. And the First Amendment won't protect you for shit. Give me a gun and I'll feel better.*

*From behind us, I hear someone shouting. Iraqis are near the front gate of the military compound, trying to flank the Marines.*


They called me Paperboy. It was a small joke in a small war. I'm a newspaper reporter. One of the journalists "embedded" with U.S. troops during the invasion of Iraq. I went to the Middle East with a battalion of U.S. Marines out of Camp Pendleton, California. And stayed with them as they crossed the border into Iraq, fought in places like Basra, Diwaniyah, Kut, and finally Baghdad. These were the Marines who pulled down the statue of Saddam Hussein, the image flashed around the world. The moment that effectively signaled the end of the war. Well, the invasion part of the war. A lot more troops would fight and die later. But that's another story.

I don't like war, but it fascinates me. It must be the part of my male brain that harkens to the Stone Age. We dress up and act civilized these days, but there's still something primal in our brains. We seek conflict. We want to dominate, whether it's other males, females, the world in general.

You can see it in gang warfare, in a thousand conflicts around the world, and in the corporate boardrooms. I don't understand it. I can't explain it or quantify it. But I know it's out there.

I saw it when I served in the Marines. Some guys just want to kill. But I joined the Corps during peacetime. Not long after Vietnam. And later I became a newspaperman. I've seen some death in my work, but not all that much. The bodies are usually gone by the time I get to an accident or murder. Not always.

But I'd never seen death on a large scale. And I'd never seen anyone die. So when I had the chance for a seat on the 50-yard line in Iraq, I took it. I rode along with the 3rd Battalion, 4th Marine Regiment.

They were led by Lieutenant Colonel Bryan P. McCoy. Radio call sign: Darkside.

It's a joking reference to the movie *Star Wars*. As in Darth Vader's "Come over to the dark side." But deep down, it's a state of mind. That part of the brain that goes back to the cave man, to life and death and protecting what's yours.

It's the kid who picks up a stick and pretends it's a machine gun. It's playing war or Cowboys and Indians. It's the love of movies with guns and bombs and car chases. It's the tingle at the start of a fight, or a football game.

Darkside understands it. As a Marine battalion commander, he has studied it, trained for it and applied it to a thousand men in his command. And then he put it to use in Iraq.

In addition to moving his thousand Marines across the battlefield and keeping them fed and healthy, Darkside had to control the violence of his men. He had to unleash it for battle, and then carefully put it away in a safe place when the shooting stopped. Some of this was his to control. Most was the result of training and careful selection of men who would serve in a fighting unit. Marines talk incessantly about "Rules of Engagement," whom to shoot and when to shoot them. It's not uncommon to see them killing enemy soldiers one minute, feeding candy to kids the next.

Darkside is 40. From Oklahoma. About 6 feet tall, 200 pounds. Blue eyes and light brown hair in a Marine Corps high-and-tight cut.

He's an Army brat. His dad was an officer who did two tours in Vietnam. But Army life didn't appeal to the younger McCoy. He liked the spirit and energy of the Marines. He lives the life of a modern-day Spartan. He trains hard, runs marathons, hikes long trails.

"Being a Marine is not something I do," he once told me, "it's what I am."

McCoy has studied the great generals. He can tell you whom he admires and why. William Tecumseh Sherman for his straightforward, no-muss, no-fuss approach to war. World War II's Erwin Rommel for his tactical mind. George Patton for aggressiveness. Napoleon for the ability to spot a weakness and act on it. The Spartans for warrior ethic.

His favorite quote is from Sherman: "War is cruelty. There is no use in refining it. The crueler it is, the sooner it is over."

Second favorite is Rommel: "When in doubt, attack."

A couple of days after the fall of Baghdad, McCoy and I sat in the coffee shop of the Palestine Hotel, and our thoughts drifted to the Marines who died during the war. McCoy eventually would have to send letters to their families.

I ask him how he deals with it, the knowledge that they died under his command.

"I don't know," he says. "I don't think I have dealt with it."

Darkside is a Methodist. He believes his profession and his religion are not at odds. As a Marine, he kills and orders others to kill. He sees it as a necessary evil.

"In the world, there are sheep and there are wolves," he says. "I like to think of Marines as the sheepdogs.

"Someone has to know how to fight. If it weren't for the sheepdogs, where would the sheep be?"

• • •

I spent about six months covering the buildup to war, and the invasion. Now, I've tried to put the whole experience together in a book. I've gone over the stories I wrote, and the notes I took. I've tried to come to some understanding. What did it all mean? Are there any larger truths here?

If the war had meaning, I can't find it. The invasion showed the terrible and terrific military might of the United States. I was there to see troops engaged in mortal combat, jets and helicopters delivering death and destruction from above. I watched the training and tactics, the command and control, the small unit leadership all in action. It is absolutely amazing. The U.S. Marines have nearly perfected the art of war. They can go anywhere, fight anyone under any circumstances, and win. I don't say that as a fan. Military might is not exactly the best thing to which a nation can aspire. But if you want or need a strong military, and you must use them, the Marines will do the job.

But it's also important to remember that institutions and individuals have faults. It's wrong to call every soldier or Marine a hero. That word should have a higher meaning than simply serving your country in a time of war. The Marine Corps is full of bright, intelligent people who are true believers in the United States, in patriotism, in doing the right thing. They are the majority. There are also cowards, slackers, petty thieves, and homicidal maniacs. Okay, the last one is a little harsh, but sometimes you never know what's in a man's heart until he has a gun in his hand and license to use it. I never witnessed an atrocity or any breach of the rules of war. But I know they happened. They always happen. This is not to indict the entire military, the Marines, or the battalion I was with. It's simply reality. I know others who saw or knew of bad things that happened in Iraq. I wish they hadn't happened, but that wouldn't be realistic.

Really, though, this book is about the intersection of journalism, war, and the military. I was in a good position to see the new embedding program from the ground up.

It was a radical concept. At least in the modern era. The military fully believed that the media lost the Vietnam War. And a lot of officers set out to make sure it never happened again. So in subsequent conflicts, the media were completely shut out. No one was embedded with troops at Grenada, or Panama, or the first Gulf War. The media kicked and screamed every time, but they had no power. No one in Washington much gave a damn.

But this war was different. For one thing, the Vietnam-era officer corps was all but gone. And the Pentagon faced new challenges in the war of information. Arab news networks show footage of American bombings in Afghanistan. Allegations are made in a highly political part of the world, and if no one is there to tell the truth, even a portion of the truth, life is much more difficult.

So in many ways, we embedded reporters were pawns. Of course we were. We knew that. Most of us, anyway. Personally, I didn't care. I just wanted to cover a war. And I knew I would write what I saw. I would be objective and accurate. If that played into the hands of the U.S. government, well good for them. I've never seen my job as trying to sway anyone in any direction. I don't believe in that form of journalism.

I just show what I see. I'm an idealist that way. I'll show you whatever I know, and you figure out what you want to do with the information. That's the whole point of the Fourth Estate, in my humble opinion.

Of course, readers don't believe that. Most Many think we're willing accomplices of the government. Or they think we're radical and subversive liars out to destroy the very fabric of American life. There may be some truth to both of those viewpoints.

In looking back at my work, I think I painted an accurate picture of men at war. But without the jingoism, or the cheerleading effect that we all despise. I think I could have been a little tougher sometimes. My stories could have been more critical. But that's pure hindsight.

After I got back to the States, I wrote a six-part series that ran in *The San Francisco Chronicle* several months later. Some people loved it, some hated it. But the greatest compliment I got was from a few who simply said, "Your stories take no sides. You can read this and either support the war or oppose it."

Maybe there's a better way. Maybe the true meaning of journalism is to take a side, and support it. But life is too complicated for that, and I'm not nearly smart enough.

I just tell stories. I'm a reporter. Call me Paperboy.

# CHAPTER 1

# GROWING UP

**W**hen I was a kid, I thought the United States was always at war. This was the early 1960s. All the movies and television shows were about the Wild West or about war. I watched *Combat!* on TV and *The Dirty Dozen* in the theater. I thought we were still fighting the Germans. I played with G.I. Joe and bugged my mom to buy me a real Army helmet and rapid-fire Tommy Gun with a little orange flash at the end of the barrel that made it look like it was shooting.

And then there was the nightly news. Vietnam was everywhere. At dinner, I would watch film of sweating men running through fields of grass battered by overhead helicopter blades. Or some machine gunner firing into the distance. I always wondered what he saw, who he was shooting. If anyone.

In high school, I read all about war. My favorite book was Leon Uris' *Battle Cry*. It's hard to explain. I didn't want to kill anyone. Or get killed. It was more about the camaraderie of fighting men. And manhood itself. A man goes to war, and there he tests himself. It's not about heroism. It's about doing the right thing, and handling pressure under fire.

But I grew older, and the influence started to wane. Vietnam turned to crap. It wasn't the kind of war that inspired idealism. Quite the opposite. In any case, what moves you in your childhood gives way to other interests as you grow older. Like girls. And cars. High school. Getting by. Making money. Buying beer.

I grew up in a small Nebraska town called Howells. It's in the northeast part of the state, nor far from where Johnny Carson grew up. Memorable for absolutely nothing. The landscape was rolling hills of corn and alfalfa. The people were good folk. Salt of the earth. But nothing really inspirational there, either. Modesty is the greatest virtue in the hinterland of Nebraska, and I had plenty of it.

So there I am, an aimless high school student in the middle of nowhere. What do you do with your life? My friends were mostly farm kids, and they were going to stay on the farm after high school. Others would be diesel mechanics. Or find work at the meat packing plant outside Schuyler, the county seat. A handful were headed to college. But they knew what they wanted to study. They were smart and focused. I was neither.

My dad—also John Koopman—drove a truck. He taught me how to drive an 18-wheeler when I was 16. But that life didn't appeal to me. Dad was gone all week, driving all over the country. It's not a bad job, but how would I ever get laid if I was gone all the time?

My mom, Greta, was a nurse. And you can just forget about that. First, Nebraska boys don't nurse anyone. Second, I can't stand the sight of blood. Or needles. Or hospital food.

So what's a boy to do? The military sure looked good.

I started off with the Navy. Went to see a recruiter in Grand Island. I thought I could get on a ship and see the world. I would study electronics. Not that I was much of a techno-head when I was young. It just seemed like a cool job. Poking around the innards of a radio, as opposed to swabbing a deck or digging a ditch. Listen, you bale hay every summer and then let me know how much you like manual labor. I'm too lazy. I'd do anything to get out of that kind of work.

I purposely did not see a Marine recruiter. I really loved the Marines, because of everything I had read about them. But I didn't want to go the macho route. And I didn't want to kill or be killed, which seemed damn likely if I wore Marine green.

So I just put that thought away. No sir. Join the Navy. Wear blue. Do your four years and then get a good job in electronics when you get out. That's the plan.

Except I had to pass by the Marine recruiter's office on my way to the Navy guy. And one day he saw me and stopped me. Asked me why I wanted to join the Navy. For the electronics program, I said. And, you know, see the world.

Well, you can study electronics in the Marines, he said. And there's something else, he said. You can be a Marine at the same time.

Shit. That was it. The challenge. The question. Are you man enough? Can you do it? We really are few and proud.

I just couldn't pass that by. So I went into the office. And was hooked.

Dad was not happy. "What do you think, you're going to be some kind of John Wayne?" he asked. Yelled, really. "This is no movie. You could get killed."

I wasn't expecting that of my dad. He was always this tough trucker dude. When I was four and would cry, he told me to "act like a man." He liked big trucks and loose women and beer. I wasn't trying to impress him by joining the Marines, but I thought he would understand. I didn't get his reaction at all.

But for some reason, I had the cojones to stick by my decision. I think I was more afraid of myself, my own internal thought process, and my revulsion toward giving up, than I was of disappointing him. So I suffered through the bellowing.

Mom was calmer about it. I don't recall any great arguments or explanations. She agreed to have the recruiter come over and explain things to her. And sign the papers. I was just 17.

On September 8, 1975, I officially joined the U.S. Marine Corps. That was the beginning of my senior year in high school. I joined on what they called "delayed entry," which meant I was technically a member of Uncle Sam's military machine, but boot camp was delayed until after I graduated the following May.

With my fate already determined, I proceeded to not give a shit about my classes. I took the hard courses and got bad grades. But passed. I played football. Poorly. I was on the wrestling team, and did all right. I ran track to get ready for the Marines.

I graduated. Got roaring drunk. Several times. And on June 6, 1976, I said goodbye to my mom. My best buddy in the world, Marte Mejstrik, drove me from Howells to Schuyler, 22 miles away. My dad met me at the bus station. We shook hands, and for the first time since I was a baby, we hugged. I turned to get on the bus and saw him turn away sobbing. I had never, ever, seen him cry. Many years later, after my son was born, I would understand. It's a parent thing. When my son was just a baby, someone asked if I would ever let him join the Marines. And it struck me: Fuck no! He's going to college.

With my dad's tears still in my mind, I rode the bus a couple of hours to the lovely city of Omaha. And reported to the Armed Forces Entry and Examination Station downtown. They poked and prodded us and made us duck-walk across the floor and sign a ream of papers. We spent the night in a motel, and an Air Force recruiter invited me to his place for a drink. I was pretty naïve back then. Still am. But when I had the beer in hand and saw the tiny apartment with the single bed in the corner, everything came fully into focus. I chugged my beer and got the hell out of there.

The next day, they took me to the airport, for a flight to Charleston, South Carolina.

All the seats in coach were full. For the first and only time in my life, I got bumped up to first class. The worst flight in my life and I go first class. Ha, ha, God, very funny.

But the Lord wasn't finished with his joke. I sat next to a middle-aged guy. Turns out he was in the Marines years ago, and he starts telling me horror stories about boot camp. The screaming, the beatings, the guys who went on to die in Vietnam. Oh, this is hilarious. As we were approaching Charleston, it occurred to me that no one had explained where we were to go once we got off the plane. Was there some kind of

Marine desk there? I wondered aloud to my neighbor. He laughed. Again. "Don't worry," he said. "They'll find you."

Marine drill instructors must have some kind of sixth sense about recruits. I walked off the plane, took two steps, and saw a man in dress blues. He saw me, and before I could say a word, he pointed a finger at me and pointed to a corner of the terminal. Several other young men with long hair were over there and I understood immediately. Too late to run away now.

We took a bus through the Carolina swampland. It took a couple of hours to get to Parris Island. We got in after midnight, and it was just like all the movies you've seen about boot camp. A drill instructor got on the bus, screamed at us, told us we now belonged to him and to get our sorry asses off his bus. We all ran out and stood on the yellow footprints on the pavement. There was an arch over the entrance to a building that said, "Through this portal pass the makings of the world's finest fighting force." At that point, I would have been happy to give up that title.

The rest is a blur. There was just a ton of screaming and yelling and recruits stumbling around trying to please their new masters. I was young and impressionable and did my best to do things right. A few older guys had world-wise smirks, like they were above all the nonsense. They got that slapped out of them pretty quick.

I won't bore you with all the details of boot camp. I'll just give you a few snippets that I think illustrate the point.

Before you actually start Marine training, you spend a couple of days in what they call a "receiving barracks." There were 80 of us, more or less, in an old World War II-era wooden barracks. The second day there, we sat at picnic tables set up inside the barracks and awaited our haircuts. We sat facing away from the tables. We sat at attention. We sat with back straight, feet at a 45-degree angle. A Marine guidebook held up by one hand directly in front of our faces.

On the wall facing me was a recruiting poster. And I'm thinking, "What the fuck?" Who are you going to recruit? It's a Marine in dress blues chatting with a couple of civilians with long hair. "Run!" I say silently. "Get the fuck out of there! Go to college, you morons!"

I could heard the clippers in the other room, buzzing through long hair. This was 1976. We all had hair to our shoulders. Or longer.

A young man marches up to the drill instructor's desk, which is in the middle of the room, and asks to speak. You really don't do this in boot camp. It always ends badly. But the DI says go ahead. The young man says there's been a terrible mistake. He's not supposed to be here. The drill instructor smiles and a couple of other DI's see what's going on, and they come over to the desk, too. They all smile and nod as the young man tells the story of how he was a wrestler in high school and hurt his back. But he really wanted to join the Marines, so his recruiter told him to fake his medical records. But now, the young man realizes he was wrong, and he'd like to go home.

He's a handsome young man. Pretty, even. With curly brown hair a few inches past his shoulders.

The drill instructor says, Well sure, we don't want to you to hurt yourself. We'll get you home right quick, he says.

The young man smiles and emits a grateful sigh.

But first, the DI says, you're gonna get a haircut, boy.

It's like a scene out of a prison movie. The drill instructors grab the recruit by his arms and legs. He's kicking and screaming, begging them to let him go. They drag him, literally drag him, into the adjacent barber room and hold him down on the chair. We can't see what's going on, but there's an awful racket. When he comes out, he's completely bald. And sobbing.

I never saw him again.

Boot camp is brutal in a pleasing, masochistic sort of way. They break your spirit and soul, and body, too. And then build it back up again in the Marine image. At first, it's just intense. There is no such thing as normal speech. Drill instructors yell every single word. Recruits are expected to shout whenever they are allowed to speak. So even the most insignificant chatter is done at the top of your lungs. And just to raise the stress level, as if that were necessary, they mandated that recruits were not allowed to speak in the first person or the second person. We weren't considered human enough for that. So you couldn't say, "May I speak with you for a moment, sir." Instead, it was, "Sir, the private requests permission to speak to the drill instructor. Sir."

If you messed up and said "You" to a drill instructor, he'd get in your face and scream, "Ewe? Ewe? Do I look like a female sheep? Do you want to fuck me, private?" And the Lord help you.

On our first night in the new barracks, we were ordered to sleep at attention. On our backs, hands at our sides, chest out, chin back. You'd fall asleep and move, and someone would wake you and tell you to get back to attention. All nightlong.

A lot of guys couldn't cut it. The day after we moved into our permanent barracks, some guy jumped off the third-floor stairwell. He lived, but broke his leg. Our senior drill instructor, Staff Sergeant Downey, called us to formation in the barracks and spoke softly for the first time.

"Recruits, one of your own has tried to take his own life," he said, taking off his Smokey the Bear hat and wiping the sweat from the brim. "And that ain't right. We're not here to make things so hard that you want to kill yourself. No, sir. There must be something wrong here.

"So I tell you what, if any of you feel this place is so horrible, so bad that you might kill yourself, just march on up to the quarterdeck, and we'll process you out of here. No questions asked."

Six guys marched up to the quarterdeck, the front of the squad bay between the DI office and the head. Downey motioned for the other three DI's, and they call descended upon the quitters.

"You dumb fucks!" he screamed. "Did you really think I was going to send your sorry asses home? Fuck, no! I just wanted to see who the weak ones are. And now I know. I'm going to make it twice as hard for you. Then we'll see if you still want to kill yourself. Get their names!"

There is a strange sense of relief in watching a scene like that. You just think, "Thank God that's not me."

I learned a lot at Parris Island. I learned that bravery and integrity are not limited to Marines. There was this guy who was a complete fuckup. I don't even know how he got there. He was short and fat and inept. He crapped in his pants doing pushups. After a couple of weeks of this, something snapped, and the drill instructors decided to process him out. But that would take a couple of days. So, to humiliate him even further, they set up a cot near the entrance to the head and made him sleep there. Said he wasn't fit to share bunk space with recruits. Scum of the earth that we were, he was a lower maggot form.

But he took it. The son-of-a-bitch took their shit and held firm. I don't think I could have done it. I lay on my rack one night, listening to the boy sobbing in his bunk and thinking of the pain he was going through. But I could not and would not do anything to help him. Not even offer a word of support. And I thought, "Who's got the honor? Where's *my* integrity?"

Boot camp was harsh. We were up at 4:30. The drill instructors would throw on the lights and toss a metal trash can down the center of the barracks. There was no lying there, adjusting to the day, or sleepily curling up with your pillow for another five minutes' sleep. There was no pleasure in anything. Lights on, hit the floor, and get on line, at attention. We'd count off, so they knew we were all still there. Then the DI would march us in groups into the head, where we'd line up along the trough urinals and pee in unison.

We'd go outside, stand in formation, and let the sand fleas dig into soft flesh. And God help the young recruit who scratched. Then run, pushups, pull-ups, obstacle courses, drill, classes, more drill. The days were full. There was not a moment to sit and think, or reflect. You ate fast, and everything on your tray. And it was never enough. We burned calories like hot coals in a stove.

Things slowed only a bit in the evening. We had one hour of free time. And we spent it polishing boots, shining brass, cleaning rifles, and writing letters home.

Sometimes, a drill instructor would use that time to counsel a recruit, or just fuck with them.

"Private Koopman, report to the drill instructor's office!" I heard the shout one evening. I ran to the doorway, slammed my palm against the door, and announced myself.

"What's this in your file, boy? It says you joined the Corps to learn a trade? What the fuck is that?"

"Sir? The private does not understand." But I did. We'd filled out a questionnaire at one point, and one of the questions was "Why did you join the Marines?" The correct answer was, Because I want to be a Marine, I want to protect my country, I want to kill someone. Learning a trade was not what they were looking for. I was being too literal, a trait that would hurt me my entire life. I just thought, hell, of course we're here to be Marines. But beyond that, what? Learn how to fix a radio, or drive a truck. Whatever.

Still, that earned me a lot of bends and thrusts that night. I was sweating when I finished just before lights out. It also made the drill instructors look at me differently. Like I didn't really belong.

Once we got used to the heat and the mental abuse, boot camp wasn't so awful. I was in good shape, so the physical training wasn't much. I was a good rifle shot, and scored expert at the range. Highest score of my platoon, which impressed the drill instructors and later got me my first stripe. But I found out I couldn't fight for shit. We had to learn hand-to-hand combat with pugil sticks. We wore football helmets and hit each other with big padded sticks that looked like giant-sized Q-tips. I got my ass kicked regularly. This, too, is part of growing up, and learning about life. The only guys who really know how to fight, and are any good at it, are the ones who do it all the time. Short guys, the ones who got picked on in school, fight best. Big guys aren't so tough because everyone thought they were too tough to fight. Fighting is an art form, and difficult. You have to like pain. Receiving, of course, but also giving, which is sometimes more difficult for us normal people.

You watch some of the real tough guys. The guys who grew up in the 'hood, and backwater South, and you realize, those are some bad-ass motherfuckers and you will never be that tough.

But that's all right. That knowledge keeps you from fighting and getting in trouble, because you soon learn that no matter how tough you are, or think you are, there's always some son-of-a-bitch who can kick your ass. Always.

I was one of the younger recruits. I was 17. I turned 18 the day before graduation, late August of 1976. I was a lean, mean Marine. I lived and breathed Marine Corps. The day before we graduated, we had some free time for the first time in three months. We hadn't had any candy or soda or ice cream or calls home that whole time. It was like living in ancient Sparta. I went with a couple of buddies to the PX, looking for a souvenir. I was in the aisle, and saw Sergeant Marchildon, one of our drill instructors. He was talking to another drill instructor. He saw me and said to his buddy, "Watch this. Koopman! Bend and thrust!"

I dropped to the floor and started, but he bent down and grabbed my arm. "No, never mind. I was just fucking with you. Go away."

I was now a lean, mean fighting machine. Ready to kill.

That mentality lasted for exactly two months. I went home on leave after boot camp, and then flew to southern California. I had orders to Twentynine Palms, a 900-square-mile Marine base out in the Mojave Desert. The Marines have an electronics school there, and I was going to learn how to fix radios. Yes, it was very macho. I could kill a man with an oscilloscope.

We all went there straight out of boot camp, and at first it seemed like an extension of it. We all marched around and yelled at each other as we had at Parris Island. Until we realized that this wasn't boot camp. That we weren't real hardcore Marine grunts. That we weren't going to war. And maybe all that boot camp shit was for the birds.

I don't know. But that's how it was for me. I still shined my boots and stood at attention and saluted. But I didn't feel it. I wasn't hard. I had proved that I could be, if I wanted to.

But I really didn't want to.

I spent nine months at Twentynine Palms. It's hot as hell out there, and desolate. Just sand and rocks. I came to like it after a while. There's a beauty to the desert, but you have to wait to find it. It grows on you. One day you look at those rocks in the setting sun, and it warms you. The desert has colors all its own, and hidden life.

I was there until the following summer, 1977. I learned about transistors and diodes and wavelengths, along with the finer points of puking from a beer drunk. We all learned that the worst place to go, after school, is Okinawa. Everyone hated Oki, which they called "the Rock." It was a foreign land, for one thing. Married guys couldn't take their wives. It's hot and humid and you have to work hard. Some guys at stateside bases worked 9 to 5 and went home every evening. And at that time, the Marines used the model for rotations that they had in Vietnam. Individuals were sent to a unit on the island for a one-year tour, then sent back to the United States. In Vietnam, that contributed to a breakdown in unit cohesion.

But there was no place I wanted to go. Our choices were limited to Camp Pendleton in Southern California and Camp LeJeune in North Carolina. So I asked to be sent to Okinawa. I just wanted to see what the fuss was all about. The Marine Corps was nice enough to grant my wish.

I remember nothing of my time on the Rock. We spent every non-duty hour getting drunk off base. They had B-girls who tried to get you to buy them over-priced drinks. I fell in love every week.

Christmas 1977. My first Christmas away from home. I called my folks. In those days, making an overseas call was a big deal, and expensive. It was the only call I made for the whole year.

Once I got that out of the way, my buddies and I pooled our cash and hit the bars. I don't remember any of it. New Year's Eve was more of the same, except that I had been working on a bar girl, trying to get her to go home with me. Finally, she agreed. We stumbled down the street toward her apartment. That's the last thing I remember. I woke up in the barracks the next morning, hung over like a dead man. I still don't know what happened that night.

Not long after that, I convinced one of the bar girls to go to bed with me. I was 19. She was 25. At least, that's what she told me. She was probably older. She had a five-year-old son. I moved in with them. I pretty much gave her my paycheck every month, and for that, I got to spend most evenings at her house and have sex.

It was worth every penny.

I wanted to stay in Okinawa. But at the end of my tour, the Marine Corps ordered me to go to Camp LeJeune. I was dumbfounded. No one asks to stay in Okinawa, but when I did, I was denied. I was sent to the 2nd Assault Amphibian Battalion. An Assault Amphibian Vehicle, called an AAV or Amtrack (amphibious tractor), is the armored vehicle that carries Marines from the ship to hit the beach. It was my job to keep communications working.

The great thing about working in a combat unit is that you get to volunteer for "floats." The Marines load up on Navy amphibious ships and float around certain areas, like the Caribbean or the North Atlantic. I went on a Mediterranean float with the 3rd Battalion, 8th Marine Regiment. I was nobody's idea of a picture-perfect Marine, but I was pretty good at fixing radios. And that talent was at a premium in the Marines, so they promoted me. I made sergeant in two years, ten months. I got promoted on the float, which was cool because sergeants don't have to do much physical work, and I think I've made my position clear on the whole "hard work" issue. Sergeants tell other people what to do. I could dig that.

A Med cruise lasts six months. You basically float around the Mediterranean, alternating between liberty ports, where you get drunk and look for hookers, and field exercises with NATO forces.

Our second liberty port was Barcelona. The second night there, my buddy and I went to a disco. The Bar Georgia. I see this great-looking woman with long legs. I say "hi." She doesn't speak English, and my Spanish is for *nada*. "Do you speak English?" I hear someone say behind me. It's her friend, Isabel. She speaks just a little high school English. Between the two of us, we can almost carry on a conversation.

I really liked her. We danced that night and I walked her home. She kissed me and laughed. Did I mention that I liked her? A lot.

We saw each almost every day for the two weeks my ship was in port. Then I left, like sailors and Marines always do. We wrote each other constantly. Mail was sporadic at sea. Sometimes we'd hit the beach for a week of field operations, and I'd come back to a dozen perfumed letters. I would carefully lay them out in chronological order and read them slowly. Sometimes I would re-read one, then go do something—go to chow—and savor the moment of reading the next one.

Ship life is very lonely.

Being on a cruise was about as close to combat as you could get in the late 1970s. It was the final years of the Cold War. But we spent a lot of time in the field. You'd go out for a week or two at a time. No showers. Cold combat rations eaten in the dirt. It was like camping, but without the fun.

And I learned that you can die in peacetime, too.

We were in Italy on a field exercise. At the end of the week, we drove the tracks back to the beach. The ship was offshore, and we were going to drive them out into the water and "swim" them to the ship. Except a big storm brought heavy waves, and we got to the beach late. No one was ready for us there and the Navy had a schedule to keep. And a million other things went wrong.

We get out in the water. It's dark as the inside of a cow's ass. Ten-foot waves are rocking the armored vehicles up and down. I'm inside the communications track listening to radio traffic. I hear my friend Matty, the crew chief of Amtrack B-32, yelling for help. His track was taking on water and the pumps weren't working. There was furious traffic between him, the platoon commander, and another crew chief who was trying to maneuver in the heavy seas to tow Matty's track.

They got a rope on B-32 and started towing it. But the water kept coming. I heard Matty on the radio one more time. "We're going down," was all he said. And then, radio silence. The 26-ton armored vehicle sank to the bottom. Nineteen or twenty grunts on board scrambled to get out. Three didn't make it. They found them a couple of days later. One guy, a Navy Corpsman, had gotten into the turret hatch of the towing vehicle. He was trying to pull Marines out of the water. By that time, the Navy had shown up. They sent a big landing craft out to try to get the Amtrack out of the water. The landing craft had a bow ramp, the kind they use on shore to drive vehicles on and off. The ramp was down. A big wave came along and picked it up. Dropped it right down on that turret. Doc was crushed to death.

So, four dead for a bunch of stupid mistakes.

I heard there was an inquiry. Probably the platoon commander got into a lot of trouble. In any case, his career was over. But I never did find out what happened to him, or any of the people in charge.

I got back to the States and went back to work. I had a year to go on my enlistment. I just wanted to get drunk, fix my radios, and stay out of everyone's way.

I also learned how to smoke dope. I grew up hating the stuff, like any good Nebraska boy. In the Midwest, we drink beer and whiskey. Pot is for hippie dopers and losers.

I knew a lot of guys who smoked dope. Yes, America, the young men and women who guard democracy get high all the time. Friends would offer to share a joint with me, and I would decline. At first, vehemently. Later, less so. Until one night, I'm at the enlisted club. A couple of buddies want to smoke a joint. They want to do it driving around, so they won't get caught. I volunteer to take them in my car.

They pass me the joint as I'm driving down the two-lane blacktop in the Carolina backwoods. I don't want to look like an idiot, so I take a puff. And another.

Wow. That's nice. Marijuana is great.

I never became a doper, per se, but after that, whenever I was at a party and the joints were going around, I was there. We all were. It was peacetime, not long after Vietnam. Morale sucked. No one wore a Marine uniform in town, or on leave. There was none of this "few and proud" stuff. Even the serious grunts weren't all that gung ho, or professional as they would become in later years.

It was just a different time. Not a good one in the history of U.S. military service.

Meanwhile, Isabel and I kept writing each other. And now we could call sometimes. I had to see her again. So I bugged my boss to let me go on another Med float. It meant extending my enlistment for two months, but I didn't care. You could say I went a long way for a pretty smile. And it was worth it. I saw her twice on that second float. I got to meet her family. Which was a hoot, because I'm a Marine from Nebraska, the son of conservative Republicans going way back. Her family were all Euro-socialists. Her grandfather had been a Communist, run out of Spain under a death order by Francisco Franco. They say opposites attract. I'm living proof.

I got back from that second float with a real attitude. I was sick of all things military. I was a salty old sergeant. Twenty-one years old. If I would have had another couple of months to stay in the Corps, I would have been court-martialed for insubordination. I'm sure of it.

A sergeant major met me on the beach when we got back to Camp LeJeune. Did I want to re-enlist? Uh, no offense, sergeant major, but hell no. I'm going to be a civilian.

A couple of weeks later, I processed out of the Marines. Dumped all my crap in my car and drove out the back gate. I stopped a quarter-mile down the road, just to savor the sight of the gate in my rear-view mirror. Then headed to Nebraska.

# CHAPTER 2

# JOURNALISM

I never wanted to be a reporter. Where I grew up, journalism was not considered a serious profession. It was performed by small men with little honor. People who would call a widow in the middle of the night. Reporters did not participate in life; they simply wrote about it. And criticized it.

But I could write. Not that anyone ever told me that, or encouraged me in that direction when I was young. I never had any of those teachers you hear about, the ones who "see" something in a student and motivate them. Maybe we just had crappy teachers. Maybe I just wasn't very smart.

I got out of the Marines and moved back to Nebraska. Not for any reason. Just had nowhere else to go. My electronics background got me a job as an instrument technician at an aviation company in Lincoln, Nebraska. I wore a white shirt with my name over the pocket and punched a time card. I spent my days upside down in Lear jet cockpits, trying to pull faulty altimeters from control panels.

I hated it. Mostly, I think, I missed the excitement of being in the Marines. Not that I cared for the military crap. But in the Marines, I was running around Rome and making radios work in the field, under impossible conditions. My buddies and I were stealing antennas from NATO officers so that our own radios would work. That kind of stuff. The excitement had gotten into my blood.

I decided to go to the University of Nebraska on the GI Bill. Six months later, in January 1981, I went to my first class. I wanted to study electrical engineering. Makes sense, right? Sure, and after two semesters of calculus, physics, and chemistry, I wanted to shoot myself. This was too much like work. Plus, when I looked down the road, I saw myself in an office, poring over electrical schematics and wishing to hell I could do something fun.

I was working at the Veterans Administration as a work-study clerk. I knew a counselor there, and he offered to help me through a guidance process. We talked about my likes and dislikes, what I had done in high school and the Marines. I told him I had worked on our high school paper. It was a monthly sheet run off on mimeograph paper. Not exactly journalism as we know it. But we started talking about journalism, and I started thinking about a job where I could go out every day and see people. A job where no two days would be the same. A job that requires curiosity but no real intellectual weight. No hard work.

He made me go talk to some journalism teachers. I picked their brains a couple of times and the more I saw, the more I thought I wanted that life. So I switched majors.

What really motivated me was the idealism of journalism. I liked the idea of media as watchdog. I dug the First Amendment. I never figured to be Woodward or Bernstein, but I liked how journalism gave me a license to snoop. And I liked to write.

Isabel and I kept writing and phoning. I spent a summer in Barcelona, and she came to Nebraska for a month. On June 6, 1982, we got married in a Catholic church near her apartment in Barcelona. I stayed a week and then went back to Nebraska for summer school. She went through all the paperwork at the American Embassy and then bought a ticket to the States. She arrived on the 4th of July, 1982.

I studied a lot. Journalism was harder than I expected. I took classes in photography, the history of mass media, communications law, all that. But most important were the writing and reporting classes taught by two funny, tough, hard-nosed former reporters. Dick Streckfuss and

Al Pagel. They were best friends at the journalism school and terrors to their students. They demanded perfection and rarely got it. Not from me, certainly. Dick had a cardboard box outside his office. We were supposed to put our stories there and make sure we met the deadline. Dick would stand next to that box, eyes on the clock. He'd snatch it up as the second hand passed deadline, and God help you if you were even steps away come deadline time.

I loved those guys. Dick died of cancer a couple of years ago. Al went on to become the department chair, but now he's retired. He still teaches a class a semester, and ruins young minds.

By the time I graduated, I really loved journalism. What a great job. You get to go out and see fun stuff, and they pay you for it.

I took a job in West Palm Beach, Florida, and soon hated journalism. I hated deadlines, I hated talking to city officials, I hated fuckhead editors who butchered my copy.

That started a roller-coaster ride that I'm on today: I hate my job, I love my job. It never ends.

In any case, I hated Florida, too. I knew people at the *Omaha World-Herald*, and was able to convince them to hire me. So it was back to Nebraska, to the heat and the cold and the Midwestern blandness that I disliked and my new wife hated with a passion. But the job was better.

I started covering higher education. It sucked. What I really wanted was excitement. Adventure. I wanted to do big stories from exotic foreign lands. Of course, I wasn't much good at my job yet, but that never stopped me from dreaming.

In 1987, I got my chance at international reporting. War reporting, in a sense. And I totally screwed it up.

It happened like this:

I'm covering the University of Nebraska system. At the Omaha campus, there is the Center for Afghanistan Studies. It's run by a former Peace Corps volunteer named Tom Goutierre. He, of course, is in big demand in the '80s because of the Soviet occupation of Afghanistan. No one in the State Department could even find Afghanistan on the map, but the Russians were fighting a proxy war there. So they called on Tom for advice and counsel.

Tom negotiates with the U.S. Agency for International Development and gets a $14 million contract to provide educational support to Afghan refugees in Pakistan, and in the unoccupied areas of Afghanistan. A couple of professors are going to Peshawar, a huge refugee city near the Khyber Pass, to administer the grant.

I proposed a reporting trip. I would go with Tom to Pakistan to set up the office. I would write stories about the project and how it would affect the Afghans. And I would get to know the Afghan Mujahideen. I would get one of the rebel groups to escort me into Afghanistan and find some of the schools Tom was helping to build. And write stories about it.

It wasn't exactly war reporting, but it was pretty close. A war was going on. Afghans were fighting and dying. I figured I could write about the education project and still see some fighting, write some stories about combat.

It was a sound plan. I give, a good plan. Follow through, not so much.

The first trip went well. I got great stories. Front-page stuff with a Pakistan dateline. I met some fierce Afghan tribesmen. Guys who had lost hands and legs fighting the Russians. I made some contacts, and one of the groups invited me back to go into Afghanistan.

A couple of months later, I went back, along with photographer Bill Batson. We bought some Afghan clothing, a couple of packs, and a lot of canned tuna to take on the trip. We would be going by foot and mule over rugged terrain. To an area south of Kabul, where schools supposedly had been built. I thought I was ready for this. I hoped I was.

Bill and I got to Peshawar and waited. The Mujahideen took reporters into Afghanistan all the time, but they were never organized. After a week of sitting around, we got a call to meet at a certain plaza the next morning. Early. We showed up and met our contact, who introduced us to a 21-year-old law student who was to be our interpreter and guide.

It all seemed a little too casual. We were a couple of Americans sneaking into the most battle-scarred country in the world. Where the evil Soviet Union had thousands of troops and combat helicopters and tanks and fighter-bomber jets unleashing death and destruction. And we were going there with a law student in a Toyota. But I figured they'd done this before and knew what they were doing.

First rule in journalism: Never assume.

The Pakistanis had a bus service from Peshawar to a border village near the city of Quetta. It was a six- or seven-hour drive. The "bus" was a large Toyota van, and carried about 15 people. We crammed in with our translator and took off.

It was hot. Damn hot. Sear-the-flesh-off-your-face hot. Bill and I wore Pakistani clothes. Loose-fitting pants, like pajama bottoms, and a shirt that goes down to your knees. We also had the typical Afghan head-gear called a "Chitrali hat." It's got a flat top, and the sides are rolled up to the top. It's like a ski cap but with a flat top.

We're drinking water from our canteens and trying to stay cool. The window is open, and the air feels like a blast furnace.

Hour after hour we bump along the cruddy roads. Every once in a while, we stop at a police checkpoint. The translator tells us to keep our heads down, so they don't spot the Americans.

At some point, we cross into the territory of the Pathan tribes. This is a semi-autonomous region that straddles the Afghanistan-Pakistan border. The Pathans run the border patrol, and we are not allowed in this area. Which shouldn't be a problem. Journalists have been crossing for years. And we have bribe money.

We come to the last border checkpoint before our final destination. I think Bill and I were both pretty bleary-eyed by then, and maybe we didn't hide it well enough. Or maybe one of the Pakistanis gave us up. In any case, I hear shouting, and the van doors open. Our translator is telling us to get outside, the border patrol wants to talk to us.

Fuck.

We stumble out of the van. A dozen young men are pointing AK-47s at our faces. I have my hands up. Trying to see if the safeties are on those rifles. Just no one make any sudden moves.

Shit.

The translator starts talking, but the head border patrolman is shaking his head. He motions to the van to take off. I watch the vehicle head down the road, a sick feeling coming over me.

We go to a shack and have a seat. The guns are still pointed at us. And it's real hot.

Abdullah the translator is talking a mile a minute. I'm sure he made a fine attorney. He shows the guy our money. He sits next to him on a cot, and I can tell he's begging and pleading. I'm thinking the guy will take the cash and let us go.

He does not.

I don't know why the guy was so obstinate. I don't even know what was being said. After a bit, they ordered us out. Abdullah said we had to go to the police station. We went around back to where a white pickup was parked.

Bill got in the front seat between two border guards. I got in the back with Abdullah and two other guards. All armed.

But the truck doesn't move. I can see the two guards in the front having an animated discussion. And I see we're alone out there. And it strikes me: What if they just shoot our sorry asses? Is that what they're talking about in there?

Fuck.

I look at one of the guards in back with us. He looks young and slow. I'm hot and mad. I'm no hero, and I'm not a fighter. But I'm pissed. And I'm thinking, if those guys get out of the cab, I'm going after border boy and taking his gun. I don't even know how to fire an AK, but I'll wave it around and run like a madman. I mean, anything's better than going down like sheep.

They talk for another couple of minutes. The driver starts the truck, and we take off.

In Pakistan, they say the Army is honorable but the police are corrupt. They took us to a police station. It was late afternoon by the time we got there, so they put us in a holding cell. It was about 10 by 15 feet. Had a straw mat on the floor. White walls 15 feet tall, a window, and an iron-barred door. About 12 Pakistani criminals were in there already. There was barely enough room for us to grab a piece of floor. The Pakistanis were eating some kind of spicy chicken dish in a common bucket.

I wasn't hungry.

There was no toilet. Just a short wall separating a small space. In there was a hole in the wall. You did your business there and wiped with a piece of hard dirt. Once a day, they came in with a bucket and splashed water over it, flushing the shit through the hole.

All in all, very lovely.

We still had our money, so every half-hour we would slip a bill through the bars to buy Fanta soft drinks. But those vendors left late in the evening. We lay on the hard floor, our dirty socks as pillows, and stared at the bare bulb hanging from the ceiling. Wondering what the fuck we had gotten ourselves into.

Middle of the night, I get cotton mouth something fierce. I can barely swallow. It's still 95 degrees in that place. No relief from the heat.

Outside the jail door is a metal bucket filled with water. Inside is a metal cup. All the prisoners use the same cup. I can only imagine the bacteria in that water.

Water. God, I have to have some water.

On my first trip to Pakistan, I learned never to drink the water. Use bottled water to brush your teeth. Never eat fresh fruit or vegetables because it's been washed with unclean water. And never have any dairy. I was pretty good until I forgot about the dairy thing and had some ice cream with dinner one night. Thought I was going to die. That was the only time I ever suffered from projectile vomiting. When I wasn't spewing, I was crapping.

So I knew full well what that water represented. I didn't care.

I walked over and grabbed the cup.

"Don't do it," Bill said when he saw me. "You'll get the screaming shits."

"I don't care."

I dipped into the water and brought the cup to my lips. Cool sweet water hit my tongue. I swallowed hard. It made noise in the way you do when you drink when you're really thirsty.

It never bothered me at all. Go figure.

Time moved like molasses. I never saw seconds ticks so slowly. I kept looking at my watch. 2:25. 3:10. 4:01.

I got mad at myself. I forced myself to wait for what I figured was 45 minutes. When I looked again, five minutes had passed.

Finally, a couple of cops came to get Bill and me. We'd heard stories of torture and beatings. They took us to an office. One asked questions, and the other translated.

What were we doing in the unauthorized area? Who were we? Who did we work for? Were we spies? How many children did we have? What property?

We answered truthfully, but they didn't really grasp the concept of two journalists from Omaha going to Afghanistan to do stories. Hours passed. Finally, they put us back in the pickup and took us to a house. I learned later it was the residence of a local judge. One of the cops talked to him and pointed to us. The judge came over and asked what we were doing.

Journalist, I said.

"Why do you wear Afghan clothes? You think we are stupid?" he responded.

"I do not think you are stupid. Afghan clothes are more comfortable in the heat," I lied. I took off my cap to show my blond, balding head. "I don't think I look like an Afghan. I'm not trying to fool anyone."

He scowled and turned away. Said something to the cop. I asked Abdullah what was going on.

"He says two weeks in the jail."

I thought about the horrible night we'd just spent and I about lost it.

"Two weeks!" I yelled. "I can't last two weeks in that shit hole. Tell him! Tell him there's been a mistake."

"I cannot. It is his decision. But we are not going back to the jail.

We go to the other jail. The prison. It is much more comfortable."

Prison?

We drove across town and parked in front of a huge prison structure. It had been built by the British in the time of the Raj. The walls were 3-feet thick.

"Well, I guess we can stay here for two weeks if we have to," I said. "And then we can go?"

"No," Abdullah said. "We stay two weeks and then there is a trial."

"A trial? For what?"

"For being a foreigner in an unauthorized area."

"What could we get?"

"I think two years."

Holy fucking shit.

The only thing we had going for us was the money. We kept tossing money around to anyone who would take it, asking them to call the American consulate in Peshawar.

We went into the prison. It was huge and foreboding. There were several barracks on the grounds. One of them, we were told, was death row. Behind it, a gallows.

But the guards seemed decent. And the warden came to meet us. As Americans, we were minor celebrities. Like that meant anything.

They took us to a barracks. It was a long, narrow building. Inside, in the middle, was a walkway. Along the walls was a higher level of dirt. Inmates slept there. At one end were showers and a toilet.

There were about 80 men in there. The guy who slept next to me was Afghan. He told Abdullah he had been accused of kidnapping five years ago. Never been to trial. Didn't know if or when he would ever get out.

The whole scene was so surreal, I could hardly stand it. I sat cross-legged on the dirt, rocking back and forth like a crazy man.

A couple of times a day, the inmates lined up to pray. Bill and I stood behind and to the side. Two or three guys joined us. Lapsed Muslims, I guess. One approached me and said something I couldn't understand.

Sounded like "hatchet." I shrugged and he held out his hand. In it was a ball of foil. He opened it and then I understood: Hashish.

I stumbled in my haste to get away from him. I had visions of prison guards swooping down and finding the drugs and sentencing me to life in the big house.

Night came and someone offered us space in the middle of the room, under one of the four or five ceiling fans. Abdullah explained that we were guests. And Muslims always give their guests the best of everything. But in a day or two, we would no longer be guests. We would be part of the group. And we would no longer get choice spots. Or food. He said the prison provides only wormy rice to inmates. If you're in prison, your family brings you food and some money for supplies. I could picture my mother coming to the front gate with a basket full of biscuits.

I slept about two hours that night. The strain was getting to me. The not knowing.

The next day, more of the same. And we just kept on handing out money.

Around midday, I heard a commotion outside the barracks. One of the inmates who spoke a little English said: "You are being released."

I didn't believe him. I wanted to, but I didn't want to be disappointed.

A few minutes later, the warden came over. He said he had called the U.S. consulate himself, and they had vouched for us. We were free to go.

We shook a lot of hands. The cop who had brought us came back and signed the paperwork to have us released. He didn't look too happy.

We walked out the front gate. Now what?

We were still in an unauthorized area. I didn't want to risk getting picked up again. I figured they might not be so understanding the second time around. We found a cab and paid him a couple hundred dollars to drive us to Peshawar.

We got there late at night. Went to the Hotel Intercontinental and got a couple of rooms. I stripped off my funky clothes and hit the shower. And finally relaxed.

We went back to the Mujahideen group that had sent us. They were very apologetic. They didn't understand how something like that could happen. They would try again.

The problem was, the Soviets had launched a massive offensive against rebel positions just across the border. And there were really only two ways into Afghanistan. The way we had tried and in the area of the offensive. We didn't want to go back to where we had been arrested, so we had to wait.

Bill and I went back to the hotel and waited. And waited. We went out and did a few stories about refugees. And the Soviets kept fighting.

But the truth is, I had no more courage left. It's one thing to wear a uniform, be a member of a fighting force like the Marines, and go into combat if necessary. But when you're out in the middle of nowhere, alone, don't speak the language, and people will kill you, or throw you into a shit-hole prison, courage takes flight.

I knew we weren't going to get into Afghanistan. And it crushed me. Personally and professionally. I got drunk at the hotel bar and sat in my room. I thought of how I'd dreamed of being a foreign correspondent. How I wanted travel and intrigue and danger. And when I got it, I chickened out.

I felt empty. Alone. But I had no choice. You could get killed out there. Or worse.

I called my editor. Explained the situation. He said come on home. But I knew it wasn't his decision. It was mine and it was killing me.

We left a week later. I had to walk into the *World-Herald* newsroom as a failure. People were nice. They complimented me on my other stories. But I heard none of it. Just the one word ringing in my head: Loser.

I stayed in Omaha for another two years, but I knew I would leave the first chance I could.

In 1990, I sent resumes to every newspaper in California over 100,000 circulation. The *Contra Costa Times*, in the suburbs of the east San Francisco Bay area, offered me a job. I left skid marks getting out of Omaha.

I think the memory of Pakistan stayed with me for a long time. I had lost my sense of pride. And self-esteem. So I just buried it. I tried to put the whole scene behind me and start over.

I worked for a couple of years as a reporter at the *Contra Costa Times*. Nothing special there, other than the fact that I never liked the name of the paper. If you called someone from outside the area, and said you were a reporter for the *Contra Costa Times*, you'd hear this silence. And then a question, "Contra what?" Is that some kind of Nicaragua thing?" After a time, I decided I didn't want to spend my life chasing disaster stories and school board elections. I figured I'd try to write a book, or become an editor and maybe get a better job with more money. I went to graduate school to study creative writing. About the same time, I became an assistant city editor, which meant I was supervising reporters and shaping, or destroying, young minds.

Life was good. I liked my job. I wasn't making any money, but I looked forward to going to work every day. I still thought about leaving journalism, and getting into public relations. Or garbage hauling. Something that would pay well. I wanted to buy a house and go on fishing trips and enjoy life, not just chase after stories all the time.

Then a friend hooked me up with the *San Francisco Examiner*. They needed an assistant city editor to work the night shift, 5 p.m. to 1:30 a.m. No one else wanted the job. So they gave it to me.

Phil Bronstein, the executive editor, hired me on May 16, 1997. I worked that crappy night shift for a year, then they made it worse. They transferred me to the morning shift, working 4:30 a.m. to 12:30 p.m. I suffered sleep deprivation for the next couple of years, until the Hearst Newspapers bought the *Chronicle* and merged the two staffs.

None of this is at all interesting. It just leads us to the war. I thought you'd like to know that.

In the middle of all this, I became a father. My son, Jordi, was born July 8, 1994. We called him Jordi because it's a popular name in

Catalunya (the province of Barcelona). And my mom and dad could pronounce it.

I fell in love with that little guy. I loved everything about him. The way he looked, the way he smelled, the way he smiled. I loved changing his diapers. When he peed all over my good clothes, I just laughed. I watched *Barney* and *Sesame Street*. I watched *Toy Story* at least 150 times, over and over again. I still know every line in that movie by heart.

I got to take him to the park and teach him how to spit. We played catch and soccer and flew kites. I wasn't always the greatest dad, but I loved that boy with every fiber of my being.

Fatherhood kept me going. I realized I didn't have to be the world's greatest reporter. I just had to be a good dad.

# CHAPTER 3

# PREPARATION FOR WAR

On September 11, 2001, I got ready for work and, for a change, didn't bother to turn on the morning TV news. I got in my car. Turned on the radio. Heard a rock station DJ telling people to stay calm. And not to assume anything yet about Muslims and the World Trade Center. Then played another rock song.

What the hell?

I got to the office and checked the wires. The attacks in New York City and at the Pentagon were all over the news. It was 7 a.m. our time. We had five hours to deadline for the afternoon edition.

It was a great day. That statement sounds crass and, in a way, it is. But you have to understand journalists. We live for the big, breaking-news story. The bigger the story, and tighter the deadline, the more we like it. The more intense the experience. The more adrenaline. And that's better than a drug.

I had reporters everywhere. In San Francisco. Washington, D.C. New York City. Everyone pitched in. Sports columnists stopped by my desk to ask if they could go gather quotes. Everyone smells the big story, and everyone wants in on it. This isn't even about ego. It's just the thrill of the big one.

We put together a great package. It was complete and comprehensive. But no one could compare to the front page headline on the other

San Francisco paper, the new *Examiner*. It showed a picture of the smoking building with one word above: Bastards!

We made up T-shirts with that front page on them.

A week later, the president gave a speech. It was clear he was going to attack Afghanistan. I was reluctant to revisit that nightmare, but I figured I was probably the best person to try to cover the conflict. I sent a note to the boss, suggesting that I go to Afghanistan through the north. Other reporters made the same pitch. But for reasons that were never entirely clear to me, we sent no one. The *Chronicle* eventually hired a woman from the region. She did such a great job, they hired her permanently.

I went back to my sucky little editing job and shut the hell up. Who wants to go to Afghanistan, anyway?

Around the end of the year, I got reassigned. I was no longer an editor. I was a reporter again. Working the night shift. The rewrite man. It's actually a pretty useful job for the paper, but it meant another crappy shift, no time with my son. I just felt shit on.

This was a low for me. I was mad. I thought, once again, about getting into public relations. At least the money was better.

But that would take time and energy and drive, and I had none. So I came in at 3 p.m., did my thing, and left at 11. I didn't put out any effort, and I didn't give a shit about the paper or the stories in it.

But I would sneak a peek at stories about Afghanistan. Reporters had a field day over there. There was a lot of combat and reasonable access to the rebels of the Northern Alliance. I should have been there. The rebels were led by Ahmad Shah Massoud, the Lion of the Panshir Valley. He was a legend for his guerrilla war against the Russians, and he had held out against the Taliban for years. I always wanted to meet him. Then, one day, a couple of guys posing as Arab journalists requested an interview with him and blew him up with a bomb hidden in their camera. His top aide was severely injured. The aide was Massoud Khalili. the guy who had arranged for me to go to Afghanistan many years earlier. I liked him a lot. Another Afghan I knew was caught by the Taliban and hanged.

And then stories started coming in about Iraq. Which sort of surprised me at the time. Why Iraq? The president said Saddam Hussein had weapons of mass destruction, he was a dictator who killed his own people, posed a threat to his neighbors and was a general all-around bad guy. It started slowly and then picked up steam. I kept thinking the situation would taper off, or that the War on Terror would soon take another direction. But it didn't. All signs pointed to Iraq.

Yeah, big deal. I have to rewrite a story about bridge tolls.

Meanwhile, deep inside the Pentagon, people were talking about how to make war on Iraq. Specifically, high ranking officials in the Defense Department addressed the issue of media access, who would cover the war and how.

A new word popped up: Embed.

Well, it was a new word to civilians. "Embed" is a military term for a unit, or soldier, who is attached to another, usually bigger, unit. For example, a tank platoon might be embedded in an infantry battalion.

But this was big news for reporters. The relationship between the military and media had been horrible for more than 30 years. Since Vietnam, soldiers and reporters have seldom had a great working relationship. We like to tell stories, and the military likes to keep secrets. I'm not taking sides here. There are good reasons to keep military secrets . . . sometimes. The point is, you have two institutions with diametrically opposed points of view.

Reporters had good access in World War II, Korea, and Vietnam. Especially Vietnam. Access was virtually uncontrolled. You could just hop a flight to Saigon and start traveling around the countryside with U.S. troops. Or do stories about the Vietnamese. Whatever. It was free and open.

But the war went badly, and of course the stories reflected that. And it just kept getting worse. Pretty soon, the military started blaming the media for the loss of public support back home. There have been a million stories and books written about this, and I don't want to go into the debate here. It doesn't matter who was right. The point is, after

Vietnam the military hated the press. You couldn't get anything out of them, and whenever there was any kind of fighting—like Grenada and Panama—the press was definitely not welcome.

It all came to a head during the first Gulf War. There was no good coverage of the fighting. Reporters were kept in hotels in Saudi Arabia and occasionally trucked out to the battlefield long after the shooting stopped. Some reporters found their own ways to cover the war, driving out into the desert looking for explosions. But it was a poor way for the American media to cover an American war.

When the United States went to war against Afghanistan, they did it without giving American reporters access. Journalists got into Afghanistan through the north, guests of the Northern Alliance, and they got some pretty good stuff. But it was by no means comprehensive.

So no one really expected anything better if there was a war in Iraq.

But something had changed. For one thing, there was now a thriving Arab media, specifically Al Jazeera. They had cameras and notebooks and they had access to the fighting. When American planes dropped a bomb, Al Jazeera was there, and if someone said the bomb landed on a hospital or civilians, there was no way for the United States to prove otherwise.

So with preparations commencing for a ground war in Iraq, someone had the idea to do something counter to the long-held view of the media as enemy. The new thinking was: Invite them all along. Embed them.

Some of this came from a long-time reporter who had covered the military since Vietnam. His name was Joe Galloway, and he had written a best-selling book with Hal Moore that was turned into the movie "We Were Soldiers." That book and movie included Galloway's work as a reporter with an Army battalion that was part of one of the first major battles between Americans and Communist Vietnamese forces. A lot of men on both sides died, and Galloway was right there to see and report it all . . . once the dust settled and he could get to a "phone." (Hal Moore was the Army officer who commanded the battalion in that battle. He retired from the service as a three-star general. Who says soldiers and reporters can't get along?)

Now with the Knight-Ridder News Service in Washington, D.C., Galloway lobbied for a return to full access. And the Defense Department, mindful of the propaganda war that would commence with the invasion of Iraq, thought it was a good idea.

That's where I came in.

At the *Chronicle*, we have an editor who is in charge of foreign and national news. He has a staff of editors who scan and edit wire stories from around the globe, and he has one staff reporter and dozens of stringers. But that's it. We're not a huge operation, like the *Los Angeles Times* or *Boston Globe*, who have foreign bureaus. That would be nice, but it costs a ton of money.

So, when the foreign/national editor, Andrew S. Ross, wanted people to cover the war, he went to the metro editor and asked for bodies.

The metro editor, my boss, Wendy Miller, suggested he ask me. Mostly because she knew I'd been in the Marines. And I had a little experience.

So, one day in October of 2002, Andrew calls me into his office. Would I be interested in joining the "war team," he asks?

Andrew, bless his heart, never asked me if I wanted to be an embedded reporter, or even to go cover the war. I think he didn't want to ask it, because if something happened to me, he would consider it his fault. In any case, he let me come up with that idea.

We started talking about my background and how the war team might work, and who might go cover the war. Rob Collier, he said, was angling to spend the war in Baghdad. Someone would probably cover the war from the north, through Turkey into Kurd country.

Oh, and by the way, Andrew says, word has it that the Pentagon might let reporters go with military units this time. He says, they're talking about embedding reporters with front-line units.

I told Andrew that I doubted the military would let us tag along.

"But if they do," I said. "I'd go."

"Brilliant," he said. He's a Brit. That's how they talk.

I started slow, calling the *Chronicle*'s Washington bureau. Calling the Pentagon. Checking clips. Surfing the Internet for whatever I could find on embedding. In the fall of 2002, there wasn't a lot of information. But the Pentagon did acknowledge that it was considering an embedding program if there was a war. But they didn't know which media outlets would get to go, or how people would be selected. Or anything.

I knew two things: I had to convince the Pentagon to give my paper an embedding slot. And I had to find a unit to embed with.

The first task would not be easy. The *Chronicle* is not exactly on Washington's list of favorite newspapers. We're too liberal. Our readers are too liberal. They hate the military. (Not all, of course, but that's the reputation.) And the closest significant military base is halfway to Sacramento.

We have two bureaus in Washington: The *Chron*'s bureau and the Hearst newspaper bureau. They were both bugging the Pentagon to give us a slot.

I called, too. And wrote. Every week. I was a pest, but I figured I had to make our presence known. Sometimes people give in just to shut you up.

Meanwhile, I fretted. What if we didn't get a slot? Could I go cover the war, anyway? Would I have the stones to do it? The thought would send a shudder through my colon. I hated it. I hated the fear. I hated not knowing.

Election day came around, November 2002. I worked late that night, like we all do, putting together the local election results. It's a crappy job, and only the serious political writers enjoy it. But it's kind of fun to have the whole staff in the office until well after midnight, trying to get everything perfect for the next day's paper. Welcome to the glamorous world of journalism.

After deadline, we retired to the local pub for a beer. Collier was there.

I didn't know Rob very well. Mostly by reputation. A few nods in the hallway. He's a medium-sized guy with a long chin and curly brown hair.

I asked him about his plans for Iraq. He told me the situation looked impossible. The Iraqis only allowed a few journalists into Baghdad. And they were from the *New York Times* and the *Wall Street Journal*. We had no juice over there. So he was going through the same problems as I had, except with a different set of bureaucrats.

He said he had a few ideas on how to get in. He planned to be there when the war started.

"You are one crazy motherfucker," I said. "They will bomb your ass. And if the Air Force doesn't get you, an Iraqi mob will."

"I don't think so," he said, sipping whiskey. "But anyway, that's where the stories will be."

I told him I was going to go in with the troops.

He thought I was crazy. He thought an embedded reporter wouldn't get many good stories, because the military was bound to censor us. Could be, I said. But they say they won't.

Rob looked at me and laughed. Cynical, distrustful bastard.

But we drank a toast to our respective roles. I told him we should link up in Baghdad and have a drink to mark the end of the war. Never once believing we would ever do it.

Meanwhile, I was trying to figure out how to cover a war. Who do you go with? Army or Marines? Infantry or tanks? Get close up to the front, so you can see some action? What war correspondents call "looking for boom-boom?" Or stay toward the rear so you can get a better overall view of the conflict, and interview different people from different war zones?

I picked Marines. Because I was one. But also, the 1st Marine Division is located in California. The Army has no significant presence here. I picked infantry over armor. I wasn't sure about this. Tanks had been in a lot of fights in the first Gulf War and, considering the size of Saddam's armored corps, likely would be again,.

But you can't see anything in a tank unless you're a crewman. It's not like you can ride on the back. You'd probably be in a Humvee or truck somewhere in the rear.

What I didn't know then, but would find out later, is that the Marines had already worked out a different combined forces technique. Tank companies joined infantry battalions to make reinforced units that could take on anything.

So what I wanted to find was a good, professional, well-trained Marine combat battalion. One that would fight, but do it well. And get my ass back home in one piece.

I went back to my Marine roots: Twentynine Palms. I knew the Marines had infantry units training out there. I figured those guys would be well-versed in desert warfare. I called the base public affairs officer, Captain Rob Crum. Told him I wanted to come visit, to write about Marines training in preparation for war. And that I wanted to find a unit to ride with if war came.

Crum says to come on down, there's a battalion finishing up a training exercise called Steel Knight. They're out on the ranges right now.

I flew to Southern California and rented a car for a two-hour drive out to the desert. It's harsh out there. Past Palm Springs, the land is rocky and barren. Loners and desert rats live singly among the scrub and yucca plants. Although it's hotter than hell pretty much all year, it wasn't so bad in December of 2002.

The place hadn't changed much since I left in 1977. The town was about the same size. They straightened out the curve in the road, the one where I got a speeding ticket from a California Highway Patrolman. Otherwise, the base was about the same size, a small cluster of buildings and barracks nestled under a rocky crag of a mountain.

I met *Chronicle* photographer Michael Macor at the front gate, and Crum came to escort us to the training range. We stopped at his office so he could give us each a helmet and flak jacket. You have to wear that stuff out on the ranges because they conduct live-fire exercises.

We drove over sandy winding roads through the back hills. Lizards darted out of our way. Out there, you can see deep blue sky, ivory-colored sand, and charcoal-colored rock. That's it.

We pulled up to the base of a small hill. A company of Marines milled about, some eating, some talking and joking. It was Kilo Company, 3rd Battalion, 4th Marine Regiment.

These were the guys who would go to Kuwait, cross into Iraq, fight a dozen battles, and pull down the statue of Saddam Hussein in one of the most memorable moments of the war.

Crum introduced me to the Kilo company commander, Captain Kevin Norton, a soft-spoken Pennsylvanian who had been an enlisted man in the first Gulf War. Macor eased into the background and started shooting pictures. I met the Kilo first sergeant, Jim Kirkland, a short, wiry guy whose voice was bigger than his body. He rounded up some Marines from Northern California for me to interview. You know, we're a regional paper, so you have to get people from the region into the story.

After I interviewed some Marines and made some chit-chat, Norton invited us to have lunch with him. They had MREs (Meals, Ready to Eat). I'd never had one. I was an old man—in my time, we had C-Rations. Everything in a can. I'd heard about MREs, also called Meals, Rejected by Ethiopians and all sorts of other ugly names. But the food was pretty good. I had a beef patty.

After lunch, I saw a short, tough-looking man come into the area. Norton introduced him to me. His name was David Howell and he was the battalion's most senior enlisted man, the sergeant major.

Howell was 41. Originally from St. Louis and had been in the Marines for 24 years.

I liked Dave from the start. He was the toughest, most profane individual I ever met. And funny as hell. At least, when the young Marines weren't around to witness it.

I liked that Dave was from the Midwest. We had a lot in common. Close in age, both from blue-collar families. I had joined the Marines just a couple of years before him.

"You know, if I had stayed in the Corps, I would outrank you," I told him.

"Yeah, but you'd be some pussy warrant officer running a comm shop," he said. "I wouldn't give a shit what you said."

That kind of set the tone for the rest of our friendship.

I told him why I was there. I wanted to be up front with these guys right off the bat.

"Look, I don't know if there's going to be a war, but if they do this embedding thing, I want a good seat," I said.

Dave didn't say anything. Just nodded. Soon, training got under way, and I wandered around, watching the Marines do their thing. A couple of tanks rumbled over. The grunts were working some combined arms drills. Teaching the infantry how to deal with tanks. The tank crews can't see outside very well, and those 70-ton vehicles will run over you and kill you if you're not careful.

"This tank is dangerous," barked a tank officer to the group of infantrymen surrounding him. "It will kill you. If you're behind it, and this thing starts backing up, it'll roll right over you and your weapon and not even register it.

"Stay alert."

Howell always prowled the outer edges of the formation, watching his Marines, making sure they were paying attention. As the men moved here and there, I found him at my side. Asking questions. Some innocent, about my family and San Francisco. Some more specific. About journalism. About my work and my beliefs. What I thought about the possibility of war. How I would cover it.

I told him I had no opinions.

"It is what it is," I said. "It's not my job to have opinions. I'm just here to write what I see. If it's good, it's good. If it's not, I'll write about that, too."

How do I think the American public will react, he asked, if I'm on hand to see Marines at war killing people, and I write about it?

The question stunned me. It brought home the reality of what would soon occur. A lot of death and destruction. Maybe my death. Maybe Dave's.

But to answer his question, I just said, "People will react how they'll react," I said. "I think people understand what war is all about. The question will be, how will the Marines conduct themselves? That's what people will be looking at."

We walked over to a staging area. Dave saw a Humvee approach and said, "Let me introduce you to the C.O."

The commanding officer of the battalion was Lieutenant Colonel Bryan P. McCoy.

I liked him, too, but in a different way than the sergeant major. McCoy was educated, intelligent, forceful, interesting. He's from Oklahoma and has that soft-spoken, airline pilot kind of voice. About 6 feet tall and 200 pounds. Big, but not huge. With a very commanding presence. He had the aura of a lieutenant colonel, and my old instincts as an enlisted man kicked in. I almost saluted.

McCoy and I talked. About training. About war. About football. McCoy went to high school in Nebraska, because his father was stationed at the headquarters of the Strategic Air Command south of Omaha. His family is from Oklahoma, though, and that's where he went to college.

You get a Nebraskan and an Oklahoman together and they're going to talk football. McCoy was a pretty good player in high school, and could have gotten a football scholarship. But he chose the University of Oklahoma and ROTC instead.

After a bit, he excused himself. I saw him talking to Dave. And that's when it hit me: The sergeant major had been interviewing me as much as I was interviewing him. It was a little like a job interview. I wondered how I did.

McCoy left and went to do commanding officer stuff. Not long after that, we wrapped it up, and I drove back to the public affairs office with Crum and Macor.

I wrote a story for the *Chronicle*. McCoy e-mailed me and thanked me for writing what he thought was an honest and accurate story. In our e-mail exchange, he said something that I liked a lot.

"I don't expect you to be a cheerleader for the Marines," he said. "That's not your job. Just be fair and accurate, that's all I ask. If we screw something up, I expect you to write about it. If it's something that needs to be fixed, a story will speed things up."

And that set the tone for my relationship with him. I had been worried that I would be with a commanding officer who was more concerned with his career than the truth. I worried he would try to spin my stories, or influence me somehow. Or just ride my ass every time I tried to talk to people.

But I felt comfortable with McCoy and Howell. They struck me as sharp, competent Marines. People who would do what they had to do and bring me back alive.

What more could I ask for?

A couple days later, I talked to Captain Crum. He said McCoy had told him I was welcome to ride with Three-Four in Iraq.

Everything was going according to plan. The Pentagon had my name, and I had a unit all picked out. I had gone to the division headquarters in Camp Pendleton after I left Twentynine Palms. I went to lunch with the public affairs officers and told them what I was looking for. I think they liked that I had been in the Marines, and that I took the time to meet with them. One lieutenant told me that I was the only reporter to show up in person. "The others just call and say, 'Put me on the list for embedding,'" he said. "I can tell you that you'll get priority."

After that, I waited. Waited for war. Waited for the Pentagon to parcel out embedding slots. Waited for a flight to Kuwait.


It's 11 at night. I'm in bed. Isabel is lying next to me. Time for another fight.

"Did you find out about the insurance?" she asks.

"No, not yet."

"What did they tell you?"

"They're still waiting."

"What are they waiting for?"

"The Hearst people are talking about it."

"That's ridiculous. They can't ask you to go to Iraq without insurance."

"I'm not going to Iraq without insurance. I told you."

"So why can't they tell you how much it's going to be?"

"I don't know. They're waiting."

"Well, you know, it has to be a lot. You have a son."

"I know that. It will be enough."

"I just don't know why you have to do this."

"Oh, please. Not again."

"What about Jordi?"

"I know."

"What am I going to do without you?"

We would fight every couple of nights. Sometimes there were just a few words. Sometimes it escalated into shouting and tears, and would last for an hour or more.

We would talk it out. I would apologize and make all sorts of promises, and we would make up. Until the thought of me going to war would weigh on her again. And we'd start the fight. Over and over again.

To be sure, I was the villain. I accept that. When Andrew Ross asked me if I wanted to cover the war, I knew I would do it at any cost. I had to do it. A lot of people think that's stupid. They think I was an asshole and reckless. They're right. I was. I can't explain it. I just had to see a war.

After my first discussion with Ross, I told Isabel about our conversation. I told her about the "war plan" and some of the possibilities for covering the war, if it should happen. I said they might ask me to go to the region. But that it was all up in the air. Nothing is for certain.

It was an outright lie, of course. I knew what Andrew wanted, and I knew what I wanted. I knew that if I had the chance, I would stand right in the middle of a war if the United States launched an invasion.

I knew all that, and I lied my ass off. Because I knew if I opened the topic for debate, it would be ugly. And I would lose.

So I kept things deliberately vague. We might cover the war. They might allow reporters to embed with units. If they did, I probably wouldn't do that. But I might go to Kuwait and report from there. I wouldn't be on the front lines. And if I were, it would be well after the battle.

Being vague about it meant we didn't have to confront the issue until all the decisions were made. But it meant a lot of fighting.

We would talk about it. And fight. And at the end of the fight, everything would be better. Or so I thought. The next day, or two days later, we would fight the same fight all over again. I put Isabel through hell. I wondered whether I would have to pay for it when it was all over.

Meantime, the Pentagon was putting on what they called "media boot camps." Each service hosted one. They invited 60 reporters and photographers at a time to go to a military base for a week. They taught people how to survive on the battlefield. As well as legal issues involving noncombatants, first aid, rank structure. All that good stuff.

I wasn't planning on going. I knew the difference between a major and a major general (a whole lot of pay). And I knew how to treat a sucking chest wound (yell for a medic—loudly—until one comes running). But one day I got a call from the Pentagon saying they had one slot open after a last-minute cancellation. Did I want to go?

I thought about it for a second. It meant getting away from the newsroom for a week. With pay. So I figured I would go and meet some people. What could it hurt?

My media boot camp was held at Camp McGuire, an Air Force base that's part of the Fort Dix installation in New Jersey.

It was January. In New Jersey.

Leave it to the Air Force to teach reporters how to survive in desert warfare by bringing us to New Jersey in the dead of winter. It was 7 degrees outside. And snow on the ground.

We stayed in a room-style barracks. The rooms were about 20-by-20, with ten double-decker bunks and wall lockers. We were divided into squads of ten each, with a couple of soldiers as our keepers and helpers.

I was assigned to Foxtrot squad. Foxtrot is the letter F in the phonetic alphabet used by the military. We had reporters from all over, including the *Washington Post,* United Press International, *New Orleans Times-Picayune, Omaha World-Herald,* the *Wall Street Journal,* a German TV station, and others.

We had a pretty good time, and became friends. We called ourselves "The Fearless Fuckups of Foxtrot." In truth, I learned nothing at the course, but I was glad to know the other reporters. I still keep in touch with some of those guys. It was helpful later on, in Kuwait, when we all had our heads up our asses, and wondered what we were doing. We helped each other out, passed on information, told each other where to get gear and whom to talk to. That kind of network was worth the time spent in New Jersey.

Victoria Clarke, the Pentagon spokeswoman who was involved in developing the embedding project, said: "It's in our interest to let people see for themselves, through the news media, the lies and deceptive tactics Saddam Hussein will use."

My friend, and fellow Foxtrotter, Richard Leiby of the *Washington Post,* said, "We're supposed to be the anti-Al Jazeera."

For those of us at the training session (which was nicely lampooned in the "Doonesbury" comic strip), those were academic and philosophic questions. Would we be objective? Of course. Would the Pentagon try to spin the war and control us? Of course. But we won't let them. Will we?

What really concerned us was the whole "death" thing. The soldiers, sailors, and airmen who instructed us kept harping on the dangers of the battlefield. There will be booby-traps. Don't walk into a building before it's been cleared. There will be land mines. Don't wander around the combat zone. There will be snipers. Keep you head down.

In the manner of men and women for whom danger is a byproduct of their profession, death and dismemberment were dealt with lightly.

They liked to use the term "mess up your whole day." As in, "If you step on an anti-tank mine, it will explode with enough force to rip a hole in an armored vehicle, and I guarantee that will mess up your whole day."

It didn't help that they showed a film clip from the movie *Saving Private Ryan*. The beginning scene. When Americans are dying by the bucket load on the beach.

The room got real quiet.

Because that scenario was going on in everyone's head. We all knew, logically, that we might see bombs falling, or hear bullets flying. But what if you got over there and really landed in the shit? What if your convoy got ambushed? People killing and dying all around you? And you armed with nothing more than a Bic pen?

In the barracks, there was a lot of chat about: "That bright flash on the horizon could be very unfortunate, indeed."

It got so bad that Eli Lake, a State Department correspondent for United Press International, began to wonder if it weren't a plot.

"Every time we turn around they're telling us how this can kill us and that can kill us," he said. "I think they want us to forget about (covering the war). Which isn't a bad idea."

We had physical training every morning. I found out that I was not as fit as I thought. An hour in the gym three or four times a week did not prepare me for 3-mile runs, and an hour of strenuous exercise in the frigid air. We spent a couple of days in the field, riding in the back of half-ton trucks and learning how to get out and take cover if shooting breaks out.

We learned about nuclear, biological, and chemical weapons. We had to learn to put on a gas mask, taken from a hip carrier, in nine seconds. Late in the program, the military trucked in a bunch of reporters from local TV and newspapers. I was glad I was not one of them. Imagine having to go interview a bunch of other reporters. Talk about a suck-ass assignment.

Leiby and I agreed to talk to a guy from a newspaper. I joked that I could put my mask on in 90 seconds. And that's what he wrote. Damn reporters. Humor is lost on them.

We Foxtrotters went to town every night for Philly cheese-steak sandwiches and beer. We had fun with the lingo. Leiby kept telling everyone, "Keep your head on a swivel." Wes Allison from the *St. Petersburg Times* liked the Air Force term for anything cool or fancy: "High Speed." As in, "I like that watch, it's really high speed."

After the course wrapped up, I stopped in New York to visit my friend, Takae Miller. She took me down to Ground Zero, where the World Trade Center used to be. I was awed by the hole in the ground. And the memorials all around. It seemed fitting, since so much of the rhetoric for war involved 9-11.

I got back to San Francisco and talked with Andrew about the trip to Kuwait. We weren't really sure when to go. It was January. The weapons inspectors were in Iraq, and it looked like they would be there for a while. We figured we had some time. Troops kept flying over there and gathering in Kuwait. And it didn't look like there would be a surprise attack. The president kept saying the United States would do this, or that, before launching an invasion.

I started wondering what my role would be in all this. Every time something could shift course, it didn't. Every time something could derail the war, or my participation, it all stayed on course. I'm not a superstitious person. I don't really believe in fate. But important things don't usually happen to me. Not this way. I can go on a ride-along with cops in a dangerous neighborhood on Saturday night, and the worst that will happen is someone gets a parking ticket.

I'm not saying I'm glad there was a war. Personally, I despise the concept of war. I'm about one degree away from being a pacifist. But professionally, I wanted to do this and all the chips fell neatly into place.

But why? Why me? Why was I going? Did it mean something, or was I just thinking too much?

Would I be with the unit that found weapons of mass destruction? Would I witness something historic? A battle? A massacre? What was my role in this historic event?

It's 11 p.m. I'm lying in bed. Isabel lies next to me. Time for another fight.

But I'm tired of this argument. I've had enough.

"Listen," I tell her. "I've made my decision. I'm going. I know it's wrong. I know you're against it. I know. I know all this."

"Then why are you doing it?"

"Because I have to."

"You don't have to do anything. No one will say a thing if you tell them you can't go."

"I know, but I want to do it. I'm sorry, I just do. Anyway, here's the thing. I need you behind me on this."

"I don't think I can do it," she says, exasperated with me.

"You have to. I'm going. You have to either be with me or against me on this. There is no middle ground."

Silence.

"I'm not asking you to support my decision," I said. "But stop arguing. Stop fighting. Be with me. We'll work things out when I get back. But I'm going."

I didn't know what that kind of talk would bring. She was about an inch away from kicking my ass out of the house. No one would have blamed her. I was a shit.

I think we had another fight or two, but the intensity was dissipating. After another couple of days, the fighting stopped. I didn't want to give my wife an ultimatum, but I couldn't fight another minute. She was 100 percent right, and I was a selfish asshole. But in my mind, as time got nearer, I had to think about me. I was putting my life on the line. It was scary and harsh and difficult enough without thinking about how my death would affect my wife. Or my son.

The Marines of Three-Four flew out in January. I got a call from the division. Did I want to fly out with them?

I declined. Mostly because we figured the war wouldn't start for another month or so. And no sense in sitting in Kuwait, waiting that long.

Plus, we still hadn't heard from the Pentagon regarding embed slots. I worried every day. What if they ignored us? What if they gave us a crappy assignment? Would I still want to go?

I kept calling the division public affairs officer, Captain Joe Plenzler. Joe wasn't a typical public affairs guy. He was a hard-core infantry officer at heart. But he had this assignment, and I think he did a great job. Joe never BS'd you. He gave straight answers, and he called you back.

I asked him if he heard who was going with whom. He told me to stop worrying. He said I should go to Kuwait and wait for the war. Even if the Pentagon didn't give us a slot with the division, he said, I could go anyway. If the war started before the embedding thing was in place, he said, he'd just pick me up and take me out to the battalion.

"Possession in nine-tenths of the law, John," he said. "What are they going to say if we just take you along? Hell, if you're here when the war starts, I'll just give you a call and tell you to meet me at Starbucks. And we'll go from there."

I felt pretty good about that until I saw a news story in which an Army spokesman said all "side deals" made with unit commanders were null and void, and that officers who made deals should rescind them. I called Joe again. He laughed. No way the Army would tell the Marines what to do, he said.

We heard from the *Houston Chronicle* that they were getting some good slots, but that the rest of Hearst was not. That about sent me into clinical depression.

Finally, an e-mail. The *San Francisco Chronicle* had four spots. One with the Navy, one with the Army and two with the Marines. One Marine slot, the one I wanted, simply said "Marine Division."

We were good to go.

# CHAPTER 4

# LEAVING HOME

*January 23, 2003*
*To Whom It May Concern at San Francisco Chronicle:*
*My son is a Marine stationed at the 29 Palms Marine Corps base in Southern California. Some time ago, he mentioned to me that a* San Francisco Chronicle *reporter had done a story on his battalion (3rd Battalion/4th Marines), and that he might be traveling with the battalion in the event of a war in Iraq.*
*I would very much like to make contact with this reporter. Can you send me his name and e-mail address.*
*Karen Gentrup*
*San Jose, California*

Karen was the first one. There would be hundreds of others. Mothers, fathers, sisters, brothers. Some aunts and uncles.

## THE CORPS

To really understand all this, we have to go back in time. For me, it was only a few decades ago. For the Marines, it started in 1775. For those of you who did not spend time wearing a green uniform, I'll give you the very condensed history of the Marine Corps.

The Corps was born on November 10, at Tun Tavern in Philadelphia.

The Marines have always had swagger. It comes from the way the Corps was born and raised. Originally, there were no Marines. There was just the Navy for the seas and the Army for land.

On the big wooden ships, fighting could be fierce, and close-up. So the captains would go looking for the biggest, toughest sailors on the ship and make them into an elite fighting unit. They would be the first ones over the side, and onto an enemy ship, for hand-to-hand fighting. When the captain needed to row ashore for anything, he would take his handpicked fighters with him. They had to be expert shots, too, because he would sometimes send them into the rigging with muskets, to shoot down upon the decks of opposing ships.

These were Marines, taking their name from the Latin, which meant, essentially, Sea Soldiers.

No one thought much about the Marines before the twentieth century, although they were involved in some great battles. That's how the Marines hymn got its passages, "From the Halls of Montezuma" (Mexican War) to the "Shores of Tripoli" (fighting Mediterranean bandits).

World War I brought the Marines to the public attention. They were sent to Europe in 1917, along with the Army's doughboys, to fight the Germans. The Marines fought so fiercely, especially at the Battle of Belleau Wood, the Germans nicknamed them "Devil Dogs." The name stuck. Marines still get tattoos of a dog with that slogan underneath.

In World War II, the Marines fought up and down the Pacific. From Guadalcanal to Tarawa, From Saipan to Okinawa.

At the battle of Iwo Jima, foot-by-foot some of the most expensive real estate ever in terms of human life lost, a rag-tag bunch of Marines reached the top of Mount Suribachi. They put a small flag on a pole and tried to plant it in the rocky soil. The wind was heavy, and so several men had to get together for the task.

A photographer for the Associated Press was there to snap the picture. "The flag raising on Mount Suribachi" flashed around the world. Something about it struck a public nerve. The photo won a Pulitzer Prize. Later, a monument was built in Washington, D.C., to honor the flag raising.

After that, the Marines' place in American life was sealed. There were always a few members of Congress who wondered why the United States needed an Army and Marine Corps. They do the same job. They fight with the same equipment. Their uniforms are similar. There was a time when the Marines specialized in amphibious warfare. They still do, but we've seen with recent conflicts that amphibious landings are nothing special. Vertical insertions (from helicopters) are all the rage. That, or driving inland with tanks and Humvees.

But the talk of merging the Army and Marines has never gone anywhere, primarily because of what Harry Truman once called the public relations arm of the Marines. By that, he meant those of us who once wore the uniform.

The Marines fought famously in Korea and Vietnam, even if those wars were not as glamorous as the ones that preceded them. No war ever will be again, I think. Life, and the world, is too complicated.

In any case, young men and women continue to join the Marines and get indoctrinated into the history and lore. I've talked with soldiers and sailors, but none of them has any strong sense of the history of his branch. People know about wars and famous battles, but not with the passion and intensity of Marines. I think part of it is the size of the Corps. It's a small service, running at around 200,000 people at any one time. So it's a close-knit family. And because it was small and vulnerable in the early days, there developed a greater sense of camaraderie, of esprit de corps.

Two guys can meet, and they might mention that they had been in the Army. That might elicit a discussion about the units they served in, or the jobs and training they had. But two former Marines will get animated about it. They might know the same people. In any case, there is an instant bond. It's like a fraternity that way.

## THE BATTALION

The 3rd Battalion, 4th Marine Regiment, was activated on October 1, 1925. They were sent to Shanghai, China, in 1927 and served there as members of the famous "China Marines" until 1934 when the battalion was deactivated. Reactivated in May 1941 the battalion was sent to the Philippines, destination Corregidor. In early May 1942 the 3rd Battalion was lost along with the rest of the 4th Marines with the conquest of "the Rock" by overwhelming Japanese forces.

The battalion rose from the ashes in February of 1944 on Guadalcanal. They fought in the Solomon Islands, Guam, and Okinawa. After the Japanese surrender, the 4th Marines bounced around from brigade to division, spent more time in China, and then deactivated again in 1947.

The regiment was reactivated for the Korean War. They were sent to Japan, then to Korea, and later Hawaii.

During Vietnam, the 4th Marines were made part of the 3rd Marine Division, which is permanently located in Okinawa. The Fourth fought at Hue, Quang Tri, and Khe Sanh. All legendary Marine battles, now taught to young Marines in boot camp.

After Vietnam, the 4th Marines continued to be shuffled around. They were given to the 2nd Marine Division in the early 1980s, and they deployed to the Mediterranean and once again to Korea. A reinforced rifle company helped security forces in Panama in 1988.

And then, in September of 1988, they were deactivated again.

The 3rd Battalion, 4th Marine Regiment, returned to life in 1994 to assume its latest incarnation. The regiment is headquartered in Okinawa, but its three battalions are scattered among other regiments of the 1st Marine Division.

The 3rd Battalion, 4th Marine Regiment, is now the fourth infantry battalion of the 7th Marine Regiment. This is a little difficult to understand from the outside. Normally, a unit is designated by a compound number derived from the battalion and regimental designation. In other words, the 1st Battalion of the 7th Marine Regiment is known as "One-Seven." The 2nd Battalion of the 5th Marine Regiment is known as "Two-Five."

But Three-Four is part of the 7th Marines. From this point on it's just Three-Four.

They live at Twentynine Palms, California, year-round. It's hot, dirty, dusty, and dry. But the base has 900 square miles of sand and rock. So training goes on all the time, and the jets, artillery, tanks, and everything in the arsenal can shoot and blow shit up without concern for neighbors.

## THE COMMANDING OFFICER

Bryan McCoy was 40 when he led his battalion into battle in Iraq.

He was born June 21, 1962, in Norman, Oklahoma.

His father was a career Army officer. He did two tours in Vietnam, and also served at a variety of posts around the world. One of those duty stations was the headquarters of the Strategic Air Command in Bellevue, Nebraska.

McCoy went to high school there. But he's an Oklahoman. When it came time to pick a college, McCoy chose the University of Oklahoma. He also decided he wanted a career in the military.

But McCoy didn't want the bureaucracy and blandness of Army life. He'd gotten hooked on the Marines. They appealed to his sense of adventure. They were tough, and hardcore. He signed up for ROTC (Reserve Officer Training Corps). He was commissioned on May 10, 1984.

After McCoy finished his various officer training, he was assigned to the 3rd Battalion, 5th Marines, in Camp Pendleton in Southern California. He was a rifle platoon commander, and later ran the weapons platoon and the 81 mm mortars platoon. This is where young lieutenants learn how to lead, and start forming opinions about how war can and should be fought.

The military bug struck McCoy hard. He probably should have gone to one of the military academies, Annapolis or West Point. He had that kind of grasp of military history and modern warfare.

In any case, he started down a path that could take him to great heights in the military world. Certainly, he'll wear a star on his collar someday. Maybe several.

After Camp Pendleton, McCoy went to the Marine Barracks in Washington, D.C. This is a plum assignment for a young officer. He gets to meet important people, and his Marines are showcased to high-ranking politicians and visiting dignitaries.

He served first as a platoon commander, and after his promotion to captain, he commanded A Company.

He was there when Saddam Hussein invaded Kuwait in 1990. Because Marines fight, no matter what their normal duties, McCoy took his D.C. Marines to Saudi Arabia and waited for war.

The war came, but it was an air and armor battle. Very few infantry troops were used, other than mop-up. They would have been used extensively if the president had decided to go on into Baghdad. But he didn't. He stopped the fight as the Iraqis were running through the desert, and then he sealed the borders.

But McCoy watched what happened, and he put it all into context. From what he knew of Iraq and the region, he figured it was just a matter of time before he went back. The question was not if, but when.

At least, that's what he told me.

After the war, McCoy went to the School of Amphibious Warfare and then served as company commander with the 8th Marine Regiment in Camp Lejeune, North Carolina. Then there was more hop scotching around the Corps. He was with the 2nd Light Armored Reconnaissance Battalion for a couple of years, and then he was picked to be the Marine Aide to the Chief of Naval Operations in Washington.

Later, he went to the command and staff college. He likes to joke that he went there on a football scholarship.

In July 2001, McCoy was transferred to the 7th Marine Regiment. He served as operations officer while waiting for a battalion command to open up.

On May 30, 2002, less than a year away from the invasion of Iraq, he took command of Three-Four.

In the middle of all this, McCoy was married and had two boys. The marriage did not last

He got married a second time. His wife, Kerry, is an Army officer and West Pointer, who works in medical engineering. She's based in Washington, D.C., and the distance has been a strain. But when McCoy had the opportunity to take command of an infantry battalion, he couldn't say no. Being the commanding officer of an infantry battalion is the pinnacle of a military officer's career, especially if there is a war on. The battalion commander is in the field, and he can actually be in the fight even as he's directing the action. He commands a thousand men, and he's semi-autonomous. He is the lord and king of the battalion and whatever the battalion's mission happens to be.

"It's good to be king," he says.

His radio call sign: Darkside. For reasons that will become clear.

## THE SERGEANT MAJOR

Dave Howell grew up in a middle-class home in a middle-class city: St. Louis. Like a lot of kids, he never really had a handle on what he wanted to do with his life. In high school, he smoked and drank. After high school, he smoked and drank some more. And worked at a factory.

He got laid off, and while looking for work, stumbled upon the Marines. On a whim, he joined up.

Howell is one of those perfect examples of how the Marines will change a man. He thrived on the order and discipline of the Marine

Corps. When other Marines were grumbling about going on forced marches, or running a field exercise, Howell looked forward to more.

He went to the infantry school and soon after he volunteered for Recon. The Marines don't have Green Berets or SEALs or any of that stuff. Their elite units are the reconnaissance battalions. In Recon, you get to go to all the same schools as the SEALs and Green Berets, though. You go to jump school and dive school and jungle warfare training. All the good stuff.

More importantly, Recon usually acts alone. They don't do a lot of the mundane military stuff you find in the regular battalions. They go jumping out of airplanes, spend weeks on land navigation and survival training, and then limp back to base to get ready for more.

That was Howell's world for many years. He got promoted to sergeant, ran his own platoon, and then got promoted again. Howell liked this time in the Marines best. He was at the top of his game, physically and mentally. He was highly trained, motivated, and liked his work.

Later came more stripes. He went to Chicago as a recruiter. Had some success, but recruiting wasn't Howell's passion. He's too blunt, too outspoken. He's like a hard-working father. He's got no time for nonsense, and he can never understand why people don't do what they're supposed to do, when they're supposed to do it.

Howell served in Salt Lake City, on what they call "Inspector and Instructor" duty with a reserve unit. While the reservists came for their weekend drills, Howell and the rest of the I & I staff worked full-time, maintaining equipment, doing paperwork, training, and such.

Howell loves the outdoors and snow country. He likes mountain climbing. So he loved Utah. It had more mountains than he could climb in a lifetime.

With 20 years in the Marines, Howell earned his last stripe. He was a sergeant major. And there is no better job in the Corps.

For one thing, there is no higher enlisted rank. He could become a warrant officer, or even a commissioned officer, but that's not what he's about. He's a professional Marine with the stripes and star of someone who's been around for a while. When he speaks, Marines listen. Especially the young sergeants and lieutenants.

He and McCoy complemented each other perfectly. They both had a sense of mission. They had a mutual passion for hiking, mountain climbing, and working out.

McCoy brought his leadership skills and his perspective on tactics and warfare. Howell is the guy who would make it all happen. His mission was to make sure the commanding officers will and orders were carried out.

His radio call sign: Eyes Two. "Eyes" because he is McCoy's eyes in the field. "Two" because the battalion weapons officer, a warrant officer, already had the call sign "Eyes One."


Three-Four sat out in the desert in 2002, listening to the word out of Washington like the rest of us. Wondering what the War on Terrorism would mean to them. For most people, it's just words. Rhetoric. Something to debate, to support or oppose.

To the Marines, it meant life or death.

McCoy and Howell ran the battalion hard, especially in the last part of the year. As war seemed more and more inevitable, training became all-important. That's the difficulty of being a leader. You lie awake at night and wonder if you've done enough, if you've prepared your troops properly. Because, in your case, people could die if you didn't.

So the Marines were out in the field pretty much all the time. But there was little complaining. The work and training was no longer about the possible, it was about something real and tangible. When they pulled triggers out in the sand, the Marines knew they might well be pulling triggers on flesh-and-blood human beings soon.

Still, despite the urgency and threat, money remained a problem for Marine training. The Marines, because they're the bastard stepchildren of the Defense Department, don't get the money or equipment the Army does. So they have to make do. McCoy had a budget for ammunition. He spent a year's worth of ammo money in a couple of months. He figured that if he was right, and he was about to lead men into battle, they would need the extra training. If he was wrong, he might be in trouble with his superiors. But that wasn't the worst thing that could happen.

As the days ticked by, training rose to a fever pitch. In December, the battalion got the word: They were going to Kuwait with the rest of the 1st Marine Division.

Twentynine Palms and Camp Pendleton turned upside down. Marines scrambled to put their affairs in order. Wills were drawn up, powers of attorney signed, cars sold, wives and kids went back to home-towns, or made sure their housing allowances were enough for them to stay on, or near, base.

The chaplains became very popular.

In mid-January of 2003, the Marines flew to Kuwait City. From there, they were trucked to the middle of the desert, in the north, where Kuwaitis had erected tent cities for their guests.

It was a lot better than the Marines expected. They imagined they would sleep on the ground, in fighting holes, in miserable conditions.

Life was no picnic in Kuwait. The junior enlisted men shared huge tents with wooden floors. They grabbed a spot on the floor, unrolled their sleeping bags, and parked their gear.

Out back was a long row of green portable toilets. The kind that are hard to write on, so there wasn't much graffiti. But the Marines did put up informational posters, like how to spot an Iraqi tank by its shape. And how to avoid land mines. Pleasant reading when you're trying to take a crap.

There were wooden tables behind the toilets, and a trench dug around them. That's where you shaved and got cleaned up in the morn-ing. Take an MRE pouch full of water, set it on the table, and shave. Brush your teeth. Dump the dirty water in the trench. No hot water out there, but it wasn't too bad once you got used to it.

Later, they put up portable showers, and the guys could get a luke-warm shower about once a week.

They ate MREs at first, and later there came mess tents. Usually, they got two hot meals a day.

And training picked up anew. Sandstorms swept the countryside as tanks and trucks rolled over flat terrain of Kuwait.


## HEADING OVER

I left for Kuwait on February 17. Saying goodbye was tough. Jordi cried. He hugged me tightly around the waist and asked me not to go. I almost didn't.

Isabel stepped up. She took Jordi and said everything would be all right. That daddy had a job to do and he would come back soon.

I ran to the cab. I smiled and waved, but inside I was torn up. What was I doing to my son? Would I still be married when this was all over?

Of course, the same scene was being played out all over the United States. Except, most of the fathers and mothers leaving home wore a uniform. And most didn't have the option of saying no. Some did have the opportunity, but went anyway. Because a lot of Marines and soldiers want to go to war. Sometimes for good reasons; sometimes not.

I flew to Kuwait City. We arrived late in the evening. I was bleary-eyed and had no idea where I was going in the airport. I followed a group of people to one immigration line and then another. It took an hour to get to the desk. Finally, I gave my passport, with Kuwaiti visa, to an officer. He took the passport, read it, looked at me and back at the passport. Called a colleague over. And they talked.

"You come with me," he said.

My heart dropped into my stomach. What now? Was there a problem? I started having visions of Pakistan. And a holding cell. The man asked me to have a seat and he took my passport into an office. I sat for a half-hour. Sweating. And then a Kuwaiti man in a uniform came out, gave me my passport and wished me luck.

Twenty minutes later I was at the Crowne Plaza hotel. Four stars. Room service, cable TV. Going to war is nice.

• • •

The troops called Kuwait "The 'Wait." And all we did was wait. And wait. And wait.

The first thing I did was call Joe Plenzler, the division public affairs officer. A couple of days later, Plenzler arranged for me to visit McCoy and the battalion out in the desert.

The camps were in North Central Iraq, about 30 miles from the Iraqi border. If you stood on the northern edge of camp, you could look on the horizon and see for miles. It was dark and foreboding. How many troops were there? How prepared were they? How would the coming apocalypse look?

Marines stood watch out there. Some told stories of dark-skinned men flying by in jeeps and SUVs. Or sometimes they saw special ops guys heading out there to do whatever they did across the border. It was all very mysterious.

I drove out to meet Plenzler at the gate to Tactical Area Coyote. Marines with body armor and fully loaded weapons stood at the gate. There were rolls and rolls of concertina wire, and they searched every person and every vehicle. Every time.

Inside the gate, we headed to Camp Ripper, named after the commanding officer of the 7th Marines, Colonel Steve Hummer. Radio call sign: Ripper.

There I met Simon Robinson and Bob Nickelsburg, a reporter and a photographer from *Time* magazine. They would also be embedding with Three-Four. I was wary at first. Journalists are a territorial bunch. We thrive on competition, but we hate it. Two journalists get together and there's always going to be a lot of sniffing and scratching, trying to figure out whether the other guy is good or bad. Is he likely to steal your story ideas? Or worse, will he write things that you should be writing, and will your bosses call and say, "Why can't you do what so-and-so is doing?"

Simon's a tall lanky Australian who worked out of South Africa. Bob's a thin, wiry New Yorker who'd been shooting overseas in various trouble spots for years.

I wasn't too happy about sharing "my" battalion, but Simon and Bob were pretty cool. And because they worked for a magazine, they weren't really competition for me.

So I let them live. Just kidding.

We stood out in the desert while the Marines piddled around. They're always piddling around, talking on the phone or radio. So you have to wait. It was my first time out in the desert. The land is flat. I mean, table-top flat. Featureless. A khaki-colored land as far as the eye can see.

What there is, is sand.

Not just sand, like beach sand, but a fine, dry, dusty sand that goes everywhere and gets into everything.

It's just one of the reasons they call Kuwait "the big sandbox."

Joe Plenzler dropped us off at the Three-Four headquarters. Lieutenant Eric Gentrup greeted us. Gentrup was the adjutant for the battalion, which means he dealt with legal issues. McCoy gave him the added responsibility of being our guide, our liaison to the Marines.

I liked Gentrup. He was from San Jose, and so a hometown boy for the *Chronicle*. Plus, his father grew up in Nebraska, about 20 miles from my hometown. And Eric went to the University of Nebraska. Had a big Husker flag hanging over his sleeping bag in his tent.

In some units, the commanding officer was so worried about the embedded media, he or she would assign someone to do nothing but watch and take care of the reporters. Not McCoy. He figured we ought to be able to roam freely. I told him once how the Army had assigned a young private to be the "bodyguard" for a colleague of mine. McCoy laughed and said I didn't need a bodyguard. I had a thousand of them, he said. McCoy didn't want to control us. His philosophy was to let us do our jobs and stay out of the way.

It was good to see McCoy again, and Dave. Captain Norton was there, and a handful of Marines I'd met in Twentynine Palms. It was nice to see familiar faces in such an uninviting place.

Eric and Dave Howell got some Marines to put up a four-man tent for me, Simon, and Bob. I spent the weekend talking to people and scoping out the area.

The thing that struck me was the sky. An opaque haze hung there constantly. It was the dust of thousands of Marines swarming the Kuwaiti desert, kicking up an eternal cloud.

Machine guns rattled in the distance, and tanks rumbled and creaked as they drove by. A percussive boom smacked the air as artillery fired real, explosive, cannon shells.

There was no TV, no movies, no snack shop, no grocery store, no beer, and precious few cigarettes.

"We don't have much free time," explained Corporal Richard Scoggins, of Birmingham, Alabama. "We mostly sleep and train."

McCoy said his men were ready, if they were told to go to war. They called it "going north," or "crossing the berm," referring to a built-up earthen line that runs along the Iraqi border.

In addition to all the technical aspects of preparing for war, McCoy and his staff worked on the emotional. McCoy wanted the men to be prepared to kill and maybe to die. He wanted their affairs in order back in the States. Family issues should be resolved. And, more importantly, the Marines should make their peace with God.

"I need them to fight with a happy heart," he said. "They've already asked forgiveness for what they're going to do to the Iraqi army."

Training seemed constant, as squads, fire teams, trucks, and tanks moved from place to place, day and night. One afternoon, rifle squads practiced medical evacuations for wounded Marines. That night, trucks and Humvees moved around the desert to practice driving under black-out conditions.

Nearby, a squad was in the sand, prone, aiming at nothing, pretending the enemy was approaching.

"Dammit, get your fucking muzzle up out of the sand," a sergeant barked at a young private.

Here and there, spaced among the armored personnel carriers, young Marines stood guard. Not training, just watching, their M-16s held ready, as their buddies ran through drills. These were called "Guardian Angels." Something like regular guard duty, but the Marines infused it with a higher calling, protecting your buddies from harm, even from petty theft. *Teamwork* and *togetherness* were the watchwords.

If anyone wanted to go to war, they never said so openly. Most everyone wished the whole Iraqi issue would go away, so they could get home to their families. No one really wanted to go north.

At least, that's the way they present it to the media. In truth, I knew there were some guys who wanted war. It's impossible to know or understand, but there is a Neanderthal instinct in some men. It's what develops the alpha male. He wants to be lord over all he surveys. He wants the women. He wants to dominate. Killing is the ultimate domination. And the ultimate societal taboo. There is only one place on earth where you can kill and get away with it.

But the sentiment for most was, if war is necessary, let's do it and get it over with.

I found Staff Sergeant Ira Taylor of Jacksonville, Florida, sitting atop an Amtrack one afternoon. I asked if I could join him. He said yes, and I climbed up. You could get a good view from up there, even though it was only about 9 feet off the ground.

I asked him about war, and whether some of the guys wanted it too much. He said he heard guys talking about how they want to go to war, but he wondered if it was real.

"Some guys are like 'kill, kill, kill,' but is that what they're really thinking, or is it a confidence-building thing for them?" he wondered.

Taylor wasn't sure there would even be a war.

"I feel that it will [happen] but pray that it won't," he said.

I went around the camp, trying to get a feel for these young Marines. They reminded me of me. When I was young and invincible. Marines are a cocky bunch. They'll tell you what's on their mind. For the most part, I found their morale to be high.

So I wrote my first story with a Kuwait dateline. I spent the evening in the radio shack. There was a table and light in there. When I finished, I opened up my nifty new satellite phone on the trunk of my rental car. I pointed the big rectangular antenna to the south and phoned home. Then, transmitted the story.

Technology is great. This was way better than having to dictate the story, or find a phone somewhere out in the wilderness. With the sat phone, I could call anywhere, any time, and I had instant Internet access.

The story ran on Sunday. Front page. Nice play for a story that basically said, "The Marines are waiting for war."

The next day, Sunday, I saw a couple hundred Marines at a church service in the sand. It seemed especially poignant to me: these men finding faith, or confirming their faith, in the shadow of war.

A popular Catholic priest, Father Bill Devine, started off Mass with the hymn "Be Not Afraid." Later, he asked God to "protect us from men of violence and keep us safe from weapons of hate."

He also prayed for peace. And no war.

Every Marine at the service carried some kind of weapon, and a gas mask. They never went anywhere without them.

Later, at the Protestant service, eight Marines were baptized. A hole had been dug in the sand, and lined with a plastic sheet. It was filled with water to about thigh-deep, and the men climbed in one at a time for immersion baptisms.

Navy corpsman P. J. Dunbar of San Francisco was one of them. He said he didn't believe that killing, in the context of Iraq, was wrong.

"That's just what we have to do," he said. "God can't see it that way (as a sin)."

Bob Grove, the Three-Four chaplain, had been in the chaplain corps for just four months. The 36-year-old from Uniontown, Pennsylvania, decided after September 11 that he should do something for his country. So he went from running a church to ministering to the Marines.

"I have some anxiety myself," he said. "I don't know how I'm going to handle seeing casualties, but God will get me through it."

A few weeks later, Grove would find out.


What I didn't realize at the time, because I'm not that sharp, is that technology would alter the way this war was seen. It was the first Internet war. E-mail was in its infancy in 1990, as was the Web overall.

So while my story might appear on the inky pages of the *Chronicle*, on your doorstep Sunday morning, anyone with an Internet connection could read it online.

The e-mails started flooding in. Wives, parents, husbands, sisters, brothers would run searches for anything having to do with their Marines' units. And so my story popped up. It didn't matter if their Marine was with Three-Four or not. I got messages from parents who just liked reading a story from someone who was in the vicinity of their son or daughter.

It was touching.

*Dear Mr. Koopman, I have been reading your articles yesterday and today in the Chronicle from Tactical Area Coyote, Kuwait. You have no idea how your articles have moved us, brought us to tears, informed us, encouraged us and brought Matt a little closer to us. We miss him and worry about him and wonder constantly what his days must be like. Thanks to you we have had a glimpse into his world, as sad as it is. It has been strangely comforting to read your well written words. We pray for peace and the safety of all of you over there. May you all return home soon. Thank you so much for your articles, be safe and if you see Matt please send him our love. Thanks again.*

*I have a son with the Third Battalion - First Marine Division- India Company - 2nd platoon. If you see him, please tell him that I think of him constantly and that I love him. Thank you for giving me a sense of his life in Kuwait.*

*It seems you're with my husband's unit. If you happen to run across \*\*\*, could you PLEASE tell him that his wife loves him? Thanks. You are the envy of hundreds of lonely wives right now, enjoy it! Give him a pinch for me. And thank you for being there, we appreciate you!*

There are a thousand men, more or less, in a Marine infantry battalion. The most feared, respected, loved, and hated man is the sergeant major.

He is the senior enlisted man in the battalion. There are nine enlisted ranks in the military and ten officer ranks. Enlisted starts with private, then private first class, and lance corporal. Those are the young guys, the ones who do most of the fighting and dying in war.

Then come the noncommissioned officers, the corporals and sergeants. The higher-ranking sergeants add "rockers," semicircular stripes, beneath their sergeant stripes when they get promoted. A staff sergeant has three stripes up and one rocker underneath. A gunnery sergeant has two.

The sergeant major has four rockers. A sergeant major typically has served 20 or so years and been in units around the globe.

A Marine sergeant major provides order and discipline among the enlisted ranks, and he teaches lieutenants about life in the Corps.

I thought Dave Howell was the perfect sergeant major.

He has a bullet-shaped head and a thick chest. He seems taller than he is because he yells so much. He can chew up and spit out a misbehaving private one minute and tell a dirty joke the next.

Howell liked to come over to the reporters' tent in the evening, after everything had settled down. And fuck with us. He'd tease Simon about his girlfriend. And when I say "tease," what I mean is, ask him about sex. Dave, like everyone, had gone without for a long time.

Or he'd offer suggestions on gear. What to carry, how to carry it. Or tell stories. Howell could tell raunchy stories about ex-girlfriends better than anyone. His stories of dating Mormon women in Utah were hysterical.

Most of his stories are unprintable, or the people in them could be identified. But the funniest ends with the line: "Peg leg? What peg leg?"

You had to be there.

What I started to see in Dave was a depth, a complexity that I wouldn't have guessed from our previous encounter. He was a tough guy, from solid Midwestern roots, but he was incredibly smart. And well-read. I don't think he liked people to know, but he read the *Atlantic Monthly* and *Vanity Fair*. Much later, I came upon his bunk and found Cervantes' *Don Quixote* and Dante's *Inferno*.

I started hanging out more with Dave. I liked Simon and Bob a lot, but sometimes I wanted to get away from journalists. McCoy was always busy. Dave was, too, but his tent was nearby, and he always had a stool where I could sit and bullshit with him.

*It is such a treat for me to hear from you. Even though we've never met, knowing that you have been in the same place as \*\*\* gives me something tangible to hold on to. And I must tell you that you have become quite the topic of conversation back here on base. I've heard that you are getting quite a few emails from grateful Marine wives.*

*You're our new best friend! Maybe you don't believe me, but I'm being honest when I tell you that your articles are like manna from Heaven for us. Your hard work and kind words are giving more comfort and hope to a group of worried wives than you will ever know.*

*I'm sure you've heard the saying that in the Marine Corps we take care of our own. Well, as long as you're with 3/4, suffering and enduring and working alongside our husbands and friends you are one of ours. So if there is anything you need, please let me know. You'd be amazed at how resourceful and creative a military spouse can be!*

*Thank you again for being there and for reminding the nation that this conflict is not just a topic of debate, that it is not some abstract intellectual exercise. Thank you for reminding them that there are real men over there, real men who are putting their lives on the line because they want to serve their country.*

*It was kind of you to offer to look up my husband, but I know you must be terribly busy and finding one marine at Camp Coyote must be like looking for a needle in a cammied up haystack. If you do, maybe he'll show you a picture of our baby girl. He's such a proud Daddy.*

In the middle of all this, I'm trying to figure out how to cover the war. The point of embedding is to get reporters as close to the action as possible. But what does that mean as a practical matter? Ride in the lead vehicle? In the last? Go with a squad of Marines? What if the squad never sees any action? You could have some great personal stories, but not about combat.

And there is the question of safety. Go up front and expose yourself, but get a better story? Or hold back and interview Marines after the fact?

I'm looking at Kilo Company and thinking I should ride with them.

The battalion has been reconfigured for this conflict. Normally, there are three rifle companies. In Three-Four, there's Kilo, India, and Lima. Lima has been "traded" to the 1st Tank Battalion, so they can have infantry support for whatever tank battles they may have. Under the circumstances tank battles are considered quite likely.

In exchange, a company of tanks, Bravo Company, has been given to McCoy.

The tanks will see the most action, but it's hard to ride with them.

You'd have to be inside the tank, assuming there was an extra seat, and you couldn't see much outside.

Of the two rifle companies, Kilo is considered the best. The toughest. Kickass Kilo, they call themselves.

But Simon and Bob are talking about going with Kilo. So where does that leave me?

I sat down with Dave Howell and asked him about it.

He said McCoy would figure out who goes with whom. But that it looked like Simon and Bob would go with Kilo. I said I wasn't sure how close I wanted to get. I have an 8-year-old son I'd like to survive to see. But I want to do the right thing.

What about riding with Howell?

"No way," he said. "I'm going to be wherever the worst of the fighting will be. You don't want to be there. No one rides with me."

Well, shit. I have no idea what to do.

But it's time to go back to the hotel, anyway. More journalists have to cycle in and out of the camps, and I've had my time. It's just as well. I'd rather have room service while waiting for the war to start. Better than sitting in the dirt. Plenty of time for that later.

*My son, \*\*\*, is in the 3rd Bat 4th Marines out of 29 Palms, so he must be around you there somewhere!!! If you run across him, tell him his mama loves him and says hello! Thanks and have a great day!!!*

In Kuwait City, the military set up a press office at the Hilton Hotel. What a perfect excuse to move into the Hilton. The hotel was on the beach at the extreme south end of the city. It was beautiful. Palm trees and white sand outside. A pool. Marble bathrooms. Cable TV. High-speed Internet access.

There wasn't a lot to do. I wrote a story about Kuwait, and the Kuwaitis' reaction to the military buildup. Kuwait is a beautiful city.

Reminds me a lot of Los Angeles. Multilane freeways. Palm trees. Sunny and hazy. Nice cars.

Kuwait is oil-rich, and the citizens live well. One joke going around among reporters was, "Kuwaitis drive their Mercedes' until they run out of gas and then buy a new one."

That's not far from the truth. The good news for us American types was that the place was full of Burger Kings and Kentucky Fried Chickens. Starbucks had a concession at the Hilton.

The only problem, and it was a huge problem, was that Kuwait was dry as a bone. Not a drop of liquor could be found. The best thing for a journalist was to get invited to a party at the CNN room. They knew how to smuggle in booze in their camera equipment.

As February drew to a close, hundreds of reporters descended on the city. Friends from media boot camp showed up. We shared cabs to go to hardware stores and sporting goods stores to get supplies for our grand camping trip.

By now, I was getting flooded with e-mails from mothers and wives of Marines. There were some fathers, some brothers, but mostly it was mothers. There's something about the mother/son bond, especially when a war is at hand.

Brenda Freeman started a Yahoo group devoted to the families of Three-Four Marines. It still exists. She wrote me about her son, Eric, a young private first class. And I stayed in touch.

I wrote a story about how parents in general, but mothers specifically, worry about their loved ones.

"There are times when I feel like I can't breathe," Brenda told me. "I find myself doing meaningless things when I have other things that need to be done. I just can't get this out of my mind."

"I'm really, really proud of him," she said. "He's doing something incredibly difficult, and he's not complaining about the possibility of having to go to war.

"He's a thoughtful kid, very loving," she said, her voice lowering a bit. "He's everything I knew he could be."

Diane Carrington was the last one in her family to find out her son was shipping out to Kuwait. He knew it would hurt her.

"A lot of different things are going on in my mind," she said. "I'm concerned for him, and I'm worried for all the other moms and families out there. There's a lot of hardship when a Marine deploys."

She said it was easier for him to go to Kuwait than for her to let him go.

"He's been trained," she said. "I haven't."

And the e-mails kept coming. They were poignant and endearing.

"In case you should run into him please tell him that his parents are very proud of him and all the other service men over there," wrote one mother. "We miss and love him very much and are praying for him for a speedy return home."

A father wrote: "Should circumstances bring you face to face with my sons you might remind them that they are uppermost in our thoughts, profoundly missed and for us life starts and stops with the murmurs of war."

Stephanie Hildy of Morris, Illinois, had a 19-year-old son in the Marines: Ryan Kennelly.

"War is very different for a mom," she said. "We gave birth.

"You teach them and they grow up and you have to let them go."

Hildy also spoke of the "overwhelming pride" she feels for her son for being willing to fight for his country. But that pride comes with a lot of worry. "I've worn my floors out praying," she said.

Steve Matthews of Las Vegas wrote messages about his son that really choked me up.

"I know this sounds morbid, but I am not very confident he will return home alive, if we go to war with Iraq," he wrote in an e-mail.

"If I am one of the fortunate fathers to welcome home his brave warrior son," he wrote, "it will be a tender time with warm embraces, tears of joy, and words of gratitude to the almighty, and I am not sure I will let him out of my grasp for a very long time."

It got so that I was spending a couple hours a day responding to e-mails. But I had to do it. I felt like it was my duty.

• • •

I wrote to Isabel, and to Jordi, almost every day. And I called. I didn't talk to Jordi every time. It was too difficult. For both of us. When we did talk, I'd hear his little voice and I'd get choked up. He got a little emotional sometimes. He asked when I was coming home. And he told me to be careful.

"Are you scared?" he asked once.

"No, buddy, everything is fine. I have all the Marines taking care of me."

"Come on, Dad. You can tell me the truth. I can handle it."

My boy was growing up.

Isabel was my link to my family during this time. She had to be, because I did them wrong, too. Before I left for Kuwait, I called my parents and told them I was going to cover the war. But I totally punked out. I said I was going to be in the region, and cover the fighting from the rear. From the headquarters in Kuwait, or some other country. At one point, my father read something about embedding and said he was glad I wasn't going to do that. I lied and said, "Yeah, don't worry about that." And that's how I left it. I'm not proud of this at all. I just couldn't bring myself to tell them the truth. Possibly because it meant having to face some hard facts myself. But, mostly, I just didn't want to worry them. So I took the coward's way out.

I have to stop doing that.

So I didn't call my mom or dad from Kuwait. I would tell Isabel what was going on, and she passed the news on to my folks. Mom and Dad are divorced, so it took two calls.

Once, when she was talking to my father, he mentioned me and said, "I guess a man's got to do what a man's got to do."

"No," she corrected him, rather firmly I understand. "A man doesn't have to do what a man has to do. A man has to take care of his family."

But she wasn't giving me a hard time anymore. She had accepted that I was going to cover the war. Even if she didn't agree with it.

. . .

*Thank you for writing about us and our love for our sons. It was said by someone that I don't recall the name but it went something like this, Once you become a mother your heart no longer is in your body. It lives outside of your body and your heart is your children. This I find is very true. So, as mothers, our hearts are in Kuwait and you are so blessed to be with our hearts Mr. Koopman and also in our prayers for your safe return also.*

*I just have to throw this in. . . . If you see my heart tell him Happy Birthday it will be March 12. He is \*\*\* with India.(assault) OOOOOHRAAAAAH I am very proud of him!*

*Have a wonderful day!*

Every morning I went down to the media center to check for updates, messages, anything important about the start of the war. The clock kept ticking down. The president kept talking about war. It all seemed so inevitable. Theoretically, Saddam Hussein could have done something to stop it, or President Bush could have. But you had 130,000 troops massed in Kuwait. They were like a loaded gun, and the president had cocked it. All that remained was for the trigger to be pulled.

The military public affairs people held daily, off-the-record briefings. I always liked those. They would start by asking everyone to turn off their cell phones. Seconds later, phones would ring and ring and ring. Reporters hate to take orders.

Joe Plenzler became a legend in those briefings. He was so blunt and so tough. Not like most public affairs people. Definitely not like the Army. One day, a reporter asked about access to the troops and fighting, once the invasion started. How close would we come to the fighting? What might we see?

"Sir, if you want to be there with the Marines when they're sticking bayonets into hearts, you're welcome to it," he said. A shocked silence followed.

Joe had a tendency to speak his mind, something most of us loved. But he could scare the shit out of you, too. The discussion turned to equipment and gear. The question among reporters was, should you dress more or less like a soldier, or try to stand apart, to identify more as a noncombatant?

"Well sir, I'll just tell you what my first sergeant used to say about things like this, on the battlefield," Joe responded. "If it looks different, kill it."

As it happened, the question became moot. With the threat of chemical or biological weapons, the military issued every reporter a gas mask and chemical protective suit. So we would all dress alike, whether we wanted to or not.

The suits were charcoal-lined and came in woodland or desert camouflage. In typical military fashion, the Marines went to Kuwait with their desert camouflage uniforms, but were given woodland camouflage chemical suits. The Army, which always has the best of everything, had the latest suits, in desert cammo.

The Army gave me a protective suit, so mine was desert cammo. Which meant I stood out among the Marines. Joe's comment kept going through my head.

So there we were, a couple hundred reporters and photographers lining up to get our protective gear. You had the charcoal-lined pants and matching jacket with hood. You had rubber boots, like galoshes, and rubber gloves. The ensemble was completed with a rubber gas mask.

We spent the afternoon learning how to put everything on and how to operate with it.

This was no easy task. It's not like getting dressed. You have to put things on in order, so that the top overlaps the bottom, drawstrings pulled tight. Boots laced or snapped.

You had to get the correct fit with the mask. No beards or you wouldn't get a proper seal with the mask around your face. You'd pull on the mask, hold it in place, and blow air out. Then suck in to make sure the mask held firm with no leaks.

The mask had a small tube you could grab with your lips on the inside, and insert into a canteen outside. Which meant we all had to have the proper canteen caps, otherwise you'd just die of dehydration in that suit.

The eyepieces were just clear plastic. And the mask was too tight to allow you to wear glasses. So if you needed glasses—and everyone did—you had to buy glass inserts with your prescription.

We learned how to put on the mask in nine seconds. I had been through this before, so it was no big thing. But some people freaked out. At least one reporter quit the whole program because the chemical protective stuff was too much. And it would be for many people. Those instructors would talk about how to clear vomit from your mask, if you should upchuck inside of it.

They also taught us about various chemical and biological agents we might face. They gave us syringes of chemicals to counteract nerve gas. You had to jam that needle into your thigh. Twice if you got a good dose. You'd probably froth at the mouth and quiver, and you still might die a slow, horrible death. But it was your only chance.

This war shit was getting complicated.

About the same time, the military offered us inoculations for anthrax and small pox. There was some concern over side effects, but I got both shots anyway. I wanted to be prepared.

Finally, I trucked all this gear to my room and tried to figure out how to pack it all. That might have been the most difficult decision we had before the war: what to take and how to carry it? They told us we would be riding in a vehicle, but you still had to be able to carry all your stuff at one time.

I had a big backpack. It was stuffed full and weighed more than 100 pounds. And I had a smaller pack that contained my laptop, satellite phone, and assorted cables and cords.

I had no idea how I was going to lug all that stuff.

*If, by any chance, you encounter my son \*\*\* please tell him that we are thinking about him constantly and love him very much.*

And then, we waited for the final embed lists. Who was going with which unit. I knew I was supposed to go with McCoy's Marines, but I spent enough time in the Corps to know things don't always go as planned.

But my worries were unfounded. The list came out, and I got what I wanted. Which is more than I can say for a lot of reporters. The Pentagon wanted journalists with units all over the theater. That meant frontline combat units as well as supply and maintenance companies far to the rear.

But most reporters didn't understand the military organization, and didn't know there would be such a huge difference. So they hadn't planned ahead, and found a good unit.

Oh, the screeching and pleading when the list came out. Reporters assigned to helicopter maintenance units demanded to go with elite special forces. People assigned to go with the fuel trucks stuttered and stammered. Simon and I laughed. We knew we had it made.

What we didn't know was if our choice was to prove fatal?

On March 11, I checked out of the Hilton and dragged my gear to the parking lot. More than 100 reporters and photographers were out there, waiting to get on a dozen buses that would take us to the desert.

I had my two packs, Kevlar helmet, and 20 pounds of body armor strapped to my chest. The only luxury I allowed myself was a small folding chair I bought in the Kuwait City Ace Hardware store.

We drove to one camp, spent the night and moved on. The buses dropped people off along the way. Finally, Simon, Bob, and I found ourselves in the dirt next to McCoy's tent.

"Gentlemen, welcome to paradise," he said.

We met the fourth embedded reporter in our group: Gary Scurka. Gary was a producer/reporter for *National Geographic* television. He had hundreds of pounds of camera and sound equipment. I felt sorry for him. All I really needed was a pen, notebook, and phone.

We set up in the reporters' tent. And waited for war.

Rumors run rampant. When you're wondering if you're going to war, and you don't know when, you look for any and all signs. If a general shows up, what does that mean? If the air is suddenly filled with aircraft, does that signify that an air war is imminent?

The rumor mill gets so rampant, a lot of people refuse to believe anything. And some have fun with it.

Take J. Lo.

One day, I was in the chow tent and a couple of young Marines stopped to ask me if what they had heard was true. Was Jennifer Lopez dead? Rumor had it she was killed in a car accident and that her boyfriend, Ben Affleck, was in a coma.

I told them I had heard nothing of it, but would check. I saw nothing on the Internet when I checked later, and shrugged it off.

Two days later, I was in the chow line with a couple of senior sergeants. Staff Sergeant Jack Coughlin was laughing about a practical joke he and his buddies had started, telling people that J. Lo was dead. Killed in a car accident. That Ben Affleck was in jail for vehicular manslaughter. And they were about to punch it up by saying Matt Damon planned to cryogenically preserve her body.

But people started to pay more attention to rumors as the weekend came around. Everyone knew that the president was meeting in the Azores with other allied leaders, and everyone expected some kind of news to come out of it.

So they watched and waited, looking for activity around camp, and in the air. None materialized, other than the increased frequency of chemical attack drills. Then, later in the evening came word about a general's comments regarding the start of the air war.

Some discounted it, but others thought the timing seemed about right, because they expected the president to announce Monday night that war would soon commence.

Nothing, of course, could be confirmed.

But I did hear a rumor earlier in the day. Someone said Ted Danson had been killed.

*Thank you so much for your coverage of 3rd Bn 4th Marines, your articles give me good insight on what my husband must be experiencing. If you get the chance, please tell him his wife misses him terribly and loves him very much and is awaiting his return. He's a tank mechanic, \*\*\*, now attached with 3/4. Also, thanks for helping to keep track of rumors! My husband actually wrote and asked if it's true that Al Pacino died in a car accident. Well, yes, as the character he plays in the new movie Insomnia! Well, anyway thanks for your writing and thanks for your time, and be careful and safe!*

It's 4 a.m. Kilo Company is getting up. Their tents are near the reporters' tent, called a "hootch," so when the company gunny starts rousting people, you know it.

Kilo is going on a five-mile march this morning. First Sergeant Jim Kirkland has invited the reporters to go along. I'm thinking, five miles: I can march that far.

Except the company commander, Captain Kevin Norton, likes surprises. War is full of them, he reasons. So, then, must be training.

In the predawn dark, we start off on a fast walk, everyone wearing flak jackets, helmets, weapons, and ammunition. Norton is at the front of the column. After a half-mile, he breaks into a run. The grunts shake their heads, give a loud "Oooh-rah!" and they're off.

The infantry types dig this stuff. Less so with the tank crews and the guys who drive the armored personnel carriers. They don't spend that much time on the ground.

The column moves like an accordion as people slow down and then speed up.

Someone starts singing "Highway to Hell," and there are laughs. Except from the guys sucking wind.

First Sergeant Kirkland runs up and down the line, shouting encouragement to some and threatening others if they should dare to drop out.

Machine gunners and mortar men have it worst. They have to carry heavy tripods and gun tubes. Some have to pass off their weapons to a buddy, but that comes at a price. They are hooted and shunned until they take back their loads.

We leave the camp and we're now out in the sand. Norton slows the pace to a walk, and some sigh with relief. It doesn't last long. After another half-mile, Norton breaks into a trot. It's lighter now, and we can see the camp to one side and nothing but open sand to the other. Across that wide expanse, everyone knows, is Iraq.

We run and then we walk. Run and then walk. Run. Walk. Norton growls at the people behind him to keep up. He's carrying all his gear, but it's not enough. As we pass by an abandoned sentry post, he snatched up a sand bag and tosses it over his shoulder. He needs some extra weight.

I'm running just a few yards behind Norton. I don't have a weapon, just my notebook and a handful of pens. And I don't have to carry a full load of equipment and ammunition like the Marines. Just my helmet and body armor, which are bad enough. The armor bounces and chafes as we run, the sweat seeps into the raw wounds and burns. Sometimes we go through thick sand; it's like running in molasses. I want to quit and go get some breakfast, but I'm not going to stop or fall back. I don't want the Marines to see me like that.

I don't know what happened to Simon, Bob, and Gary. They've fallen back, and are interspersed in the long column. Every once in a while, I have a huffing and puffing chat with whichever Marine is running alongside me. I meet a young lieutenant, and ask where he went to school. The University of Nebraska, he says.

Small world.

The company works its way around the entire camp over a period of about an hour and then makes a right onto the main road into camp just after sunup. As other Marines come out of their hootches and prepare for chow, Kilo Company is running past, drenched in sweat, singing cadence.

"The guys love that stuff," Norton says with a grin. "They want everyone to know who's the toughest."

Back at the Three-Four tents, Kilo has a morning formation. Then Norton calls his men around him and gives a pep talk. He talks about motivation, training, preparedness, and war.

"All it takes is one guy over there in a fox hole with a machine gun who decides to make a stand," he says. "One motivated individual can hurt you if you're not prepared, if you're not thinking, all the time."

Later, at an Iraqi city known as Al Kut, that lesson will be learned the hard way.

*Thanks so much for the offer to say hi to my son. If you happen to find him on March 4, you may as well say "Happy Birthday," too! He will be 20. He likes to say that he will be a combat veteran before he is old enough to buy a beer, which is all too true! His name is \*\*\* and he's a machine gunner with Kilo. If you do see him, tell him his mom says she wants him to come home and be an accountant. Then he'll know you really talked with me because we've had a running joke about that for a long time. If there is one thing he would never choose to be, it is an accountant! He's a perfect Marine, and even though I worry, I feel good about his choice. Today (the 25th) is his one-year anniversary in the Corps. Geez, pardon me for running on and on, but that's a risk you take when you ask a mom to talk about her son!*

• • •

Normally, when warriors prepare to do battle they build up an intense hatred for their enemy. It's hard to kill another human being without it.

But in the desert of Kuwait, as U.S. troops prepared for a possible battle with Iraqi forces, a different emotion seemed to be taking hold: pity.

There were no derogatory names for the Iraqis. At least, not openly. The only name I heard for Iraqis, and indeed Kuwaitis, was "Haji." It's a word for Muslims who make the pilgrimage to Mecca, called "the Haj." From what I remember, it was the name of Johnny Quest's sidekick.

It's not like the term "gook" they used in Vietnam. Gook was always derogatory. In every context, Haji didn't have the same meanness associated with it. There was no invective in it. I suppose there was at times. But no one used it that way around me. I never heard "Sand Nigger" or "Towel Head" either. But most Marines knew when the reporter was around.

A lot of Marines told me they had nothing against the Iraqis. They said they were there to do a job, to liberate Iraq and get rid of Saddam Hussein. Nothing personal against the troops who might fight back.

"We're trying to instill in them that there is no sense of triumphalism in this," McCoy told me.

Perhaps it's because the Iraqis rolled over last time around. Perhaps it's because the U.S. forces were not trying to evict an invader, as they were last time around.

One training exercise was a case in point. The Marines do a lot of "round robin" training, going from classes on first aid to gunnery to loading helicopters. And one of their classes was in Arabic.

They were taught how to talk to prisoners of war, how to say "drop your weapon" and "do you need medical attention." From the Marines came an occasional wisecrack, like "how do you tell them to shut the hell up?" But then one voice came out of the back.

"How do you say, 'It's Okay. You're safe?'"

If anything, there is concern that the troops are a little too dismissive of the Iraqis because of their routing in the first Gulf War.

"I know a lot of guys say 'they ran before and they'll run again,' but that kind of thinking worries me," said Lance Corporal. Jeremy Davis, a 23-year-old Amtrack crewman. "What if they don't?"

Everyone in camp carried a gun. Everyone. Everywhere. If they weren't armed, they were within sight of someone who was, and who was specifically watching over them.

Part of it is the possible war. The Marines want their men, and women, to constantly have their weapons ready. Part of it is the threat of a terrorist act. A couple of Marines were shot and killed by a Kuwaiti early in the deployment, and there have been other attacks on U.S. troops.

Everyone carried an M16-A2 rifle with 30 rounds of ammunition. And the officers and senior enlisted men had 9 mm pistols, too.

"If someone would attack this place, the best thing to do, if you're a Marine, is hit the deck," one officer told me, "because there will be eight hundred 18-year-olds with itchy trigger fingers firing like mad. You just want to get out of the way."

Occasionally, there was an accidental discharge. A couple of soldiers and Marines were hit by gunfire. Everyone knew the story of the Marine whose rifle went off, and the bullet zipped through several tents, but miraculously hit no one.

Meanwhile, the guns went everywhere. When the Marines ran in the morning, they carried their rifles. When they went to the chow hall, they took their guns. When they went to the portable toilets, the weapons were right there with them.

One day, McCoy called the embedded reporters together for a briefing. We talked about reporting and security and all sorts of things related to embedding. And then Dave Howell announced assignments.

Gary from *National Geographic* would ride with India Company. He'd be in an armored assault vehicle, the AAVs called Amtracks.

Simon and Bob would ride with Kilo. Also in Amtracks.

"John, you'll ride with the Main," Dave said. "You'll be safe there."

I felt totally deflated. I was not going to witness combat.

A Marine battalion covers a lot of ground on the battlefield. They're led by tanks, and the platoons of the rifle companies. The infantry ride in the Amtracks, and dismount to fight. To the rear of that is the tactical center. All the intelligence and operations officers, and forward air observers who call in air strikes. They ride in Amtracks, too. To the rear of them is the Main. The supply vehicles, communications, and logistical support.

Going with the Main meant I could hear the battle, and listen to it over the radio. And later I could go talk to the people involved. It was a nice, safe place to be, and I wouldn't get killed. Any sane person would love it.

I hated it.

Once again, I was letting my personal fears override my passion to get a great story.

But I didn't say anything. Not then. I figured I would check things out, see how it all worked out, and try to come up with a plan.

*Dear John,*

*I have followed some of your informational articles on Kuwait as it appears you are traveling with someone of great importance to me. I had pondered the idea of sending you an email in the past however dismissed the idea because I was concerned about the appropriateness of the matter. In a recent article you noted that other people had sent you such mail in hopes that you would pass a long a simple "hello" or "you are in our thoughts and prayers" to the people that you may come in contact with on a daily basis. I too would like to ask that favor. Knowing what to think back home has become very difficult. You read so much of the coverage and wonder where to draw the line between fact and fiction. The delay in mail time also makes it difficult to deal with "the unknown." I am finding the letters I am sending to your camp are taking between 7 and 14 days. The return letters are getting to me in about 3 to 4 weeks. I scour the web and news constantly to catch bits and pieces of what you are all living with on a daily basis. I give you so much credit for having the courage and will to place yourself in such an uncertain area in such an uncertain time. I wish you all of the best. I thank you for bringing to loved ones that little bit of hope at the end of a day of concern and worry.*

*Cpl. \*\*\* is part of the Marines you are touring with. He is the better half of my soul and it appears he is there with you. If you do come in contact with him would you please tell him that I love him and I miss him dearly. We are all at home praying for him and waiting for the day that he can be back here with us again. We all love him and are so proud of him.*

On March 15, we went to sleep knowing that the president would address the nation the next morning about 4 a.m. Kuwait time. At 5 a.m., I woke to the sound of a camp coming apart.

The president had given Saddam Hussein 48 hours to leave town. War was imminent.

Duffel bags were filled and packs readjusted. Canteens topped off. Humvees gassed. The tent city looked like a beehive hit by a broomstick.

Everyone had a solemn look. Camp was over. People shook hands, nodded, gave each other a "good luck" and "stay safe." Then they parted to make final equipment and weapons checks before going to the fight.

Someone started a bonfire in a pit. Everything that wasn't going north went into the pit. Books, extra clothing, letters. You didn't want to take a letter from home because the enemy might find it if you were captured or killed. They would know your address; they could send letters to your family, or whatever.

Some guys took finished letters and tucked them into their packs, or gave them to friends. These were the "death letters." Messages to wives, kids, parents. Telling them whatever they needed to say in what might be their final hours on earth. No one shared those letters, and I didn't ask to see them. Some things you just don't do.

In mid-afternoon, McCoy calls a battalion formation. The companies gather in a U shape around an Amtrack with its back ramp half down and parallel to the earth, a couple feet high. The sergeant major orders the companies to attention, turns and salutes McCoy. The C.O. jumps onto the ramp of the Amtrack. "At ease!" he barks, then calls the men over to circle around him.

McCoy looks at his men. There's a good chance some won't come back. Maybe a lot won't. He has practiced this speech for weeks.

It is, perhaps, the most important thing he will ever say.

"You're ready," he says, nodding. "You've trained hard."

He tells the men to expect fear. "That's normal," he says. "Accept it. Just know you're not out there alone. These will be some of the most memorable days in your lives. Friends you make here will be friends for life. He will be your brother forever."

McCoy talks about the battalion's first mission. They're going to Basra, to engage an entire mechanized division, the Iraqi 51st. Which means they're going against tanks and infantry. Intelligence indicates thousands of soldiers in the division, though no one knows if it's at full strength. Still, the reports suggest the battalion might be outnumbered 6-to-1. Maybe 8-to-1.

"We're going to slaughter the 51st Mechanized Division," McCoy says. "We're going to kill them and make an example out of them. If other Iraqi units see what happens to them, they might just go ahead and surrender."

It will not be a fair fight, he says.

"My idea of a fair fight is clubbing baby harp seals. We will hit them with everything we have."

McCoy reads a message from the commanding general of the 1st Marine Division, Jim Mattis, who talks about the reasons for war, about Saddam Hussein, and the weapons of mass destruction. The general reminds the Marines that the Iraqi people are not the enemy, that the Marines are not to think of themselves as invaders.

The general urges the men to remain sharp, and be smart. "Engage your brain before you engage your weapon," he writes.

"Be the hunter, not the hunted."

In this war, maybe more so than others, the military worries about atrocities. The Marine Corps has its own hymn, and there's a line in it: "Keep our honor clean." Do that, McCoy says.

And then it's over. Darkside jumps off the armored vehicle. The battalion goes back to work. Gear is stowed. Weapons oiled. In the midday heat, someone cranks up a boombox, loud, to the metal song "Hells Bells."

Late in the afternoon, vehicles move out. North. It's a long line, and it takes forever for all the tanks, trucks, Amtracks, and Humvees to split.

I've been assigned a seat in the communications officer's Humvee. It's loaded with radio gear and I can listen to orders and conversations. We're the last ones out of camp, though, which means we sit and sit and sit while every other vehicle in the battalion moves out. A plume of smoke rises from the bonfire pit. We stop by the headquarters company tent. There are thousands of bottles of water in there. They just couldn't take them all.

It's getting late, and I'm getting nervous. We're on the brink of war.

Finally, around nightfall, we move out. The moon is full, and it's chilly outside. I wrap my light Goretex jacket around me and nod off as we bump along the sandy road.

We reach the main tactical center late, maybe midnight. The moon is still out, but there are no lights anywhere. We're under strict blackout conditions.

I get out my sleeping bag and stretch out next to the Humvee.

In the morning we move again. And again. Closer to the border. The Marines are setting up the division for a coordinated attack as soon as they get the word to go.

We're a couple of miles south of Iraq, next to Highway 80, which leads to the Kuwait border town of Abdaly. At night, we see cars driving down the road.

"You think those people would shit themselves if they knew what was out here?" asks Warrant Officer Gene Coughlin, better known as Gunner.

A Marine infantry battalion has enough firepower to level a small city.

Bravo Company has 15 M1A1 Abrams battle tanks. The battalion also has a platoon of Amtracks to carry Marine infantry. The AAVs (Assault Amphibian Vehicles) are about 8 feet tall and 20 feet long and can carry 20 Marines. They are tracked vehicles and can roll along at 40 miles per hour on a hard surface. They're larger than the Army's Bradley Fighting Vehicles, carry more men, but have less armor and firepower. The AAV has a turret with two guns, a .50-caliber machine gun and a 40 mm automatic grenade launcher.

The battalion has combat engineers, mortars, scout vehicles with .50-caliber machine guns in turrets, and anti-tank missiles.

They have forward air observers and artillery officers who can call in fire from jets, helicopter gunships, or the big 155 mm howitzers that are usually just on the other side of the horizon.

The Marines hear about SCUD missiles being fired on Kuwait, and early in the day hear the sound of artillery coming from the north. Word was, the sound was that of Iraqi artillery being zeroed in. When the invasion started, those rounds would be aimed at us.

Marine artillery got permission to fire "counter-battery" salvos. Throughout the day, the sound of thunder rolled across the desert as the high-explosive rounds exploded in Iraq.

Before the battle, the Marines were mostly calm, and ready to go.

"It's kind of like game day," Eric Gentrup said. "We made the team and we practiced and practiced and practiced. This is our Super Bowl."

Still, he said, people are understandably a little nervous. "They're getting jacked up," he said. "The adrenaline is flowing."

In the dusk that night, McCoy gathers his officers for a briefing. He reminds them to be leaders. That their conduct in battle would be important to their men. "When things are at their worst, you need to be seen the most," he says.

He points to the sun, setting behind the veil of a fine dust mist. "Look at that sunset," he says. "Remember it. That might be the last sunset some people see."

Then he grins, and quotes a line from the Bill Murray comedy about Army life called *Stripes*.

"Lighten up, Francis."

# CHAPTER 5

# INVASION

**W**e waited in the desert for the war to start. A sand storm kicked up. Visibility was 20 feet. Sand and dust and dirt got into every crevice, every weapon, food and water. Marines put up camouflage netting over the Amtracks, but I couldn't figure how anyone could see them in the swirling sand.

I was still thinking of asking to ride with Kilo. But I saw that Simon and Bob were stuck in the back of an Amtrack, where it's hot, loud, and cramped. They couldn't see anything when they were moving down the road. And I was still thinking of my safety. Amtracks are big targets for an Iraqi with an RPG (rocket-propelled grenade). And I was pretty sure that aluminum armor would open up like a can of Spam if it took a hit.

Then it occurred to me: ride with McCoy. Darkside had his own Humvee. He wasn't tied to the tactical center. He rides around the battlefield. He's got radios. I can listen to what's going on, and ask him questions as the need arises.

I told Eric Gentrup about my request and he passed it on. A little while later, McCoy came over to where I was enjoying a delicious MRE.

"You sure you want to ride with me?" he asked. "It could get pretty hairy."

"You're not going to let anything happen to me," I said. "Think of your career."

McCoy laughed. "Don't worry, I'll get promoted if I get one of you knocked off."

"Listen," I said. "I don't want to be in anyone's way. I just thought it would be a good place to ride, if you have the room."

"That's no problem. I'm happy to have you. Take your gear over and tell Monge you're coming with us."

And for the first time, I felt good about my plans. I wasn't going to see Marines sticking bayonets in hearts, but I would be close to the action. I could get a good story.

I'm picking up my stuff and starting to move, and I see McCoy talking to the XO.

"I'll never get shot," he says. "People will get killed all around me, but I'll never get hit."

"Aw, shit. The way it works is, people get killed around *me*. I'm charmed. Not you."

But I took my gear to his vehicle. His driver, Corporal Omar Monge, cleared space in the back for me. The way it worked was, Monge drove, McCoy sat in the front passenger seat next to a couple of vehicle-mounted radios. Lance Corporal Garfield Shealy was McCoy's radio operator, and he sat in the rear behind Darkside.

Lance Corporal Samuel Baynes rode in the turret hatch, manning a 7.62-caliber machine gun.

We waited in the blowing sand.

We're under a communications blackout. Everyone knows the invasion is imminent, but the Defense Department asked that all embedded reporters stay off the phone, no calls, no e-mails.

The unembedded journalists do not have this restriction, and so continue to communicate with their editors back home. This causes some concern for my family, and the *Chronicle*. They had no idea where I was, or what I was doing. My wife called the paper, nervous and wondering. The big boss, Phil Bronstein, called her back.

Lieutenant Colonel Bryan McCoy in the desert the morning the war started. *John Koopman*

David Howell, battalion sergeant major, 3rd Battalion, 4th Marine Regiment. *Bryan Mangan*

John Koopman, staff writer for the *San Francisco Chronicle*, writes a story inside the reporters' tent in Kuwait, just prior to the invasion. *John Koopman*

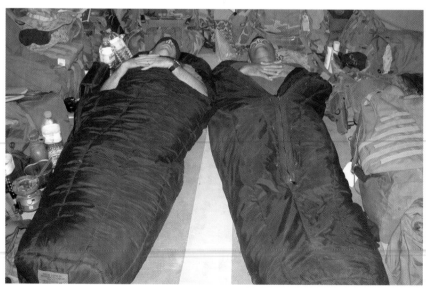

Two Marine staff NCOs catch some sleep in their tent in Kuwait before the war. *Bryan Mangan*

Reporters and photographers cram the parking lot of the Kuwait City Hilton the day they are taken to the desert to be embedded. In the foreground is *Chronicle* photographer Michael Macor. *John Koopman*

The reporters and their guide. From left, *Time* magazine reporter Simon Robinson, John Koopman of the *San Francisco Chronicle*, First Lieutenant Eric Gentrup, and *Time* photographer Bob Nickelsberg. *John Koopman*

A Marine stands watch in the Kuwaiti desert in the days before the invasion. *Bryan Mangan*

A squad of Marines trains for urban warfare by using boards in the dirt to simulate walls. *John Koopman*

First Lieutenant Paul Keener, communications officer, helps supervise the dismantling of the Marines' tent city on the eve of the invasion. *Bryan Mangan*

Lieutenant Colonel Bryan McCoy checks a map on the hood of his Humvee the morning of the invasion. *John Koopman*

Lance Corporal Samuel Baynes, machine gunner on McCoy's Humvee, stands watch and scans the distance during a sandstorm a few miles past Basra. *John Koopman*

Chief Warrant Officer 2 Gene Coughlin (left) and First Lieutenant Jojo Chames take a break during a sandstorm on the way to Baghdad. *John Koopman*

Marines set up security outside an Amtrack during a raid in the city of Afak. *John Koopman.*

Major Martin Wetterauer, battalion operations officer, checks out the view from the top of a Marine Amtrack. *Bryan Mangan*

Dave Howell monitors radio traffic inside an Amtrack on the way back from a raid on Afak and Al Budyr. *John Koopman*

Lieutenant Colonel Bryan McCoy takes a short nap outside the city of Diwaniyah. *Bryan Mangan*

He said he didn't know anything, but as soon as he got word, he would call. He gave her his cell phone number and said to call if she needed anything. I thought that was a classy thing to do.

This was also the time when a lot of us dealt with the military about the issue of security. Before embedding, we signed a contract indicating what things we could and could not report. Most of it was general stuff. Don't report the names of dead or wounded until their families are notified. And don't report on tactics, or future operations. Keep locations vague.

Senior military officials had said off the record that we might want to let the commanding officers of our units read our stories before they were filed. This is a big no-no in the business. It looks like you're giving a source the right to edit you.

But the reasoning was, we might make a trade. The commanding officer would give us information not for release, but for our own edification, and allow us into sensitive areas, like the tactical centers. In exchange, they would see what we wrote beforehand.

I don't know if any other reporters made that deal. I did not. I had no need for any of the information they dangled in front of me. I was there to write about Marines and fighting.

Still, I talked about it with McCoy. He scoffed. He'd already let me into the tactical center, and told me a lot of things he wasn't supposed to. He figured I knew enough to play right.

He said he didn't need to see my stories ahead of time. All he asked was for me to wait until we crossed the border before writing or filing anything. After that, he said, it was all fair game.

I could live with that.

*I am a very proud Marine mother of \*\*\*. I will never forget the day when he called me at work and asked me if I could leave for awhile and go to his high school. I said, "Why, what did you do?" He said that it wasn't anything he* *did but what he wanted to do, but he needed my permission. He told me where to meet him, so I went. He introduced me to 3 Marine recruiters. I was shocked. My son said that this is what he decided to do with himself. I was so PROUD of him. Of course this was October 1999. He was only 17. With him in Kuwait, I ponder the thought of "what if he doesn't come home?" Will it be my fault? No it won't.*

*I belong to a wonderful Marine Moms support group with over 4,000 members as of today. Every one of us moms, dads, wives, sisters, brothers, grandmas and grandpas or just friends support each other in every way imaginable. We are all a big extended family. I am so very proud of my son and his choice to defend our country, not just for all of us but for the children of the future. Let me tell you he is ready, they ALL are ready to defend our freedom. I love my son and miss him terribly. Let us all pray for OUR U. S. MARINE CORPS–THE FEW, THE PROUD, THE MARINES!!! OOH RAH and SEMPER FI.*

## GAS

Every couple of hours, we heard the alarm: "Gas, gas, gas!" We'd scramble for the gas masks strapped to our hips and drag them over our heads. You can't breathe well in a gas mask. Air comes in through a filter on the side. Sweat drips down your cheeks and down your neck.

Everyone in the military trains for chemical, biological, and nuclear attack. This has been going on for decades, since I was a young Marine. But it's taken on new urgency with this war.

People talked about how and when Saddam would use chemical or biological weapons. Most figured he'd wait until the noose was tight on Baghdad, and he was about to go down in flames. Because it was a given that his army couldn't beat the U.S. military.

Even so, every time an Iraqi farted on the other side of the border, the gas alert went off. We stayed masked for 10 minutes, 15, sometimes up to an hour, before the all-clear sounded. Some guys fell asleep wearing their masks.

The concern over a chemical or biological attack was so strong, the brass ordered everyone to wear the chemical protective suits. All the time. So most of the time, we wore the pants and jackets, with the boots and gloves in our packs and gas masks strapped to our hips. When the gas alert sounded, we put on the mask and waited to see if we needed the boots and gloves.

We wore shorts and T-shirts under the suits. It was still cool in Kuwait and Iraq, but those suits were warm inside.

"I'd like to beat the hell out of whoever came up with the idea of chemical weapons to begin with," says Sergeant Kevin Smith after one alert.

Smith is a long-faced Southern boy who likes chewing tobacco and dirty jokes. He was one of my best friends in the battalion.

Late one afternoon, I found Kevin sitting on a dirt mound, opening an MRE.

"Please, join me, Mr. Koopman," he said. "I'm Kevin, and I'll be your waiter this evening."

I sat down, and Smith opened one of the tan plastic bags. "Our special this evening is beef steak with savory gravy," he says. "For dessert, we have a lovely pound cake."

"Where's my napkin?" I asked.

Smith handed me a rolled-up MRE toilet-paper ration and asked if I'd like to see the wine list.

We shared the tepid water from his canteen and watched the dirt swirl.

*Hello, John:*
*Thank you so much for taking interest in those of us left behind by sons, daughters, friends and family who*

*have been deployed. I am so proud of my son, a US Marine stationed somewhere in Kuwait. He was always one with a strong sense of justice and compassion. Occasionally throughout high school he would casually mention how he and his friends counseled a young man to "knock it off" when found to be mistreating a young lady. More than once he also reprimanded fellow students for exhibiting "rude" behavior in the classroom. He joined the Marines to make a difference for good, because he said "Somebody needs to stand up for freedom, and I'm that Somebody." It pains me and other parents so much to hear that most of the news reaching my son and others overseas consists of anti-war coverage. They have heard how Vietnam veterans were disrespected upon returning from Asia. Please be so kind as to remind our fellow citizens that no matter what their political views over going to war or not, these brave young (very, very young) people are doing their best to fulfill a promise they made. If you ask a Marine, Sailor, Soldier, Coastie, National Guardsman or Airman what he or she thinks of the anti-war, anti-military views being broadcast over every form of media, their response would most likely be "God Bless America" or Voltaire's quote "I don't believe in a word you say, but I'll defend to the death your right to say it."*

## THE NIGHT BEFORE WAR

The artillery fire continued. Helicopters buzzed back and forth across the border. Inside the battalion tactical center, radios crackled and squawked. Engineers on the border were coming under Iraqi mortar attack. A Marine tank has been hit by a Hellfire missile, fired from a Cobra gunship, in the first friendly fire incident of the war. It's getting tense.

I've never seen a war start before.

Marines find humor everywhere. Word came down that the missile knocked out the tank, but the crewmen survived the hit. "Someone got his bell rung," someone said.

No one knows what's going on to the north. No one knows whether the Iraqi army will hit hard or fade away.

An intelligence report says the Medina Division of Iraq's Republican Guard has secretly moved from Baghdad to the border.

The Medina Division is about the only Iraqi unit that the Marines respect. And now, allegedly, here they are, ready to get down to business.

The news scares the hell out of me. Have the Iraqis developed a plan to ambush the Marines? It doesn't seem possible that the Iraqi military could win this, or any fight. But they could kill a lot of people. I have thoughts of a bloodbath. I picture hundreds of Iraqi tanks dug into ambush positions. I picture the battalion caught in the middle, explosions all around, people dying, and me trying to crawl into a hole.

The battalion staff stays up all night rewriting the battle plan. They have one night to redo what the division has worked on for months. No one gets much sleep.

If anyone is worried, they don't show it.

"Looks like the Republican Guard is going to come out and play," McCoy says in the morning. "Well, good on 'em. We'll slaughter them, too."

*Whatever happens to him he keeps telling me is his destiny! We have been through the pain before and I don't know if that makes it better or worse now! I know what it feels like to almost lose him and I cry tears of joy for having him and then tears of pain thinking it might happen again! We are so proud of him and feel he has been strong in the past and will be now! War seems inevitable now and so we go on with our prayers and pain.*

*Thank you so much for being there to report! You are an angel! I'm not sure why I am sending this to you. It is just good to share and helps me through this nerve wracking times! Helps me affirm that God has bigger plans for \*\*\* since he has seen him through so much . I know no matter what I do besides pray, I can't help him now! I truly believe he will be safe in God's hands!*

## HOGAN'S ALLEY

The war starts in the morning.

The order to move comes from Ripper 6, the regimental commander, Colonel Steve Hummer. McCoy's boss.

Pretty much the entire 1st Marine Division starts forward toward Iraq. The land is flat and sandy. You can see thick smoke on the horizon to the west and north.

The movement is slow. The border between Iraq and Kuwait is strung with long lines of concertina wire, with a deep trench and a long earthen berm. Engineers were there the night before to blow holes in the wire and make sure roads crossed the trenches. The result, however, is that Marine tanks and trucks bottleneck trying to get over the border quickly.

We're stuck behind a supply convoy. How the hell did that happen? This is Three-Four, they're supposed to be at the front of the fight.

McCoy gets on the radio, looking for a way over, through or around the column. He taps his radio handset impatiently against his helmet. "Go! Go! We've got to get past this!" he says to no one in particular.

Finally, the battalion picks up speed. I see the rolls of wire and a path cutting across it. We drive over the trench. Into Iraq.

Now it's for real.

But there are no Iraqis. The battalion's tanks and AAVs pick up speed, cruising over bumps and berms north toward Basra, Iraq's second largest city. There's no shooting, no bombs going off. Where is everyone?

About a half-hour after crossing the border, I see Iraqis. They live in low mud huts encircled by low mud walls. The terrain is greener here than in Kuwait. There are plowed fields and scrub brush.

People have hung white flags on their rooftops. They gather in courtyards to watch the tanks and trucks rumble past. Some wave. Most do not.

The Marines are on constant alert. At every stop, they dismount and set up defensive positions in the dirt. No one knows when or from where an attack might come.

There is none. The reports that the Iraqi Medina Division was readying for a border fight were false.

And then, we're at Basra.

Three-Four is ordered to attack and secure bridges on the outskirts of town, to attack and defeat the 51st Mechanized Infantry Division, which has its garrison on the southeast side of the city, and to secure the Basra International Airport.

There is almost no fighting. Only scattered skirmishes, when some unlucky, or hardheaded, Iraqi soldier decides to dig in and make a fight of it.

"We had guys out there killing the enemy," McCoy says. "A lot of Iraqis surrendered, but there were a few out there who decided to make a stand. You've got to respect them for that."

I sit in the back of the Humvee and try to take it all in. McCoy is constantly busy, on the radio, checking map coordinates. Sometimes I ask a question; sometimes he just tells me what's going on. The view is great. I can hear all the radio traffic, so I know who is doing what. And so far, no one has shot at us.

We drive and stop, drive and stop. Everyone looks around wildly, waiting for gunfire. None comes. A goat looks at the Marines with their weapons ready, and turns away.

McCoy drives around the battlefield, looking for any place Iraqis might put up a fight. He goes to the garrison where the Iraqi division had been located. The garrison is a skanky looking building outside the city. There is a grove of trees nearby, a road, and an open field beyond that.

Marine tanks prowl the roadway, their turrets turning to and fro, looking like robotic dinosaurs. They fire at Iraqi armored vehicles in the distance. You can see the rounds hit. Sparks shower the horizon to the sound of a distant "boom."

Most of the Iraqi armor appears to be abandoned and, in many cases, non-functional. But the tankers blow holes through them, just in case.

The road becomes known among the Marines as "Hogan's Alley." It's a reference to a training area at Quantico, Virginia, run by the FBI, where cops and Marines and soldiers practice "fire/don't-fire" exercises.

In this case, the Marines have Iraqi civilians in the distance, surrendering Iraqi soldiers alongside the various tanks and armored vehicles, as well as the occasional soldier who wants to fight.

The tanks move on the left side of the road. Their cannon blasts raise huge dust clouds. The concussion is tremendous. If you're within two city blocks of a tank cannon, the blast hits you in the chest like a two-by-four.

Across the ditch to the left is a family of sheep herders. Two young men, a boy, three women, and a donkey. They're terrified.

The tank guns fire over them, slightly to the left and right.

Marine tank commanders get out of their top hatches and motion for the family to stay put and stay down.

"I was real worried for that family," Captain Bryan Lewis, commander of the tank company, says later. "I was really quite proud that we got through there and did our job, and they didn't have a scratch on them when we left."

It's at Hogan's Alley that the legend of Darkside grows.

As the tanks fire to the left, McCoy's Humvee crawls along behind them to the right. McCoy gets out his binoculars and tries to make out hits in the distance. The Humvee stops and McCoy looks to his right.

There, about 50 yards away, is an Iraqi T-55 tank. It's been dug into the dirt. Its turret is above ground and its machine gun visible. If someone is inside that tank, he has only to traverse the turret and shoot us at point-blank range.

McCoy jumps out of the Humvee with his M-16, followed by Shealy, the radio operator. The two men run over to the tank, pointing their rifles into the ditches and trenches dug next to it, looking for Iraqi soldiers. They find none.

McCoy jumps onto the tank and tries the hatch. It's "battle-hatched," or locked from the inside. Which means there's probably a crew inside.

The two Marines run back to the Humvee. McCoy yells, "Light it up." The colonel and Shealy fire their M-16s at the tank. The turret gunner, Baynes, opens up with his machine gun. The bullets bounce harmlessly off the armor, knocking around the machine gun. Darkside is trying to rattle whoever's inside. Considering how close we are to the tank, this does not seem to be the best idea.

McCoy grabs a fragmentation grenade—called a "frag"—from his vest and runs toward the tank. He throws the grenade into the trench next to the turret and hits the deck. The grenade goes off, dust and dirt bounce 3 feet into the air.

Still nothing. We drive off. McCoy calls the Marine tank commander and tells him to hit the Iraqi tank. And I'm thinking, there's someone in there. Maybe a couple of guys. If so, they're dead moments later when a Marine tank round blasts the turret.

Word gets around. Not only among the men of Three-Four but the entire regiment: Darkside is a hard-charger. He gets up to where the fighting is. And he frags tanks.

"I can't let the lance corporals have all the fun," McCoy says.

He wasn't being entirely impetuous. Darkside also wanted to motivate his men. And he did.

As the Marines mop up around the garrison, it becomes clear that the Iraqis have no fight in them. The barracks are empty because the Iraqis have run. And now, Iraqi soldiers start surrendering in groups.

Mostly, the Marines let the Iraqis go. There are not enough of them to be an effective fighting force, and they appear to have no fight in them. The Marines were told this might happen, that the Iraqi soldiers in the south were mostly conscripts, and not in favor with Saddam. So they weren't likely to die for him.

The Marines don't want to take everyone prisoner. When that happens, a whole series of laws and regulations kicks in, mandating how the prisoners are treated and by whom. Better to leave them by the side of the road. Some of the Iraqis can't believe it. They walk toward the Marines with hands held high, shirts off, or used as flags. The grim-faced Marines just ignore them and keep driving.

I've always wondered if a lot of these guys didn't join the resistance later.

As the Marines drive down dirt roads, they find uniforms scattered everywhere. Helmets and AK-47s are in the ditches. At first, the Marines stop and pick up the weapons. Sometimes they keep them. Later, they strip out the bolts and toss them in drainage canals. Later, they just drive over them, hope to break them up and make them unusable. There are just too many.

*I have a nephew who is with the 3rd Battalion, 4th Marines that you are with. Reading your articles gives me a better understanding of what he is experiencing. I know that the men and women are unable to write home as often as they would like and this allows those of us at home to have something to connect to.*

*Thanks you again. And please tell the men and women you are with that we are proud of them and are praying for them all the time. May God hold them in the palm of his hand.*

## THE AIRPORT

The battalion now turns its attention to the airport.

McCoy gets on the radio to put his infantry and tanks together for a fast strike. Night has fallen, but that means nothing. Everyone has night-vision goggles. They wear them on their helmets and look like alien creatures.

But swampy land and the fog of war slow things down. In the middle of the night, the Marines swing around to the edge of the airport, but not everyone is in place, so the attack waits until dawn.

Monge parks the Humvee on the side of a dirt road. I have to write a story from the day's fighting. Monge and Shealy put blackout curtains on the windows, and I got out my laptop. I sat in the backseat and balanced the computer on my knees. I had no elbow room, so had to peck the keys with two fingers. It took about an hour.

I set up the satellite phone on the hood and made contact with civilization. I called the metro desk in San Francisco and let them know I was all right. It was my first contact with them. I'd been too busy to think much about how my absence would go over. Not with my family or my friends.

But I didn't have time to chat, either. I asked the editor to call my wife and then hung up, so I could file my story, and sent my story off.

I got back in the Humvee. There's no room back there. Only about three inches of leg room. I sleep sitting upright, my body armor pushed up around my neck to keep my head from lolling to the side.

As the sun comes up, the Marines move in from the south. It's a civilian airport, but there is a large military compound adjacent to it. That's the target. McCoy lets everyone know they are to leave the civilian portion of the airport alone. The U.S. military doesn't want to have to rebuild the area after the war.

A couple of low buildings, and an earthen berm encircle an empty stretch of ground the size of a football field. Tanks and Amtracks set up about 300 yards from the complex and pour machine-gun fire into it. Sparks fly from the buildings as the big .50-cals walk up and down the compound. From the distance, you see figures of men running. And falling under the hail of half-inch-thick bullets.

Then it's quiet. No targets present themselves. The buildings are shot to hell. The Marine turrets move left and right, looking for something, anything, to shoot.

This is the first combat I witness. It is anticlimactic. But the war has just begun.

A man appears in the distance. He's alone. Holding a white flag. He's wearing the green shirt and trousers of a regular army soldier, but no hat, and carrying no weapon. I keep thinking someone's going to cut him down. There's nothing but automatic weapons out there and a lot of twitchy trigger fingers.

"Keep your gun on him," McCoy tells Baynes, in the turret. The man walks slowly toward the colonel's Humvee. The driver, Monge, gets out and motions for the man to lie face down in the dirt.

Monge kneels on the man's back and frisks him, twisting his torso to one side and then the other to search his pockets. He finds nothing but cash. A big wad of bills, all Iraqi dinars. Which means the whole stack might buy one good lunch in Baghdad.

"He said everyone is deserting," Monge reports. "He said he went to sleep last night dug in with his unit over by the bridge, and when he woke up everyone had gone but three of them. His buddy was too afraid to come out. He told this guy to go over and surrender and if he lived through it, the other guy would come, too."

We sit for a while. I ask McCoy if I can file a story. Sure thing, he says.

I got out the satellite phone and set it in the dirt. I got a signal and sent the story. Then I called home. Isabel cried when she heard my voice. I couldn't understand it at the time. But that's how it works. When you're at home, thinking about the war or anything you've not actually experienced, the not knowing is what kills you. When you're there, and you can touch and feel the dirt, and see other people, and understand the risk and threat, it's not so bad.

I ask McCoy if I can let Monge call home. The colonel smiles and says go ahead.

That's what I came to look forward to in the war: the look on a Marine's face when I handed him the handset and told him to call his mom.

Monge called his girlfriend. He went behind the Humvee and spoke in a low voice for a while. No one bothered him.

The radio crackles. Tan-colored vehicles are crossing a bridge to the north, heading toward the airport. Iraqi reinforcements.

Inside his AAV, the Kilo Company commander, Captain Kevin Norton, sees the Iraqis. He calls in artillery. The bridge and adjacent woods are engulfed in smoke as big shells scream in and lay waste to everything.

An old Sheraton Hotel separates the military compound from the civilian side of the airport. Marines move into the lobby. Gunshots ring out, and explosions spark through the windows as grenades go off inside.

It's here that the only Marine injuries occur. A couple of guys throw grenades into rooms, to clear them, and they bounce back, fragging the throwers. But no one is hurt badly.

And so the Basra airport falls. At the terminal building, a dozen Iraqi civilians come out to greet the Marines. They're fearful, first of the Marines, and then, when it becomes obvious they won't be shot, for their families. They've seen Marine artillery shells landing in the city, in the direction of their homes. Artillery makes a god-awful blast. It scares everyone.

I try to talk to some of them. Their English is poor, and they seem terrified to me. Plus, I'm wearing a uniform. For all they know, I'm a Marine, too. So I give it up.

But it's weird to stand at the curb of a modern airport with the smell of smoke and gunpowder in the air. Shealy said it was nice that we could park in the loading area and security would leave us alone.

Yeah, or you'd kill them.

The battalion moves down the road. People are exhausted. Captain Norton, the Kilo Company commander, has a glazed look in his eyes. He can't focus. He has been without sleep for three days. He has killed Iraqis, coordinated his troops. Finally, incoherent, he put his executive officer in charge and takes a nap.

"Norton's in the zone," McCoy says after a briefing. "It's the feeling you get when you run a marathon. Late in the game, you're past exhausted. Your brain stops functioning, and you run on pure adrenaline. It's a scary place."

McCoy has orders to turns control of the airport over to British troops. The Brits will stay in Basra and fight a guerrilla war. Probably with the same troops who dropped their uniforms and guns along the side of the road.

People will look at Basra as a place where the Iraqis fought hard, harder than many imagined.

But not at first. Not against the Marines.

McCoy shows the Brits around the airport perimeter and then heads out to rejoin the rest of the battalion, which is camped outside the city. Getting ready to move out, toward Baghdad.

On the way out the front gate, McCoy stops to cut down an Iraqi flag. It's on a flagpole at the entrance to the airport. The flagpole is adjacent to a huge poster of Saddam's face. McCoy uses his bayonet to cut off Saddam's mustache. Two guard shacks flank the entrance. Parked next to one shack are two vehicles, riddled with holes. One is a pickup, and it's black from fire. It has an anti-aircraft gun attached to a trailer hitch.

As we drive past the pickup, I see the body of a man, maybe the driver. He's lying on his side in the charred vehicle. He's burned beyond recognition. The skin on his face is burned off to expose teeth locked in an eternal grimace.

"Man, that dude's fucked up," Shealy says.

It the first dead body I've seen close up. I've seen others, accident victims, murder victims. This is my first war dead. I imagine the guy sitting in his truck, hanging out, waiting to get off duty and go home. And then a helicopter gunship swoops in, sees the anti-aircraft gun, and lights him up.

I see a Marine approach the pickup, holding a camera. I'm thinking, Don't take that picture. Don't take that picture.

He takes the picture.

Darkside is on the radio, talking to Ripper 6. The Marines are on their way to Baghdad. Orders have them driving to the east side of the city. There, they are to engage another mechanized division.

The plan has the 3rd Battalion taking a bridge, crossing it, and fighting and harassing the Iraqi tanks until Marine tanks can get across and blast the hell out of them. In McCoy's words, Three-Four will "grab the tiger by the tail" until the tanks get across.

"Gents, you're about to make history," McCoy tells the Marines in his Humvee.

This plan sounds suspiciously dangerous. But the Marines, once again, are nothing but optimistic. They're still looking for a good fight.

But first, there's about 300 miles of desert.

# CHAPTER 6

# ON THE MARCH

We've been on the road for a week. No one's had a shower for a couple of weeks. Fingernails are cracked and caked with dirt. The only relief is the occasional baby-wipe bath.

These are the dark days of the war in Iraq. We still don't know how tough the Republican Guard will be. The Marines suspect the Iraqis are sandbagging, holding their armor and hard-core infantry in reserve, waiting to hit hard when least expected. This could be a bloodbath.

The drive from Basra starts off well. It's hardtop for many miles, and we're making good time.

I like riding with Darkside. I like knowing what's going on, and where we're going. He and I talk more, and I feel less like an outsider. I'm just another body in the vehicle.

Bryan makes coffee in the morning, with a filthy little percolator atop a small gas stove. Just about every vehicle has one of these stoves. They're hard to light and hard to use. I can never get the hang of it. Someone gave me an extra one, and I messed it up so bad I had to throw it away. Fortunately, Bryan usually makes more than he needs, and he gives me a cup.

I listen to reports of the war on a small radio I brought with me. It's a crappy little plastic thing I got at Heathrow Airport on the way over here. But it seems hardly anyone else has this luxury. I become the unofficial battalion crier. Guys come up to me, McCoy does it too, and ask what's the latest news. All they know is what's directly in front of them. It was not uncommon for something big to happen a couple of miles away, and we never knew about it until much later.

I come to hate listening to the radio. I get a lot of Arabic stations, and I wonder what they're saying. "Death to the Americans!" for example. Or they're using the open frequencies to arrange ambushes, or other attacks. Who would know? I don't speak Arabic, and I didn't meet anyone else out there who did, other than the interpreter.

The radio picks up some Christian station in English. It fades in and out, as does Voice of America and the BBC. It's a little irritating. Why the hell can't the signal come in loud and clear? Not that it would help much. The BBC is all war all the time. It's like watching the news on election night. Just the same stories over and over again. And when you've heard it once, hearing it the second time just pisses you off. Plus, I'm hungry for other news. What's going on in the world? Who's getting married, or divorced, in Hollywood? I think I just wanted to know that life went on, even if I was sleeping in the dirt and eating shit every day.

I came to despise the BBC news readers. I imagined them to be nice and clean, freshly showered and just having driven from their homes. Sitting in a nice clean office reading into a microphone. Bastards. Why do they have it so good when I'm sweating and living like an animal? I want a shower and a cold beer. Or hot coffee. I want to sit and relax, just for a little while.

News of the war is not good. In Nasiriyah, an Army maintenance unit took a wrong turn and ran into an ambush. The Iraqis killed a bunch of them and took five prisoners. This is the infamous Jessica Lynch story. Only we don't know it yet. But I get sick listening to the story. I know what it's like to be a prisoner, and under conditions less severe than those soldiers. My stomach churns at the thought. I hear the newsman say the Iraqis show pictures of dead soldiers, some shot in the head at close range. And I think, this is a bloody, nasty war that can get a lot worse.

The Marines, too, get a little somber when I mention it to them. It's almost as if they would prefer a quick death in battle to being a prisoner. Especially in Iraq, in a place where we are the invaders. God know what the Iraqis might do to an American soldier or Marine.

About the same time, we hear a report that Iraqis had used a fake surrender ploy. Everyone had seen the Iraqis giving up in Basra, and so the idea that some of them might fake it is on everyone's mind. The story went like this: A Marine unit spotted a group of Iraqis holding a white flag and went to disarm them. When the Marines got close, the Iraqis pulled out AK-47s and RPGs and lit them up. We hear nine dead, maybe 30. It doesn't matter.

That sets the tone for future operations.

Late the next night, the operations officer, Major Martin Wetterauer, gathers the battalion staff around for a briefing. At the end, he tells them what he knows about the fake surrender.

He reminds the officers that the proper procedure is to keep rifles and machine guns trained on potential prisoners and to have them come to the Marines.

But some prisoners of war approach with their rifles held high. He said the Marines should order them to drop their weapons. If for any reason they don't, fire a couple of rounds in the dirt at their feet.

"What do you do if he still doesn't drop the weapon?" the major asks.

From the rear of the group comes a voice: "You light him up."

*Dear Mr. Koopman,*

*I hope this letter finds you safe and well. Are you still traveling with the 3rd Battalion, 4th Marines? We have heard that they have not been receiving very much mail from home. Our son, \*\*\*, is in the 3/4. If you know him, or* *see him, could you please tell him that his Dad, Mom, sisters and critters all send their love and prayers? We are proud of him and the rest of the troops, and we are confident that they will get the job done, and be home soon.*

*Wishing you all a safe, speedy return.*

*Thank you,*

*MOM*

## CIGARS AND SKITTLES

In the back of McCoy's Humvee is an old green ammo box with a Three-Four decal. Inside are McCoy's personal gear and items for survival: coffee pot and cigars.

Every morning, after briefings and orders or when he has moments to spare, McCoy gets the box and takes out the dirty, battered percolator. He sets up a small camp stove. Puts water and grounds in the pot and sets it atop the flame. He drinks a cup and pours the rest in an equally battered, dirty thermos.

And then he lights a cigar. It's a morning ritual, especially on the morning of a day in battle. He's partial to Cubans, but anything will do. Simon, the *Time* magazine reporter, brought him Cohibas from Kuwait City. I have Montecristos.

He snips the end off and lights up with a Zippo. He keeps the cigar going for more than an hour. Just don't tell his wife. She hates cigars. Darkside can fight a war, but he fears his wife. Well, more like he doesn't want to disappoint her.

For some reason, just before battle, he gets the same song stuck in his head: "The Girl from Ipanema." He has no idea why.

Now I've seen war. I've seen dead soldiers, and I've seen at least one man die.

I'm still afraid. The future looks bleak. We're in the middle of Iraq. The Republican Guard is between the Marines and Baghdad.

I miss Jordi. I've been gone too long. He's 8 years old, and he misses his daddy. I think about him when I bed down at night. I think about how I would tuck him in at night, or cuddle with him. The thought tears me up.

Worse are the days when I get Skittles in my MRE.

MRE stands for Meals, Ready to Eat. Combat rations, the constant butt of jokes.

But they're not so bad, considering we're in the middle of nowhere. You get about 1,200 calories per meal. The food comes in plastic pouches. You warm them with another pouch that contains a dry chemical that heats up when you add water.

Inside the MREs are snacks. You can get M&Ms, peanut butter, hard candies. And Skittles.

My son loves Skittles. After school, I take him to the corner store for a treat sometimes and he asks for Skittles.

So now, I get my Skittles in the meal and I think about my boy and it hurts. I know my wife was right, that my leaving hurt him. I am a bad dad.

> *Just wanted to thank you for your coverage, as you have been one of the key ways I have found out what is going on over there. My little brother \*\*\* is one of the Marines you are with, and joined the Marines after the attack on Sept. 11th. I am very proud of him and worried as well. Please let the Marines around you know that most all of us support them, and what they are doing.*
>
> *Thanks and good luck,*

## THE STORM

After several miles of hardtop, the road dissolves into dirt paths and small hills. It's like a motocross course. We bump up and down, the tires and tracks spewing dust into the air.

We move well into the Euphrates River valley. I'm told Saddam drained a lot of this area long ago. To persecute the locals, or just because he's an asshole. Doesn't matter. What's left is a fine dust, a powder-like substance akin to talcum. Walk in it and you sink down to your ankle.

A wind sweeps down from the north. It's God-awful. At 50 miles an hour, the wind whips up the fine dust and darkens the sun. The air is orange. Breathing is hard.

The 1st Marine Division is moving along this stretch; a thousand vehicles churn the dust, which whips in the wind and sometimes blackens the sky. McCoy moves up and down the convoy, making sure all the vehicles are set up and in place. There are other battalions here, and the convoys are trying to move at the same time.

We stop near regimental headquarters and I get out of McCoy's Humvee. There are a half dozen civilian vehicles here, with tape on the sides to indicate they're friendly.

I see reporters and photographers milling about. They are unilaterals, Pentagon-speak for non-embedded reporters. I had a lot of respect for those reporters and photographers; these are some crazy dudes. They crossed the border right behind U.S. forces, but not as part of a unit. Their plan was to move freely about the war zone. Which meant they could report anything and everything; they could interview Iraqis and have a better sense of the death and destruction caused by the war. But they were on their own. They had no security. As far as I knew, they carried no weapons or any kind of gear that might suggest they were part of the American war machine.

People have said I was nuts for being an embedded reporter, but you had to be a total head case to drive around Iraq during a war.

Anyway, these guys crossed the border and soon found themselves in a tough spot. As the Marines had moved north, fighting had increased in the south. We heard reports that a British TV crew was shot up by a U.S. tank when they got caught in the crossfire of a battle. We heard one dead and others missing. So they couldn't go south, and to the north was the Republican Guard, with more fighting on the way.

And now they're stuck in a fierce sandstorm. Without much food and gas.

I know a couple of them, guys I met in Kuwait before the invasion. Kit Roane is there. He's a writer for *U.S. News and World Report.* A very funny guy. Also Kuni Takahashi from the *Boston Herald,* who would take some of the best shots of the war. Gary Knight from *Newsweek,* a veteran war photographer. Some French guys, an Associated Press reporter, and a writer with the *New York Times Magazine.*

The last time I saw Kit, we were having dinner at the Hilton. Now he looked dirty and hungry.

He and I chat for a bit. It's obvious these people are in a bad way. My first thought is, I don't want any other reporters around here. I know, that sucks. But there was some animosity between the embedded reporters and the unilaterals. The unilaterals considered us to be working with the military. There was always a slight hint of collusion. And now here they are, looking for help.

But I like Kit a lot. He's a great guy, and I know the Marines will help them, if asked. I suggest they talk to McCoy. As he comes back from his meeting with regiment, I introduce him to the unilaterals. Darkside is cool, and he feels for them. He tells them they can tag along at the rear of the column. As long as they don't get in the way, he'll protect them and provide whatever food and gas he can spare.

"You'll have to abide by our security precautions, though," he says. "We're under blackout conditions, so no lights at night."

Another Marine asks if they have night vision devices, so that they can travel at night, without lights, as the Marines do. Of course, no one has any.

"What do you suggest we do?" one of the reporters asks McCoy.

"I suggest you pray we don't move at night," he says.

But even as he says this, he's turning to another officer and conferring in a low voice. I know they're talking about how to make it work. There was no way Bryan would let those journalists go in harm's way. It's not his style.

Meantime, the wind has gotten worse. We get back in the Humvees and drive on, but soon visibility is down to nothing. It's a clusterfuck out there, with the entire regiment trying to move through whirling sand. We get another couple of miles down the road and then pull over for the night.

The wind dies down just a bit, so I get out the laptop and put together a story about the day's movement. I sit cross-legged in the dirt and peck at the keyboard. The computer is covered with duct tape to keep out the sand. I'm thinking, as I sit there, that I am not paid nearly enough.

Sand fleas are eating me alive. My buddy Kevin sees me scratching and swatting, and brings me some bug spray. I don't see Kevin that much anymore. He rides with the tactical center. But it's nice to see his smiling face.

The light dies, and I still have to finish my story. So I crawl on my belly into my sleeping bag to keep the light of the monitor from giving away my position. I type with two fingers until I'm done, then connect the sat phone and file.

Once the story is in, I call the office. Gail Bensinger answers. My friend, my editor, my lifeline to the outside world, I love Gail. We used to work together back at the old *Examiner,* and now she's deputy foreign editor. When I went to Iraq, she designated herself as my personal editor, and I love her forever for it. She treated my stories with care, and made sure I had everything I needed. She'll never know how much that meant to me, sitting out there in the dirt, feeling isolated much of the time.

After that, sleep. That fine dust makes a nice sleeping surface.

In the morning, I call the office again. That's the routine. I file at night, my time. Which is morning back home. So the people at the paper have all day to mess with my story. I call in the morning, my time, to see if they have any questions. Sometimes I dictate a couple more paragraphs to freshen up the story.

I call and get the night editor, who passes me to the night reporter, my best friend, Suzanne Herel. Suzanne watches out for me, too. By the time I call, she has a copy of my story and has scanned the wires to see if there's anything missing, or if the editors want something more.

So we go through the story first, and then I spend a few blissful minutes asking about work, what's going on in the office. Who's doing whom, and where. Who's about to be fired. Hell, from Iraq, I want to know about her cats, Barney and Vesper, and how much it costs to fix her car.

She asks about Iraq, but I can't say too much, because there's too much to say. How do you describe that place in a few words over a sat phone? It would take a book.

I hang up and stow my gear in Darkside's Humvee.

The wind is even worse than yesterday. We move on down the road at a snail's pace. Start, stop, start, stop. All day long. It's maddening.

The wind grew and I heard someone on the radio call it the "Mother of all sandstorms." Saddam said it was evidence that God didn't want Americans in Iraq. I was beginning to believe that was true.

By late afternoon, you couldn't see a thing. The entire battalion pulls off to the side of the road to wait it out. It's hot inside the Humvee and dangerous outside. You don't dare walk far off, you might not find your way back. I sit in the backseat for five or six hours. Darkside is on the radio much of the time, making sure that everyone is accounted for. That security is out. That the refueling trucks are on their way. Every so often, the four of us chat. About the war, what we've seen of Iraq so far, family. But even talking gets to be a drag after a while. The inside of the Humvee is thick with dust. It comes through every crack and hangs there, like cigar smoke.

We're sweating and uncomfortable. I have a scarf over my face. It keeps out a bit of the dirt, but it makes breathing difficult. My back and legs are cramped.

In the middle of all this, we hear a call from Kilo Company that a Marine has fallen from an Amtrack and hurt his back. He can't move his legs.

No one can move in this storm, so there is no med-evac. His buddies have to keep him still and wait for morning.

Time creeps by. My body is on fire. Finally, I get out of the Humvee and stand in the wind. I stretch and moan. I can't help myself. I moan like an animal. I lie on my back in the dirt. The wind roars past me. Flying sand and small pebbles blast bare skin raw. But it's worth it.

A couple of miles away, an officer and enlisted man with the 5th Marines bed down in their sleeping bags. In the middle of the night, a bulldozer runs over them. A major is killed and an NCO severely injured.

Everyone is on edge. The sergeant major wonders if Iraqis will use the sandstorm as cover for an ambush. Marines have their rifles ready, but they're not much use. Visibility is an inch past the end of your nose. The only consolation is that the Iraqis have it just as bad.

About 3 a.m. the wind dies down. Followed by rain. Big, fat dollops of rain that collect dust on the way down and make a muddy "splat" when they land. The rain turns the desert to mud. The mud is the consistency of wet concrete. I can't kick it off my boots.

McCoy is on the radio, setting up a refueling point. The trucks and Humvees churn in the mud, but at least people can see again.

And we're back on the move.

*Hello, you're traveling with my brother's group of Marines (3rd Battalion 4th Marines). I know you probably don't really care and I have no idea how many guys there are exactly that you may be keeping up with, but I was wondering if maybe you could tell him I love him and miss him and that I'm praying for him. I just really miss my brother. I can't even hardly put together words right now—sorry, I just want all this to hurry up and get over with. Thanks. God speed to you.*

The Marines are moving slowly north.
There's talk about killing and dying.

Basra was a good little fight because the battalion got blooded. Marines shot and killed the enemy. You can train for it, and practice it, and think about it. But pulling the trigger and watching another human being die is not a natural act. No one knows if he can do it until the time comes.

Some people are repulsed and horrified. But the dirty little secret is that others are precariously thrilled. After Basra, some who killed, or were shot at, wear that like a badge of honor. Others are jealous. Those who had not been involved in firefights spoke wistfully of those who did. Those guys had been blooded: they had proven they could fight a battle and survive.

Dave Howell doesn't like the talk. As far as he's concerned, killing is the unfortunate result of military action.

"There is no joy in the taking of human life," he says. "This is not a game."

Much of this is a generation gap. The privates and lance corporals, the riflemen and machine gunners, are kids. They're 18, 19, maybe 20 years old. Full of machismo and hard-charging. Death and dying are abstract concepts to the young. Even killing doesn't mean much, because they haven't really thought about how they will live with it later if they have to take a human life now.

"I'm 20 years old and already I've been in combat," one Marine noted, idly musing to himself during a lull afterward.

"You're lucky. I had to wait until I was 28 to see combat," responded an officer who overheard.

I ask Baynes about it. He's McCoy's turret gunner.

"I want to be in a firefight," he says. "I swore an oath that I would fight for my country, and that's what I want to do."

It's a strange phenomenon for most civilians, and even some in the military, to fathom: the allure of combat.

There is a primeval need, or desire, among some people to prove oneself as a man. As a warrior. There are a lot of guys like that in the Marines.

Major Martin Wetterauer, the battalion operations officer, said some young men grew up listening to their fathers or uncles talk about fighting in World War II and they want to show they, too, have what it takes.

Some, he said, are enthralled by action movies or TV shows that glorify violence. And they are often disillusioned when they see the reality.

Others are just adrenaline junkies. They like the rush they get by going into a violent situation, and living through it.

Wetterauer said he pretty much falls into the latter category. He's a 35-year-old from Baton Rouge, Louisiana, who likes to cook and restore classic cars, but he can't really imagine having a job where he doesn't have a gun strapped to his hip.

"There's something about facing your fears, and responding to a situation," he said. "There's no other feeling quite like it."

In the back of every Marine's mind, Howell said, is the desire to test himself. There is no other arena in which to do that but combat.

"At the same time, they want to believe they are doing something worthwhile," Howell said. "They want to do something to make the world better."

In fact, Baynes said his main desire in entering combat is to rid the world of Saddam Hussein, whom he views as a tyrant.

"I want to get him in my sights, there in Baghdad," he said. "Him and Osama bin Laden, shaking hands or something, so I can get them both at the same time."

I'm feeling more comfortable in the field. You fear most what you don't know, or can't see. Now that I've seen fighting, I figure I might make it out alive. And then, I get news that I won't be riding with Darkside anymore.

My friend Simon, the *Time* magazine reporter, has had enough of the Amtracks, and he has asked to ride with the colonel.

I'm going to ride with the sergeant major.

I haven seen Dave much since the invasion. He would attend the staff meetings that McCoy held every day, and sometimes we had time for a short chat. But that was it. When Eric Gentrup told me I'd be riding with Dave, I had mixed emotions. I like him a lot, and think of him as a friend. But I know he's likely to go into hot spots. Riding with Dave is probably the most dangerous place to be. The fear returns. But now, it's mixed with a sense of excitement.

Howell rides in a Humvee that's set up like a pickup. It's open in the back, with bench seats along the sides. The doors are made of canvas. I'll be riding in the back.

He has a sniper team with him. Staff Sergeant Dino Moreno of El Paso, Texas, is the shooter. A young corporal from Burlington, Vermont, named Mark Evnin, is the spotter. Evnin doubles as the sergeant major's driver.

Moreno is a quiet, laid-back guy with dark hair and a soft voice. Evnin is a kid who sports wrap-around shades and a smirk. He looks like he's on his way to a fraternity party.

I go to Howell's Humvee and load my gear. The back is full of confiscated AK-47s, anti-tank missiles, sniper rifles, ammunition, water, and food. You can't climb in from the rear. You go to the front of the vehicle, grab the brush guard and fling yourself onto the hood, then climb over the roof and drop down into the back.

I hear Howell on the radio, and ask him about his call sign, "Eyes Two."

"Hey, I want a cool radio call sign," I tell him. "It ought to be something like Reporter 1, don't you think?"

"Oh, we already have a call sign for you," he said. "You're 'Paperboy.'"

"Paperboy? That's not cool," I say. "How about 'Writer One?' Or 'The General?'"

"No, you're Paperboy."

We sit in the desert the rest of the day and wait. What we really want is news that the war is moving along. We know the Army's headed toward Baghdad from the southwest. We keep waiting to hear they've engaged the Republican Guard. Then comes news that the Army is slowing it down. They say the Army supply lines are too thin. And they, too, worry that the Iraqis will ambush supply columns.

So the Marines slow down. And fume.

McCoy meets with Ripper 6–Colonel Hummer–and comes back with a mission. The 1st Marine Division is advancing on Baghdad from the southeast. It's split into two columns, running roughly parallel to each other. A road links the two routes and there are Iraqis–militia types or the Fedayeen–in those towns. Three-Four is to drive through those towns and flush them out. The idea is to beat down the Fedayeen, and keep them from attacking the two columns, and maybe developing into another Nasiriyah.

There are two civilians with us now, Ray Smith, a former Marine two-star general, and Bing West, a writer and former Marine officer who once served as assistant secretary of defense. They're observing, and working on a book about the war. Both are hardened combat vets. Bing has talked with intelligence guys about this area, and says the towns will be bad news. They're filled with dedicated irregulars who like to mix it up with the Americans. He compares them to villages in Vietnam. You never knew where the VC were, or when they would show up in force.

"I think you're crazy for going in there," he says. "Better to go around."

But the Marines are itching for a fight.

*Thank you for your continuing coverage of the 3/4. My son is there with you. You continually give a very detailed story of their daily life. I can close my eyes and visualize what is happening. Thank you and continue to be safe . . .(with all those young Marines with you, I'm sure you feel safe!!)*

However, some e-mails expressed a different sentiment.

• • •

*This is all well and good, John, but what's to say your story hasn't been sanitized by Iraq Central Command in which case it's just pulp fiction?*

And.

*How about getting embedded with the Iraqi people and charting their "perilous journeys" through daily life???!!!*

We get up before dawn to prepare for the raid. I go over to talk to McCoy, and the executive officer, Major Matt Baker, approaches.

"Sorry to interrupt, but I have some bad news," Baker tells McCoy. "We lost a man last night."

Lance Corporal William White was in a Humvee the night before, and a couple of guys were moving it around for departure in the morning. In the dark, the vehicle plunged into a canal. The water was cold, and White was trapped inside for too long. Other Marines pulled him out, and the doc worked on him. But he died of hypothermia.

I walked away. I knew McCoy and Baker had to deal with this. It isn't something you can learn in the States. No amount of training can prepare you. As a civilian manager, you have to learn how to deal with a million aspects of leadership and management, but having one of your people killed isn't one of them.

But McCoy didn't slow down a bit. We talked about that later, many times. He always said his mission and his responsibility to his men came first. There would be time to think about the dead later.

I go back to Dave's Humvee, and he tells me he isn't taking his vehicle. The mission is too dangerous for soft-covered vehicles, like his with the canvas doors. We have to move into an Amtrack.

The battalion tactical center moves around the battlefield in a special Amtrack. The bench seats were removed and captain chairs installed, along with banks of radios and crypto gear. It's lightly armed, and so a second vehicle, a personnel carrier with turret-mounted .50-cal, goes with it.

We all pile into the personnel carrier. It's crammed with backpacks, ammunition cans, food, clothes, extra fuel. There's no place to sit, and time's running short. Smith and West are piling in, and I'm scrunched in the middle. Howell kicks an empty can and roars, "Who's in charge of this piece of shit?"

A sergeant steps forward.

"Why is this thing full of crap? Get this shit out of here. Clean up in the rear and make some room. We have to get five more people on this thing."

Marines scramble, shuffling packs and boxes and cans.

"We have to open up the top hatches so we can get 360-degree security," Howell says, looking at the tents and camouflage netting tied to the top of the trak. "Get that shit off the top so we can open it up."

"That's impossible," a young lance corporal says.

Ray Smith, the former general nicknamed E-tool, turns three shades of purple and roars: "Nothing's impossible! Get your ass up there and take down that netting." Smith is as civilian as I am, but nobody argues with a general.

Howell is getting madder by the second. His rage feeds on itself. He orders everyone off the Amtrack, including officers. When the sergeant major gets wound up, rank means nothing.

"You people are walking around here like you're back in Twentynine Palms," he shouts. "You're in Iraq. There are people out there who want to kill you. So you all better get your asses in gear and start acting like you're in combat. If you don't, you're going to end up like those other poor bastards who got killed in Nasiriyah. I want everything off this vehicle and repacked. You have five minutes."

And then, an afterthought: "Just pack what you need and leave the rest. I don't care what you have to leave behind. For this mission, if it doesn't have to do with killing Iraqis, it doesn't go."

The Marines toss a half ton of supplies, and we all reboard the vehicle. A few minutes later, we're on the road.

It's a scary trip. The Marines call it Indian country. There's no cover, just flat fields and drainage canals all the way to the horizon. There's no backup, no other Marine units that could come quickly to the rescue. You can always call in artillery or aerial bombardment; still, you like to know the cavalry is available if you need it.

The roads are in good shape and clear of traffic. I see farmers in their fields. They're looking at us. It's a beautiful, sunny day.

The Marines drive into the village of Hajil. The rules of engagement go like this: Shoot any Iraqi who is armed. They don't have to be threatening you.

There's some sporadic shooting at Hajil, but mostly the Marines search for weapons and information. The column moves, and stops as Marines dismount and search buildings. The sergeant major jumps out of the Humvee and puts his boot through the door of a shack. He searches buildings along the side of the road. I don't go with him. I'm worried about booby traps and land mines. Howell doesn't care. He kicks in doors, uses the barrel of his gun to push debris around.

He comes back with an armload of radios, journals written in Arabic, posters of American tanks and planes.

In a roadside schoolhouse, he finds AK-47s, journals, and a half-eaten bowl of rice. It looks like the school was used as a lookout point, possibly an ambush site.

We keep going.

Next is the city of Afak. There are about 100,000 people here, and most of them are on the side of the road. They smile and wave. Some just stand and stare. I wonder what's on their minds. I can't tell if they're smiling because they're glad to see Marines, or because they're happy about not getting shot.

I understand why they would resent the Marines' presence. I think about my hometown and how I would feel if foreign troops drove through. I can tell you this, I'd be an insurgent. I'd be shooting at anyone coming through my town with guns.

The Marines go in heavy. Tanks roll through intersections, followed by AAVs. The ramps drop and the Marines run out. They drop to their knees, rifles at the ready. Some charge into nearby houses, busting down doors, running up to rooftops.

This becomes known as an "Afak Drill."

McCoy calls the strategy "violent supremacy."

"You go in like you own the place," he says. "You make it clear to people that any violence aimed at American forces will be returned a hundredfold."

Some of the Marines toss food and money to Iraqis, especially to kids if they're smiling or giving a thumbs-up. The kids tear after the MREs and yellow humanitarian ration bags.

There's light resistance in Afak. A Cobra gunship chases down a pickup with a machine gun mounted on the hood and blows it up. Marines return fire on a few Iraqis brave enough to take shots at them.

We stop just outside the town, and an Iraqi man with a cell phone comes toward the Amtrack. Howell aims at him. "Get back!" he shouts. "Go home!"

The man keeps walking, talking into the phone. Howell fires a 5.56 mm bullet directly between his feet. The man stops, turns, and walks away.

"You should have seen the look he gave me," he says. "Like he didn't even care."

Howell figures the Iraqi is Fedayeen, and that he was on the phone describing the Marines and their weapons to his colleagues. "He was scoping us out."

Behind the Amtrack is an armored Humvee with three Army soldiers and an Iraqi, who served as translator. They have a sound system in the vehicle and a three-foot-tall speaker mounted on the roof. They play a couple different recorded messages. Usually stuff like, "The Marines are here to protect you and will stay until Saddam Hussein is gone."

The Marines move down the road to Al Budyr. The Baath Party has headquarters there. Iraqis open fire on the Marines from rooftops and palm groves. Machine guns rattle here and there. Sometimes the gunners have targets. Other times they engage in "reconnaissance by fire," shooting into a building or tree-line to see if someone shoots back. Or dies.

It is near Al Budyr that the Marines encounter a phenomenon that would be repeated throughout the war. An Iraqi man drives his pickup straight at a Marine tank. The tank commander shoots up the vehicle, thinking the driver was trying to attack. In this case, the pick-up is destroyed, the man wounded.

Inside a funky old jail, Howell finds a cache of RPG rounds. He calls for some C-4 explosive. They blow the ammo in place, and the blast hits the Amtrack like a brick. My ears ring for an hour.

Moreno the sniper goes to the top of a small jail to scope out the area through his sniper rifle. He spots a man who looks like militia. He looks like he's carrying something under his jacket.

Moreno puts pressure on the trigger. One round could fly straight and true and take the man's head off. But is he a legitimate target?

Moreno backs off and sighs.

"I'm sure it's a gun," he says. "I probably should have shot him, but I couldn't know for sure. I was thinking, 'What if he's carrying home a present for his kid, or something?'"

We stay outside Al Budyr that night. It's horrible.

I left my sleeping gear behind, in the sergeant major's Humvee. All I have are the clothes on my back and my body armor to keep me warm.

But the days are getting warmer, so I'm thinking I might be all right. I find a soft spot and lie down. Two hours later, I'm awake and freezing. I get up. Exercise will keep me warm. I do jumping jacks and then lie back down. But the ground is cold. My teeth chatter and I rub my shoulders. It's no help.

I'm not sure what to do. You can't go to a Marine and ask to use his sleeping bag.

An armored vehicle starts up. The driver is recharging the battery. I notice that the exhaust output is mounted on the side of the vehicle. About head height. I go over and stand under that hot exhaust.

It's beautiful. Hot diesel exhaust floods my head and neck. It slowly warms me, like a hot shower. I stay there for five minutes, until the driver shuts down the engine, then return to my spot on the ground. I fall asleep and awake an hour later, shaking with chills. A few minutes later, the armored vehicle fires up again and I run over to the exhaust. It's over too soon.

I take an exhaust bath three more times that night.

> *I have been following your reports because my brother, \*\*\*, is a member of 3rd Battalion, 4th Marines, India Company. I am sure you have many requests to relay messages, and there are probably so many men out there, you perhaps don't even have a way of knowing him. But if you could do so, please let him know how much we love him and how proud we are of him. He is on many prayer lists here at home, as are you all. We can't wait for this whole thing to be over and for you all to come home. Please tell him that the baby and I are doing well . . . just growing away!!*
>
> *I understand if you can not pass on these greetings. But whatever you can do would be greatly appreciated! God bless you.*

The next day we sit, bored, outside Al Budyr. I tune in the BBC to get some sense of whether the war is on or not. The colonel goes to regimental headquarters and comes back with the news: Central command has ordered a 21-day operational pause to allow supply lines to catch up and God only knows what else.

Damn. It's bad enough we have to be out here in the middle of a war zone, but now we have to sit and wait until the Army gets ready?

McCoy and his officers start drawing up plans for a mini-occupation. They will meet with the local Iraqi leaders and try to help them out in exchange for them giving up the Baathists. McCoy says he'll be the mayor of Al Budyr.

"It's good to be king," he jokes.

Fortunately, military orders often have a shelf life of minutes. Howell and I are sitting in the dirt. I'm eating an MRE cracker and he's airing his disgusting, blistered feet when the colonel's driver comes running past us.

"We gotta get back to the main road," he shouts. "We're moving out in a half- hour."

The war is on.

# CHAPTER 7

# THE ROAD TO DIWANIYAH

The Al Budyr expedition drives back to rejoin the rest of the battalion. In Afak, more people line the road, most of them smiling and waving. In the distance, I can see a bunch of kids playing soccer on a dusty field. The sun is setting, and it seems peaceful. There is no war here, it seems.

As the battalion leaves the city, reports come in that there's shooting going on to the rear of the column. At first, everyone is concerned that the Iraqis are attacking the Marines. But no one comes under fire. It could be celebratory gunfire. McCoy poses another theory: It's the persecuted attacking their tormentors. Probably the people in the Baath Party getting some payback. Could be. No one stops to ask, or confirm.

We drive back to the main road leading toward Baghdad and settle in the for the night.

In the morning, the battalion moves down the road to a cloverleaf. It's a modern traffic structure that links the main highway to the road leading to the city of Diwaniyah. The 5th Marine Regiment was here earlier, and the tail end of their units are just leaving when we get there. The Fifth took a lot of fire from this position in the previous couple of days. A corpsman was killed when an RPG slams into his Humvee. Word is, the rocket hit him in the chest and knocked him clear out of the vehicle. There wasn't much left of him.

Everyone is on edge.

We spend the day there, as McCoy confers with his superiors on upcoming movements and tactics. I'm out of the loop now. I can't even hear the radio traffic in Dave's Humvee. He has a radio, but no external speaker. He uses a handset. I ask him sometimes what's going on, but he doesn't always have a big picture view like McCoy does. He just knows what he needs to do.

Later I find out that the division likes McCoy's "violent supremacy" tactics. A lot. Three-Four is ordered to beat the shit out of the Iraqis between the highway and the outskirts of Diwaniyah. A lot more Marines have to drive down that road, and division doesn't want them under attack all the time.

Send McCoy's Marines to beat up on people, and let them know there will be no attacks on Marine convoys. Not here.

The attack is scheduled for dawn the next day.

It's nice to bed down in an area where troops have already dug in. They made deep fighting holes, dug into hard-packed earth. Must have been hard. I wouldn't know. I drop my sleeping bag into a wide, shallow hole and get comfortable.

I set up the sat phone and call home. No story tonight, so I can focus on Jordi and Isabel. Jordi cries when he hears my voice. He asks me again when I'm coming home. Soon, baby boy. Real soon.

It's good to hear Isabel's voice, too. I miss her. The memory of the fighting is gone. I know she's having a tough time, doing the work of two parents, keeping the household, working. I know I owe her a lot.

When I'm done, I offer the phone to Moreno. This is my favorite part. I love watching Marines call home. Dino called his wife. I don't know what he said to her, exactly. I just remember most conversations started with "Honey? Honey? It's me. Yes. Yes. I am in Iraq. I'm in the middle of the desert. Yes, I know. I'm calling on a reporter's satellite phone. Isn't this great? What? Oh yeah…"

And then they would turn away, voice hushed, and say the things their wives wanted to hear.

After Dino finishes, I give the phone to Mark Evnin. He tries to call his mother back in Vermont, but misses her. He leaves a message, and then calls his girlfriend.

"Hey, thanks, man," Evnin says when he's through. "That was really cool." And he grins the rest of the day.

I ask Dave if he wants to call his girlfriend. He thinks about it for a second, then declines. It wouldn't be right, he says, for him to call when so many other Marines don't have the chance.

Finally, it's time to sleep. The ground feels good after spending all day on my feet, or hunched over in the back of a Humvee. The sound of machine guns in the distance lulls us to sleep.

Iraq is beautiful at night. There is no ambient light. The sky is black, and the stars shine bright.

Sometimes American artillery fires overhead. I lie in my sleeping bag and listen to the roar of outgoing rounds. Sometimes they fire RAP. That's Rocket Assisted Projectiles. The projectile is fired from a cannon with regular gunpowder. As it's flying through the air, an on-board rocket kicks in and gives it some extra boost. In the night sky you see a bright red streak when the rocket fires. It's like a laser light show.

Wednesday, April 2, the battalion lines up next to the crossroads linking the main highway with the road to Diwaniyah. Once again, tanks lead the way, armored personnel carriers close behind.

This part of Iraq is flat and featureless, with green fields and occasional groves of trees, mostly palms. The soil is wet beneath a dry crust. Most buildings are dun-colored, both the mud huts and the apartment buildings in the city.

It's chilly and windy, but the sand isn't blowing.

The Marines lining the road into the city start moving. First contact comes about 10 minutes later. Iraqi irregulars and soldiers, dug into pits along the road, start firing. A .50-caliber machine gun atop a tank rakes the Iraqis, killing several and sending more fleeing into the countryside.

"It's like turning a light on and watching the cockroaches scurrying," McCoy says.

The column continues past mud huts and small farms. Every so often, the sound of a heavy machine gun rips the air, interspersed with the short bursts from the fully automatic grenade launchers. It sounds like "whack, whack, whack, whack," followed seconds later by impact—"thump, thump, thump, thump"—in the far woods.

Tanks spot an armored vehicle and blast it. The 120 mm turret gun goes off, and the concussion rocks everyone within 200 yards. It's difficult to spot enemy soldiers or enemy dead. They are shot or blown up far away. But you know every time you see that cannon round explode in the distance, someone probably dies.

The sergeant major drives up and down the column, checking things out. I get a good view of everything. There are homes, like little farmhouses with barns and huts in the back. A shot rings out during a lull, and Howell goes to check it out. He comes back a few minutes later.

"Some asshole shot a donkey," he says.

Another Marine walks past and points out that the Marines dumped a bunch of food at the farmer's door.

"Oh great," Howell says. "I'm sure those packages will take the place of that donkey. That was his livelihood. Yeah, we're really making friends here."

Up ahead, Kilo Company and Bravo Tanks have wedged themselves into an industrial area of the city at its outer edge. Howell has Evnin drive us up close. Machine gunners are raking a building. Someone had been firing from a window there. Can't tell if the .50 cal is having any effect, so they fire a cannon round into the side of the structure. Goddamn blast rocks everyone. It hits the side of the building, makes a small black hole, and explodes somewhere inside.

A couple hundred yards away, another drama is playing itself out. A portly man of maybe 50 is trying to surrender. He's waving a white flag. He looks terrified. He's stuck in no-man's land between a tank and its target.

The psyops team—three Army reservists and an interpreter—
motion for the man to take off his clothes and get on the ground. He
does. Wearing just boxer shorts, he crab-walks out of the line of fire.

It's a tense time. Marines have their weapons trained on the man.
One bad move and they'll riddle him.

"Everyone just back off!" Dave yells. "Put that muzzle down, asshole!" He does not want a bloodbath here.

The soldiers search him and tie his hands. The interpreter speaks
with him. The man says the local militia forced civilians to fight the
Americans. He says they were told their families would be killed if
they didn't. And they were told that once the Americans left, the
Baath Party and militia would return for revenge.

It's hard to know the truth. The military has its version of how things
work between the local militia and Baath Party officials. And the prisoners may be saying what they believe their interrogators want to hear.

In any case, the prisoner is clearly terrified and humiliated by the
circumstances. The Iraqis are poorly equipped and poorly trained.
They come at the Americans with AK-47s and RPGs, maybe an occasional mortar. The Marines respond with tank fire and 155 mm
artillery rounds. They blow the hell out of everything.

The tanks keep firing. Other Marine units call for artillery support. The rounds sound like thunder when they land in the distance.
Some hit buildings, lighting them up with a flash followed by black
smoke. Others are airbursts, going off 20 feet, 50 feet overhead. They
fire a brilliant yellow spark, which you see several seconds before the
sound reaches your ears.

I look at the groves and the buildings where the artillery hits, and
I imagine the people there.

Much of the shooting descends upon a palm grove across the
street from the city landfill. When the shooting is over, the Marines
move in and take 17 prisoners. When we pull up, the Iraqis are lying
face down in the dirt, in rows. Marines keep M-16s trained on them
as others kneel on their backs and go through their pockets. I see a

Marine pull a wad of cash from one Iraqi's pocket, shuffle through it and then try to put it in the man's hand. The man doesn't take it. He can't see it. I'm not sure if he doesn't know what's being put there or he can't believe the American wouldn't take his money. Eventually, the Iraqi takes the money, clutching it in his hand, while the Marines and the interpreter start interviewing his pals.

One of the men appears to be a Republican Guard major. They say you can tell a Republican Guard officer by the green uniform and red-tinted boots. He says nothing, but they keep him separated from the other prisoners.

Bob Nickelsberg, the *Time* photographer, tells me there are bodies in the grove. The Marines have swept through and secured the area, so it's supposed to be safe. I venture in. I see a body 30 feet away, then 20. I'm filled with dread and revulsion. I hate dead bodies. I'm not sure why. I should probably talk to a shrink about it someday. Maybe it's an overly morbid fear of death. I'm afraid I'll throw up, or God knows what.

I almost turn away, but then I think, I've got to do this. It's obscene to be here, to cover a war and write about it, and not look death in the face.

So I go to the body. He's a colonel. He's wearing the uniform of the Republican Guard. He looks to be about 40. He's got a slightly receding hairline and a Saddam mustache. There are no visible wounds on him. He might have died from the concussion of an artillery shell. The ground is littered with chunks of artillery shrapnel. I pick one up. It's about three inches long and has ragged edges, razor sharp. Artillery rounds sometimes burst in mid-air, spraying the chunks of metal into the ground below the blast. I think about what it must be like to have that raining down on me, cutting and slashing.

The man's shirt and pants are open. The sergeant major says the Marines found him still alive and tried to save him. But it was no use.

Near him is a pot of stew with red sauce and cabbage. Next to that is a moldy sack of flat bread. The attack came as the Iraqis were preparing breakfast.

I imagine guys sitting in that grove for days, maybe weeks, waiting for the Americans to come. Wondering if they would. Hoping they would not. Sleeping in bunkers and trenches. Tuning in a radio to the news. Making breakfast. Then hearing the sound of tanks and machine guns. Knowing, probably, that the end was near. The boom of artillery, and the sky opening up and swallowing them.

Near the colonel a charred car sits next to a brand-new Honda motorcycle, still upright on its kickstand, riddled with bullet holes.

The midday air is hot. Flies from a nearby landfill swarm around the dead. The landfill smells slightly sweet, slightly sour. It's a sickening smell.

*We are following your stories with great interest, good job. Can you pass a word on to \*\*\* that we are wishing him, yourself and all the troops a safe and successful conclusion to this war and the liberating of the 23 million Iraqis that have endured two and half decades of fear and subjection.*

*Tell \*\*\* that all his aunts in California love him and pray for his safe return.*

The Iraqis are taken away and the Marines start to patrol the area, looking for Fedayeen. Howell parks his Humvee on a road, several hundred yards from a set of buildings. It's the outer edge of Diwaniyah.

Moreno lies on the roof of the vehicle with his sniper rifle. Evnin is next to him with a spotter scope. They watch people in the distance, so far away I see nothing. They talk about potential targets. Evnin thinks he sees a man with an AK-47. That would be a target. The man goes into a building, comes out with no weapon. So Moreno holds his fire.

Howell watches with binoculars. He and the sniper team follow potential targets, and discuss whether to shoot. But none of the Iraqis is a valid target. No one is carrying a gun.

A Humvee pulls up, carrying another sniper team. The sniper, a staff sergeant, says he got two-and-a-half kills today. The "half" is an

Iraqi he wounded in the shoulder, who then ran. The sniper explains how the man turned just as the sniper rifle went off, so a bullet that should have gone through the chest hit a shoulder in a spurt of bright red blood.

The Marines talk matter-of-factly about these things. That's their trade. It's difficult for a civilian to listen.

McCoy's Humvee pulls up soon after, and he confers with the sergeant major. A tank arrives moments later.

The tank commander radios that he's spotted a large group of people assembling nearby. McCoy tells him to shoot if they look hostile. The tank commander says he sees no weapons. So he waits. He calls back to say the group includes women and children. So he will not shoot.

The Marines are about ready to wrap up and leave when the Iraqis do a very unfortunate thing. Some militiamen crawl up close to the armored column and fire off a half dozen RPG rounds. The rockets whoosh overhead, exploding about 20 yards behind a Humvee.

That sets the Marines off. A tank fires into a building and at a yellow bus. Moments later, the bus is ablaze; thick black smoke is curling into the sky.

Atop Darkside's Humvee, Samuel Baynes opens up with his 7.62 mm machine gun. He's the best machine gunner in the battalion, but he doesn't get many chances to let loose. Now he goes crazy. He sprays fire across the front of a warehouse, into parked cars, electrical transformers. Anything. I can't see any people but it's a fair distance away. This is recon by fire, trying to shake someone loose.

Finally, the shooting stops. The sun is getting low in the sky. The Marines head back to the cloverleaf and settle in for the night. Guards are doubled around the perimeter. Everyone thinks the Iraqis will retaliate at night, fire rockets or mortars into our position.

I'm dog tired. A thick pall hangs in the air, blacking out every shred of light. I try to dig a sleeping trench but can't seem to make my sleeping bag line up. I feel around in the dirt, in the dark. Finally I give up and sit there, trying to eat an MRE. But I can't even see what I'm putting into my mouth.

I lie down and look up. A guard patrol almost steps on my head.

"Boom!" The sound of a mortar round, from somewhere inside camp. We're under attack, I think. I should get up and find cover. But I'm too tired. I'll wait to see if the Marines get up. No one moves. All is quiet. I'm a newbie. The sound I heard was a Marine mortar, outgoing, registering fire.

I drift off. No attack comes that night.

*I want to thank you for giving me a window into my husband's life. Every day I search for your articles to get the latest news on 3/4's whereabouts—of course some times this is a blessing and some times it is hell reading about the attacks they have already weathered. You are with a well trained battalion and I can only imagine what lies ahead. And if you by chance see my husband, tell him that his family back at home loves him, his mother-in-law has drunk all of his Foster's Lager, and the price of bananas is 59 cents. We are very proud of all of our troops and again, be safe.*

Around this time, I'm hit with a strong case of déjà vu.

I wish I could remember what the thought was. But I can't. I have no memory of that thought, but it existed as sure as the sand. In fact, it might not have been a thought so much as a feeling.

I got that a lot in Iraq. It started long before. In San Francisco. I feel déjà vu every once in a great while. But when the war drums sounded, they came more frequently. They picked up in Kuwait. And by the time I got deep into Iraq, I experienced it on a regular basis. Like, a couple of times a week, as opposed to once a year or so in regular life.

I'm not terribly spiritual. I grew up Lutheran, and we went to church every Sunday. I was fairly religious in my youth. I still believe, but I'm too lazy to go to church anymore.

Still, Lutherans don't exactly include déjà vu in the Sunday school lessons. But I've read a little about other religions, and beliefs. And I started to wonder: Is this significant?

If life is just a cycle in the space-time continuum, if we relive our lives over and over again, does déjà vu represent that to us? Is it how we know we've lived this life before?

More importantly to me, in the middle of Iraq, why am I experiencing this phenomenon so frequently? And the answer I came up with was disturbing. Maybe it meant my life was coming to an end. What if strong and regular déjà vu was my soul going through a check-off process as the end neared?

I don't like the idea of death. I'd really rather not die. Strangely, though, the thought that I might soon die did not frighten me. I can't explain it. I felt okay with it, like it was a natural thing. I've lived my life, I've followed a path that took me to a war, and now I would die. I would be part of the process, I would be a casualty of war. Everyone dies. If it's preordained, there's nothing I can do about it. Just wait.

The Marines are dug in at the cloverleaf waiting for orders. The war has been going on for nearly two weeks now. Everyone is hot and tired and dirty. The enlisted men pull guard duty at night, cutting into the little sleep they would otherwise have.

Officers stay up all night working on battle plans. Sometimes they catch catnaps.

McCoy goes off to meet with regiment. He comes back he informs the staff that the battalion is heading to the city of Kut. The officers start making arrangements.

Darkside is dog tired. Fighting a war is grueling. You don't think about it in peacetime. The training and the preparations. The running and physical fitness. They're all for this moment. When you need to work 23 hours a day, for weeks at a time. When you have to push your body to a point well past its limit. If you train hard, and prepare well, you can withstand a lot.

Captain Bryan Mangan, Three-Four intelligence officer, looks for enemy troops using a Dragon Eye, a high-tech recon device made from a model airplane equipped with a camera and a transmitter. The Marines use a computer to direct the airplane, and special glasses allow them to see whatever the onboard camera sees. *John Koopman*

About halfway to Baghdad, Marines take stock of Iraqi munitions in the early morning–after having slept on them the night before. *John Koopman*

Marines from Kilo Company sweep a palm grove where Iraqis had set up an ambush outside the city of Al Kut. Corporal Mark Evnin was killed, and three other Marines were wounded. *John Koopman*

Two dead Iraqis lie in a fighting hole in the palm grove outside Al Kut. They died in the firefight following their ambush of Three-Four. *John Koopman*

An Iraqi man waves a white flag as Three-Four Marines drive toward Baghdad. The man stood next to a dead body of a man who appeared to be a relative. *John Koopman*

A Marine sergeant poses with jubilant Iraqis, who have put flowers in his protective vest, in front of the pedestal of the statue of Saddam Hussein in Baghdad's Firdous Square. *Bryan Mangan*

Another view of Firdous Square, as a crowd of Iraqis tries to pull down the Hussein statue. *Bryan Mangan*

Cheering Iraqis swarm over a Marine M-88 tank recovery vehicle as it prepares to help bring down the statue, which is adjacent to the Palestine Hotel in Baghdad. *Bryan Mangan*

Captain Brian Lewis, commanding officer of Bravo Company tanks, gets hugged by a celebrating Iraqi moments after the statue of Hussein came down. *Bryan Mangan*

Armored personnel carriers from Three-Four line the road in Baghdad on their way to Firdous Square, where the Saddam Hussein statue was toppled. *Bryan Mangan*

A ceremony for fallen Marines held outside Diwaniyah after the fall of Baghdad. *Bryan Mangan*

Marines from Three-Four pass in review of their fallen comrades during the ceremony. *Bryan Mangan*

Corporal Mark Evnin at home on leave with his mother Mindy before Three-Four deployed to Kuwait. *Mindy Evnin*

A soldier stands in the crater left by the explosion of a roadside bomb in Ramadi. The IED went off a microsecond too soon, sparing the lives of four men in a Humvee. *John Koopman*

Captain Matt Danner of 3rd Battalion, 4th Marines, shares a moment with his Iraqi police counterpart, his brother, Captain Samir of the Haditha police. *John Koopman*

Soldiers with the 1st Engineer Battalion dig up a weapons cache inside a home under construction in Ramadi. The engineers sweep through suspect neighborhoods with metal detectors and shovels to look for bombs and other weapons used against U.S. and Iraqi troops. *John Koopman*

McCoy finishes his briefing and drops to the dirt on his back. His helmet is still buckled and strapped. His armored vest, all his gear. He holds his M-16 across his chest and closes his eyes. And drifts off. All around him, men are scurrying and packing and getting ready to move. Bryan just lies there, a blissful look on his face.

Ten minutes later, someone needs his attention. He sits up, rubs his eyes, and moves on as if nothing had happened.

> *John,*
>
> *I don't know where to begin to thank you. When I sent the first e-mail to you I never expected a reply I just wanted you to know you were appreciated. When you replied I was so surprised and thankful that you had taken the time to respond. The e-mail with the message from \*\*\* meant so much to me. It is the last communication I've had with him now that all this has started. I have been reading your articles and passing them on to family and friends. Your articles make the oceans between us seem much smaller. I can't imagine what it must be like over there for y'all. I keep you all in my prayers and pray for everyone's safe return. Thank you for risking your life to bring us such valuable information.*

I'm obsessed with electricity. I run from Humvee to Humvee looking for power converters to keep my laptop and sat phone charged. There aren't many around. I find out the Army guys with the interpreter have one. I offer them all the chance to call home, and after that they let me use their converter any time I want.

The power of the phone is immense. I have contact with the outside world, and with home. Guys stop by all the time wanting to know who won the game, who won the Oscars, or whatever. I invite everyone I know to write down short messages, along with e-mail addresses. I'll send e-mails on their behalf when I have the time.

These tough killing machines get emotional when writing their mothers, or wives. They get a little sheepish when they hand me the notes. I pretend not to read them right there, so they don't have to be embarrassed.

I detect a pattern to the notes. The Marines almost never whine or complain. Invariably, they simply say they are all right. And they tell their loved one not to worry. That's important to them. No one should worry about their conditions, or the danger.

But they mostly find a way to tell the person "I love you."

*May there be a star in you crown in Heaven!! Last week you let \*\*\* send my daughter an email, and for that moment, however brief; there was happiness in her world.*
*May God Bless You and Keep You Safe.*
*Mere words cannot express my gratitude.*

Diwaniyah is good for the Marines. Fighting is always good for a combat unit. It hones skills. And it helps if none of your buddies gets killed.

But Howell isn't impressed. He wonders how the Marines will react if they really get in "the shit." The shit is when you're involved in a bad firefight, when you're shooting and killing and the enemy is too. How do you react when your buddy dies next to you, but you have to carry on the fight?

Howell is a world-class pessimist, but that's what he's paid for. He tends to imagine the worst in a given situation and if things go well, a crooked smile might break out.

Right now, he's worried about Baghdad. The Iraqi regular army and Republican Guard have not come out to fight. The sergeant major believes they're dug in at Baghdad and there will be bloody house-to-house fighting once we get there.

"It ain't over until it's over," he says to everyone who talks about

getting home soon. "It ain't over until I'm grilling a steak on my patio."
Thank you, Mr. Sunshine.

> *Thanks for your articles. I read them every day now.*
> *Don't know where our dear \*\*\* is but I read with great*
> *interest about the Diwaniyah battle and hope and pray for*
> *all of you that there were no casualties as we were assured*
> *in other reports.*
>
> *I was awake in the night thinking how lucky we are*
> *here that the planes we hear overhead are taking people to*
> *work, to play and home. How peacefully we live here with*
> *hot running water and roofs that don't leak and air condi-*
> *tioning on demand. How fortunate we are! There are flow-*
> *ers in the yard and the pool sparkles so brightly in the*
> *evening. Please know that we are thinking about you too*
> *and hoping that you will*
> *Be safe.*

Another day on the road and the battalion is outside the city of
Kut. Another morning raid.

It's about 100 miles from Baghdad. Everyone is anxious to get
there. Take Baghdad, end the war. Kut is the closest large city and
there's been fighting in and around it. Three-Four is to provide more
violent supremacy and militia suppression.

At dawn, 155 mm howitzers shake the earth. They're launching
high-explosive rounds into the outskirts of the city. The battalion
moves toward the city, following a path taken by another regiment.
Death and destruction are everywhere.

Bodies lie on the side of the road, jackets covering faces. Iraqi
military vehicles are smoking ruins. A herd of sheep lies silent, mowed
down by machine-gun fire. I can figure this one out. It was dark. The
herd moved up, near a Marine post. The Marines, thinking the sheep
were Iraqis, opened up. Only to find dead sheep when the sun rose.

The place smells of death.

For a long time, I see no live Iraqis. Armored vehicles, tanks, and artillery pieces are on the road and in nearby fields. Marine tanks blew holes in everything. Just in case.

We come upon a T-55 tank, still burning. Something inside the tank explodes. The crew hatch on the top of the turret blows off and hurtles 30 feet into the air. Following it, through the circle of steel, is a perfect smoke ring that wafts 20 feet straight up before dispersing.

It's beautiful.

For all I know, three of four Iraqis were roasted inside that tank.

We keep moving toward the center of Kut. This is an industrial area. Warehouses and repair shops. Tanks blast, and machine guns rattle now and then.

War is loud.

Howell's Humvee is right behind a tank, and I watch its turret move back and forth. I try to anticipate when the big gun will fire so I can plug my ears. The tank stops, and the turret turns to the right. Howell listens to the radio traffic, says the tanker saw movement in a building.

I plug my ears and, at the last second, see a dog in the dirt halfway between the tank and the building.

"Boom!" The explosion rocks the building, and a terrible shockwave hits the dog. The mutt howls and yelps in pain, runs around in the dirt trying to catch its own tail and then runs into the brush. A half-mile down the road, I spot the dog running with a slight limp.

## THE AMBUSH

As we move farther along, the sergeant major stops the Humvee and tells me to get in the front, in the passenger seat, so he can get in the back with his rifle. I do as I'm told, but it makes me nervous. That stupid canvas door won't stop a bullet. If we take fire from the right side, I'm in trouble.

We come to a stretch of road with a wide-open, sandy patch to the left and a palm grove to the right. The roadway is elevated, and there's a 10- to 15-foot embankment facing the grove.

It's an ambush.

The Iraqis are dug in. They let most of the tanks pass. Then open up with machine guns and rocket-propelled grenades.

I see bullets hit the last tank in the column and the Amtracks. We're directly behind the last Amtrack in the column. The fire is coming from my right side, and I know I have to get out and get cover. Evnin stops the Humvee and I run around to the back. Taking cover. It's what I do best.

Someone fires an RPG at the Amtrack closest to us. The shot comes from close range. It hits the armor, then bounces off, and explodes in mid-air. Apparently, it hit the vehicle before the warhead was armed. Otherwise, it would have opened up that AAV like a soup can.

The Amtrack pulls to the side of the road and parks at a 45-degree angle. The turret gunner starts pouring .50-caliber fire into the woods.

Evnin pulls the Humvee behind the Amtrack as I walk along behind it.

The Amtrack driver drops the rear ramp of the vehicle and 3rd Platoon of Kilo Company pours out. The Marines hit the pavement and go down that embankment, into the teeth of the Iraqi machine guns. And start to return fire.

The grove is filled with gun smoke. You can hardly see. The last two tanks in the column are still close enough to fire. They shoot their high-explosive rounds directly into the groves. The deafening blasts cut palm trees in half. All I can think is: God help anyone underneath those blasts.

I squint and peer into the grove, trying to spot Iraqi soldiers. There, behind a stump, I see movement. A head pops up. I see a teal blue shirt.

A tank gunner sees it, too. He opens up with his .50-caliber machine gun. The tree stump, a tree next to it, the dirt all around—they come alive with a flurry of bullets.

The Iraqi bounces up, then slumps over the stump. Dead. Half his face is gone.

Behind me, the sergeant major is telling Evnin to get his M203. The 203 is a hybrid weapon, an M-16 assault weapon with a 40 mm single-shot grenade launcher attached to the underside. Kind of like an over-under shotgun.

Moreno is on the roof of the Humvee with his sniper rifle, looking for targets in the smoky grove. The action is so close, he doesn't need a spotter.

Evnin gets his weapon, and the sergeant major leads him to the rear of the Amtrack in front of us.

"There's an RPK firing out of that bunker back there—try to take it out," Howell tells Evnin. But Evnin can't spot the bunker in all the smoke. Howell takes Evnin's 203 and loads one grenade round into it. He fires at a mound at the far end of the grove.

"Right there, right about where that hit," Howell yells over the din of gunshots. "You see it?"

Evnin nods and takes back the weapon. I'm standing by his side, to the right of the Amtrack, looking at the raging firefight, as he reloads. He fires a grenade into the trees and steps back behind the Amtrack to reload.

I step away and move to the other end of the AAV, keeping the vehicle between me and the shooting. I want to take a look at the battle from the left side. But I still can't see much. Too much smoke. I turn to my right, to see what Evnin is doing.

He's falling to the ground.

Evnin had stepped out to fire his grenade launcher when an Iraqi in the grove cut loose with a burst of machine-gun fire. Evnin is hit in the upper thigh and abdomen. About an inch below his protective vest.

Dave was sitting behind a small mound of dirt, about 15 yards away, when he saw Evnin get hit. Now he runs over, exposed to fire, and grabs Mark by his body armor. He drags the young corporal over the pavement back to the cover of the dirt mound.

I run over to see what's happened. Dave loosens Evnin's trousers and calls for a corpsman.

Time moves slowly and sights are blurred. I watch the sergeant major and the medic working on him. How can this be? It's Mark. He can't be shot. What the hell?

Evnin's pants are down. I see two bullet wounds, one on the right and one on the left side of his gut. Just inside his hip bones.

It doesn't look too bad. Not a lot of blood. I look away from the wounds.

Evnin is awake and alert. The corpsman tries to work on him. He opens his medic bag and the contents spill onto Mark. He groans in pain. Dave grabs the young medic and tells him to calm down. "Do your job!" he shouts. A Humvee roars to a halt on the road next to them.

Howell looks down at Mark and smiles. "Hey, Evnin. Look at the bright side. You won't have to ride with me anymore."

Evnin looks up and says, "Sergeant major, you're an asshole."

Four Marines pick up the wounded man and push him into the back of a Humvee. The vehicle speeds off to the rear, toward the battalion aid station. And, presumably, to a helicopter out of here.

By now, the Marines have pushed the Iraqis back, deeper into the palm trees. It's safe, more or less, to walk down the embankment. There, I see two other Marines who have been hit. Corpsmen take them into an abandoned trench and bandage them.

"God, it hurts," says a young Marine, gritting his teeth, his arm in a bloody sling. "Kill some of those motherfuckers for me, sergeant major."

The fight in the grove is fierce. It may have been the toughest, face-to-face, man-to-man fighting of the invasion.

Lance Corporal Dusty Ladendorf is an 18-year-old kid from Oroville, California. Later, in Baghdad, we talk about that battle. It was his first big fight. "There were two seconds of shock, and after that I just started going through the motions," he says. Just do it. Don't think about it. Get out of the track, start shooting. Cover your buddy, find the enemy, maneuver, close in on him. And kill him.

Ladendorf and the others start working their way into the palm grove. The squad comes upon a bunker. They see a hand come out holding an AK-47, spraying the area with bullets.

A Marine throws a hand grenade into the bunker. The Iraqi picks it up and throws it back. It lands seven yards from Landendorf. The grenade has a "kill zone" of five yards. It goes off. No one is hurt.

A Marine throws another hand grenade. The Iraqi throws it back, too.

Finally, someone takes a grenade, pulls the pin, and waits a couple of seconds. Then throws it.

The grenade goes off in the bunker. No one comes out.

Over the next half-hour or 45 minutes, the platoon works its way through the grove. Bob Nickelsberg runs past me, trying to get in front of the Marines to get their pictures. Crazy bastard. I admire the hell out of Bob. He has no fear. And for that reason, he shot some of the best pictures to come out of the war.

I look around. Howell is busy, there's no place for me to be. So I walk into the grove alone, about 30 meters behind the nearest Marines.

It's hot. Smoke fills the air, and I'm scared. I don't know who's dead and who's alive. There are bunkers everywhere, and I expect an Iraqi to come out of one shooting.

I pass by a large fighting hole and look inside. Two dead Iraqis are lying there, both curled into fetal positions. They're facing each other, heads almost touching. They look like friends, or brothers, sleeping together. It's intimate. Horrible.

The sun beats down on the grove and we all sweat under the heavy gear. The Marines find weapons and ammo and throw them into a pile. They set fire to it, which adds to the heat. Bullets crackle and pop as they cook off in the fire.

The platoon reaches the far end of the grove. Officers are screaming at sergeants. Sergeants are shouting at privates. Adrenaline pumps and bullets go off. Everyone yells.

Any Iraqis still alive run out the back of the grove and disappear. Some try to swim across a stream and are cut down by machine-gun fire from a Marine tank.

After a while, the shooting dies down. The only noise comes from the ammo still cooking off in the fire. The fight is over. I go back to the road, still wary of the bunkers, but more confident now. Surviving that kind of hell gives you a certain amount of self-assurance. Or stupidity.

Up on the road, two Marines bring out a prisoner, his hands bound tightly behind him. He wears green pants and a black turtleneck. Not the uniform of a regular soldier, or Republican Guard. He speaks English. Simon is there now, too, and we try to talk to the guy. But he doesn't have much to say. Just that his arm hurts. It looks broken.

Moments later, four Marines bring out another Iraqi. He's in bad shape. His left leg is twisted and turned 180 degrees. He's bleeding. He's either unconscious or dead.

The Marines drop the Iraqi on the ground next to the other prisoner. The first one raises his head and looks around. A Marine sergeant shouts at him to put his face in the dirt. He does, for a minute, then raises it up again. The sergeant grabs the prisoner's head and shoves it to the side, facing the dying man.

"Keep your fucking head down, or I'll put a sack over it!" he says.

The man nods. I can see him looking at the other man. Their faces are about a foot apart. The second one has his eyes closed. His body convulses. I think he's dead. But then he brings his arm up from his side, to his head. And lies still.

A few minutes later, both men are taken to the rear, to the aid station.

With the fight over, Howell drives back to check on Evnin. As we approach the aid station, we see a transport helicopter in a field to the right. Running toward the helo are four Marines carrying a stretcher. On it is a body bag.

God, don't let it be Evnin.

It's the Iraqi.

He's dead.

The doc at the aid station doesn't say much about Evnin. Just that he was stable when he was put on the helicopter.

But we feel okay about him. When a wounded person is alive and alert when he gets medical attention, he usually makes it.

In the Humvee, Howell sees that Moreno is wearing Evnin's pistol belt.

"It's okay," Moreno says. "Mark and I always said, if one of us gets hit, the other gets to ratfuck his gear. I told him I was going to take the holster."

"Evnin's got it made," Howell says. "He's out of this shithole."

"He'll be getting a sponge bath from a pretty nurse tonight," I add.

We drive back to the front of the column. The tanks are sitting by the side of the road.

I find McCoy in his Humvee. He says we missed a suicide run. Six or seven Iraqis had got up from their fighting holes in the sand and run across open ground toward the Marine tanks. They carried only AK-47s. The tank gunners mowed them down like wheat.

The 7.62 mm AK bullets bounced harmlessly off the heavy tank armor, barely scratching paint.

In one of the fights, the tank company commander, Captain Brian Lewis, caught a round in his hand. He was in the turret hatch when a machine gun raked his tank. The bullet entered just behind his index knuckle and came out near his wrist. It cut through tissue but didn't hit any bone or tendon.

"It hurts like a mother, but I got real lucky," Lewis says.

The fight is over. The battalion drives out the way it came in, on the highway that leads back in the direction of Baghdad. Along the road, we see hundreds, maybe thousands of young Iraqi men in civilian clothes. They are going in the opposite direction, from Baghdad toward Kut. Dino wonders if they're Iraqi soldiers who have deserted. Or maybe on their way to start a guerrilla movement.

The Iraqis are grabbing everything they can along their route. Every vehicle has a swarm of men on it, like flies, stripping wiring, steering wheels, tires.

Three-Four moves to a staging area a couple of miles down the road to spend the night.

We get to the area late and park in the middle of a hundred other Humvees, tanks, and Amtracks. I pull out an MRE and set it on the hood. Time for dinner. I'm chatting with Kevin Smith, about nothing in particular, when Dave Howell asks to speak with me in private.

We go behind the Humvee. The sun has set. It's dark.

"Evnin didn't make it," he says.

*Would you help me calm my nerves? All you would have to do is affirm that my only son \*\*\* is okay. I've been told that you are embedded with the 3/4 Lima Marines, based out of 29 Palms. If my information on you is correct and you have the desire to check on him and send him my love and admiration, it would mean very much to me. Our nation is very fortunate in having such fine young men and women risking so much for their country's safety from terrorism. Not to mention our media which is right there with them ensuring that the truth is known. Keep alert and stay safe. I hope that all of you are home soon. My thoughts and prayer go out to all.*

In the city of South Burlington, Vermont, Mindy Evnin is getting ready for bed. She's changed into a robe and slippers. She hears a knock on the door.

For a second, a thought flashes through her mind. Could this be "the knock?" The one every mother dreads? Had something happened to Mark?

Of course not, she thinks. Stop that.

But there, on her porch, are three men in uniform.

It's a bad dream, happening in slow motion.

"Just tell me if he's been wounded, dead, or missing," she says before they can get any words out.

"Could we please come inside, ma'am?" asks one of them, a Marine major.

With those words, she knows.

She vaguely remembers the major saying that Mark had been killed in Iraq. He opened a paper that had just the briefest information: time of death, location, and the letters DWRIA, "Died of Wounds Received in Action."

*My husband is with 3/4 Marines. I was thrilled to find out that you were embedded with their battalion. My husbands name is \*\*\*. At least I know that you have my fella over there somewhere. I haven't spoken to him since he left home on Jan. 30. I have gotten letters, but no phone calls. I am now 5 months pregnant, and miss him terribly, so this information makes me feel much better. I WANT TO KNOW WHAT MY MAN IS GOING THROUGH. Thank you, thank you, thank you for sacrificing yourself to go over and do what you are doing Mr. Koopman. God bless you.*

*Take care and remember all us wives are living with our dear husbands through you, that doesn't mean we don't want the truth, so just tell it like it is. We are the wives of Marines. We can handle it.*

*Semper Fi,*

# CHAPTER 8

# THE COMPOUND

Faces are grim the next morning. We leave Kut and head north-west again. This time the destination is clear: Baghdad. Iraqis continue to flood the road. Some are refugees, but many are young and well-groomed. In Iraq, American troops have long considered that a sign of military service. I'm not sure if it's true or not.

We're moving at a pretty good clip now. The roadway has been cleared, and there are no attacks. But we see the signs of battle all around. Dead bodies, burned-out buildings and vehicles. In the median strip, there is a dead body, the top half of him covered with a jacket. A dog is chewing on his leg. A Marine yells at the dog, yells again. Then shoots it. Dog and Iraqi lie dead in the dirt.

Most of the live Iraqis we see look somber, and there isn't much waving. I see one old man standing by the side of the road, waving a white flag. Next to him is a dead body. I think it must be his brother or son.

The guys are too tired and too mad to care. Losing Evnin was tough.

The sergeant major says little about Mark. It's hard to read him. He's not exactly a touchy-feely, it's-okay-to-cry kind of guy. But he'd been tough with Evnin. He rode him about his appearance, about his driving, about keeping the Humvee clean. But it was just sergeant-major stuff. Not much different than he was with any of the Marines. I got the sense Howell wondered if he'd been too rough on the kid, and now couldn't take it back.

We drive to an intersection and sit. Waiting. That's the hell of war, you wait and wait for something to happen. You wait for the column to move out, for orders to come down. It's maddening.

Three-Four drives to the outskirts of Baghdad. No resistance. McCoy gets orders to raid a military compound. This is a sprawling, forested area with new buildings and a high fence atop an earthen berm.

We wait while the combat engineers try to figure out how to get into the compound. They finally decide on a line charge. It's a long rope fired from a gun, with a hundred pounds of explosives attached to it. The line is fired and it lands on the ground, or draped over a fence or whatever, and the explosives go off.

The Marines fire the line charge over the fence. It goes off with a teeth-rattling blast. Now there's a huge hole in the fence. The vehicles file in and drive off, looking for a fight. They find nothing. Not a single person. Just a couple of old, empty armored vehicles and ancient anti-aircraft guns. The Marines pop them with thermite grenades and look around.

The search takes most of the day. It's getting hotter every day. Everyone's glad it's not summer. It gets to 130 degrees in Iraq. But it's hot enough, and we're all sweating under the body armor. Sweat drips down your face under the helmet.

Somewhere, a fire has broken out. Tracer rounds from a .50-cal apparently lit some trees on fire. A smoky haze hangs over the area. It's harsh and burns your lungs.

The Marines are about to head out when McCoy gets a call from an officer. They've found a suspicious building.

Darkside drives over, followed by the sergeant major. There in the middle of the woods, in broken-down dirty Iraq, is a nice, clean complex of buildings. What piqued the interest of the Marines was a bunch of high-tech metal lathes sitting in the sand outside of the buildings. They were surrounded by sandbags and covered with plastic sheets.

It all looked highly suspicious. Everyone was wondering where we would find the weapons of mass destruction. All the reporters hoped they would be with the unit that first discovered them. We all took it as a matter of faith that they existed. The president had assured us they were here.

And this place was a likely candidate. Nice. New. Gleaming, even. With machinery well maintained and protected.

We park outside the main office, and McCoy confers with his officers. He gets on the radio with regiment to explain what's been found and await orders.

Simon and I go exploring. The Marines show us a warehouse. Through the windows you could see piles and piles of bags filled with some kind of material. The mounds are covered by plastic sheets. The Marines are certain that the bags contained chemical or biological agents. They're terrified to even open the door, and so post guards there to wait for the chemical, biological warfare experts.

I have a thought. Why not put on my gas mask and go inside? If this stuff was a chemical agent, this would be a tremendous news story.

I tell my idea to Simon. "Are you nuts?" he asks. Then says, "Hold on, I'm going with you."

We put on the masks and go in. It's dark inside, dusk is upon us. I have a small flashlight. We look carefully at the bags, careful not to disturb anything. As best we can tell, they're just sandbags.

We go back outside and find Captain Brian Mangan, the intelligence officer, with his interpreter. They are about to go searching some of the offices and warehouses. We invite ourselves along. Mangan could have told us to shove off. I thought he would. But he's a good guy, and lets us tag along.

The offices are modern and nice. They have air conditioners, but the electricity is off. Some of the interior offices are still cool from the AC. There are pressed-wood cabinets, like you find at Home Depot. Every single work space has a painting or photograph of Saddam.

The first offices we see are completely empty except for the Saddam portraits. It's eerie inside in the dark.

We come to a wooden office door. It's locked. The interpreter kicks it. Nothing. Mangan kicks it. Still nothing. "Oh Christ," I say. "Don't you ever watch TV?" I motion them to the side, and launch a solid kick two inches to the left of the handle. The whole door explodes into the room. "Don't tell anyone you saw me do that," I say. I'm supposed to be an observer. I'm supposed to be independent. I'm not supposed to kick in doors. But I can't stop myself. This is fun, and cathartic. I need to beat on something after living through Iraq for the last couple of weeks. Plus, I'm never going to get a chance to do that at home.

Anyway, Mangan and the other Marine kick down other doors and rifle through desks and file cabinets. There's nothing in there. It's a little too clean. Not a single document. And few personal effects. But suspicious enough to be declared a "Sensitive Site."

We're going through what looks like a secretary's office. There's a refrigerator in there. It's been turned off for a couple of days. But the cold stays inside. I open it and find a six-pack of bottled water. Mangan wonders whether the Iraqis poisoned the bottles on the way out. Sometimes, paranoia is just good thinking. But I'm hot and thirsty. I figure the Iraqis couldn't have been nefarious enough to booby-trap a water bottle. So I take a sip. I'm still alive a few minutes later, so the other guys divide up the water and start drinking. It's just cold enough to be good.

We've been inside for more than an hour. Because our search is fruitless, Simon and I go back outside. The Marines are freaked. And mad. There are reports of underground tunnels in the area, and Iraqi agents. They're thinking we'd disappeared, or been captured.

Shealy sees me and says, "Oh, the sergeant major is going to have your ass."

I'm thinking, oh great, I've got to listen to Dave scream. First I stop by the tactical center to find McCoy.

"You're still alive," he says.

"Yeah, I brought you a present," I say, handing him a bottle of water. He's about to take a sip when I tell him where I got it, and he drops it on the ground. "No, thanks," he says.

"I hear the sergeant major is a little upset with me."

McCoy smiles. "He's okay, but I imagine he'll want to say a few things."

I find Howell sitting on his Humvee. He looks like he could bite through a nail.

"You don't do that again," he shouts, like I was an errant schoolboy.

I point out that I was with a Marine officer. "What else do I need from you?"

"No one knew where you were."

"Well, a Marine captain knew. He should have told someone."

"That's bullshit and you know it. And I'll talk to him later."

I tell him I understand his concern, but that I had a responsibility to investigate. If there were chemical weapons or evidence of such, better that a journalist be on hand to avoid later allegations that the goods were planted by American troops.

"Besides," I said. "It's my neck. I know the risks."

"I don't care," Howell yells. "You put Marines at risk with that kind of shit. You know we'd have to come looking for you. Someone could get hurt or killed trying to save your ass."

We keep arguing. Neither giving ground. Both too stubborn and hard-headed to give in. I'm tired and irritable and in no mood to be chewed out by a Marine. That's why I got out of the Corps a long time ago.

But I know Dave is right. We should have come out sooner. "In retrospect, one of us should have come out to let you know what we were doing," I say. "We just got carried away."

I tell him I'll leave his Humvee if he wants, and find another ride.

The sergeant major isn't used to dealing with civilians. He accepts my apology and then tells me he's sorry for yelling. There's an awkward silence, and I offer him a drink of my cold water. He accepts. I tell him where I got it and he spits it out. He asks me what we found and I describe the offices.

I'm about to leave, to go find a spot to write my story, and he stops me.

"Hey, John," he says. "One other thing. I don't want you off the vehicle. You know you're welcome to stay."

I get out the laptop and sat phone to file my story. There's an e-mail from the editor of the newspaper in Burlington, Vermont. He wants to know more about Evnin's death. So I call. The secretary tries to put me on hold. I tell her I'm calling via satellite phone from Iraq. I always like doing that, it really speeds people up. Anyway, she gives me the editor's home number, and I call him there.

It's good to talk about Mark. I tell the guy everything I remember, every detail. It's cathartic. I lie on the sidewalk in front of the compound, looking at the stars, talking on the phone to a guy 10,000 miles away about a dead Marine.

We hang up. I fall asleep among perfectly groomed rose bushes in the courtyard of the complex.

*Trying to ram democracy down the throats of the Iraqi people will never work, and anybody with half a brain can see that. Instead of filling up your webpages with Nazi propaganda, why don't you try and figure out a way to post pictures of body bags of the US troops that the US government has prohibited you from doing.*

*What are you? A bunch of scared little babies? If you had any guts you would be living up to the standards of your profession instead of roaming around embedded with the invaders and trying to glorify the killing.*

*For the record, I spent a full year in combat in Vietnam 68–69. Most of you are too young to remember that nasty episode, but what's happening here is worse.*

The next day, Three-Four sets out for Baghdad.

First stop: the bridge over the Dyala Canal. The bridge has major military implications. The entire 1st Marine Division is about to attack Baghdad from the southeast. There are only two bridges that allow access from this direction. Both have been damaged by the Iraqis. Units are dispatched to fight their way to the bridges, find a way to cross them and secure the other side. So that the rest of the division can cross and continue into Saddam's backyard. Basically, the entire division is waiting to cross. Right here, right now. The war depends on it.

McCoy's bridge has a hole in the middle; nothing can drive across. But the Marines have to take this one so engineers can build a pontoon bridge across the canal.

The battalion drives out the front gate of the military compound mid-morning. It's already hot. The main gate opens onto Route 6, which leads to the bridge a couple of miles away. And then on into Baghdad.

To the left of the road is a tall berm. On the other side, more trees. Kilo Company spreads through there and moves forward toward the bridge.

To the right of the road are buildings, houses, and shops. It's a crappy, cramped urban area. And it's swarming with Iraqi Fedayeen.

The Marines move about 100 yards down the road

I'm sitting up front again, in what I'm calling "the death seat," so Howell can have a better vantage point in the back. Up ahead, we hear shots. Rifle shots, followed by machine gun fire. The column slows while the Marines engage in a slow-moving firefight.

I'm tired. So damn tired. I could sleep. The sun is warm. More shots. My head drops. More shots. I don't care. I nod off. Right in the middle of a firefight.

Boom! An RPG round explodes mid-air above us.

That'll wake you up.

I get out of the Humvee and move around to the back. Fire comes in from the buildings. Iraqi snipers firing from rooftops. RPGs rain down like the Fourth of July. An RPG is an ugly, nasty little thing that has killed U.S. troops in every war since Vietnam. It's like a large bottle rocket, fired from a shoulder-held tube. The warhead has no tracking system. That is to say, it's not heat-seeking or anything high-tech like that. If it were, I'd be dead. The rocket just goes straight off and either explodes on impact or detonates in mid-air above a target.

You hear "pfffffssssssssstttttt" and then "boom."

Howell has run off to check on something to the rear. He has a new driver, Lance Corporal Kevin Norcross from Orange County near Los Angeles. He drives the Humvee behind an Amtrack, moving slowly down the road. I get out and walk alongside. I want to keep a lot of metal between me and whoever is shooting at us. Moreno is still in the back.

"PPffffffffssssssssssstttt! Boom!" An RPG round explodes 20 feet over our heads. There's a puff of black smoke. We hear bits of shrapnel hitting the pavement around us.

I get down and try to take cover.

PPffffffffssssssssssstttt! Boom! Another RPG goes off overhead.

Boom! And another. Boom! A fourth RPG.

"I think someone might be aiming at us," Moreno says.

"You think so?" I ask.

I hear that PPFFFFFFFFSSSSSSSSSSSTTTT again and dive straight for the dirt. Boom! Another one directly overhead.

For the first time in the war, I think I might die.

Norcross' hands are shaking as he drives the Humvee to the left side of an Amtrack, almost scraping the paint off, to get some steel between us and the RPGs. We sit there and hide.

I look up and see two Marines sitting atop the Amtrack. They're calmly firing their M-16s into the buildings. Like a couple of duck hunters. They seem neither afraid, nor desirous of cover.

"Did you see that guy in the window?" one asks.

"I saw something move. I was just shooting into the window and all around it. I was hoping."

"Yeah, he never popped back up. I think you got him."

"Could be."

They keep firing. Bullets are plinking off the armor and off the pavement. The Marines have a serene, internal calm. The violence, the threat of death all around them, seems to mean nothing. They just sit up there and shoot.

Someone told me once that the trick to keeping your wits in battle is to imagine that you're already dead. Or that you certainly will die. If you survive, all the better.

I try that now. It doesn't work.

But I am thinking I want to be one of those Marines on top of the vehicle. Give me a gun. Let me shoot back at those who are shooting at me. It's not that I want to kill anyone. I just want an equalizer. I feel completely exposed out there. And the First Amendment won't protect you for shit. Give me a gun and I'll feel better.

From behind us, I hear someone shouting. Iraqis are near the front gate of the military compound, trying to flank the Marines. A .50-cal in an Amtrack opens up and pours a stream of fire down the street. I can't tell if they hit anyone. But the shooting continues for a long time. They must have gone through a thousand rounds. Maybe more.

The column keeps moving and eventually Norcross pulls into a courtyard behind a building, on the other side of the shooting. I sit in the sand and heat. What the hell am I doing here?

McCoy comes and goes in his Humvee. He sees the fight from a higher vantage point. He's getting reports from commanders all around. And it's good. No Marines dead or wounded.

McCoy says the Iraqis are employing "Chechen-style" guerrilla tactics. Much like the resistance fighters opposing the Russian Army, they gather in seven- to ten-man "hunter-killer" teams. Armed with RPGs and machine guns, they try to set up ambushes. They aim to strike quickly, with deadly force. Then disappear.

But the Marines have studied this and trained to work against it. They're chasing down groups of Iraqi men and challenging them, and getting into firefights.

"We really put the wood to them," McCoy says. "The boys are getting some good kills."

The Marines are getting more and more tense. They see unarmed men walking around. Sometimes these men duck into a building and come out firing. The troops figure the Iraqis have weapons hidden here and there. They know, or hope, the Marines won't fire on unarmed men. The Iraqis go from cache to cache, firing, dropping weapons, firing again.

It's a rugged couple of hours. The Marines creep slowly down the roadway. Machine guns rattle and tanks blast holes in buildings. We're all sweating like animals in the chemical suits.

At times, the air is a solid wall of sound. M-16 rifles, M-60 machine guns, and .50-caliber heavy machine guns pour fire into alleys and windows. The smell of cordite fills the air.

The Marines say they killed 15 to 30 Iraqis in the neighborhood. It's impossible to get an accurate count, though. I can't see any dead. They're scattered in and among the houses and shops.

Up ahead, Marines have reached the bridge and the near bank of the canal. Iraqis are on the other side. There is a firefight across the 100-yard-wide canal. My sniper friend apparently recorded eight kills firing across the canal.

The fighting takes all day. We stop for the night, an assault on the bridge scheduled for the next day. Howell pulls his Humvee into an enclosed courtyard adjacent to a small medical clinic. The building is rectangular, with an open-air center. Simon joins us, and we go into the clinic.

Ray Smith and Bing West are already there. They've pulled a table into the center of the building and are looking for chairs. We get out some MREs and have a nice dinner together. It's not too bad. Good company. Fair food. No one shooting at us.

I look in one of the rooms and find a sink. It has running water. We all use it to wash some of the grime off our funky bodies. It's refreshing.

I lay my sleeping bag out on a concrete slab in the back, and fall asleep listening to the sound of gunfire in the distance.

*Mr. Koopman, I just wanted to send greetings to you.*

*My son is \*\*\* with the 3/4, and if you meet up with him, you won't find a finer officer (I know, all the dads tell you this.) If you do meet up with him, it would be wonderful if you gave him greetings from his dad and all that love him.*

*I'm sure you are inundated with those asking similar favors, but I will tell you that being able to read your columns helps to give a "connection" to what my son is experiencing. Keep up the great work.*

## THE BRIDGE

Finally, the bridge. The area leading up to it is a dirty, ugly part of the Baghdad metropolis. Like a slum. There's garbage on the street. Abandoned restaurants are caked with grease and dirt and smell like barnyards. Abandoned food in shops is rotting and smells sickly sweet. It's a nasty smell that gets in your nostrils and stays there.

I hear shooting coming from the bridge.

The Marines come under heavy fire from Iraqi army and militia on the other side. All evening, Marine artillery and mortar fire rain down on the Iraqi side. The Marines shoot rifles and machine guns across the canal into buildings and cars.

Private First Class Brian Outman, 20, of San Jose, tells me he almost died four times in the fight for the bridge.

"That's enough for me," he says. "I wouldn't mind going home now."

Corporal Justing Fetzer, 21, of Westfield, Wisconsin, says Iraqis kept trying to drive across the bridge, and were firing AK-47s and rockets.

"They just kept coming at us," he says.

When I finally make it to the bridge, I see a dead Iraqi on the span, close to the U.S. side. He's in civilian clothes. He's been shot in the head and chest. There's a bullet hole in his forehead. On the far side, a small Japanese-made car burns brightly. Thick, black smoke rolls from it.

On this side of the bridge is a cluster of buildings around a courtyard. In front are three shacks, at the top of the embankment leading down to the water.

A couple of tanks are parked to the left of the shacks. I'm standing inside the little building, peering out a window, the tank cannon about 10 feet away. I hear the shout, "Tank's firing." I try to duck, but the big gun goes off. The force of the blast lifts me six inches off the ground. My ears ring for an hour.

The 120 mm cannons tear holes through houses on the other side.

*May God protect you and our troops! Thank you for being there to bring us food for our yearning hearts. If you see \*\*\* please tell him his family loves him and is so proud!! (He's the tall good looking one!)*

## INCOMING

Digging my fingers into my ears, I walk into the courtyard. In that space, about 200 square feet in an L-shape, Kilo Company is getting ready for an assault on the bridge. The division commander, Major General Jim Mattis, has come to survey the scene and talk to McCoy about his planned attack. They both know how important it is for the entire attack on Baghdad.

"Don't fuck this up," Mattis says with a smile.

Marine artillery pounds the far shore. I watch the brilliant yellow flashes explode among the palms, hear the concussive boom as it comes across the river at us.

Simon and I stand in the courtyard and chat. There are about 30 Marines sitting in the courtyard, resting before the big assault.

We watch shell after shell land on the far shore. From a nearby radio speaker, I hear someone say the bridge assault will start in 15 minutes.

Then we see an artillery shell land in the water. It sends up a huge spray. I'm thinking it's an American round that fell short. A couple seconds later, another shell hits the water. Closer to us this time. A third shell lands on the U.S. side, down the canal bank to the right. I duck my head. A Marine nearby laughs at me. "You don't have to do that," he says. "If you can hear it, you're all right. If it was going to kill you, you'd never know it."

I smile and nod, thinking his words are no consolation.

And then, time stands still.

I hear—or feel—an enormous blast directly behind me. I know it's an artillery shell. I pray it's far away. I pray it doesn't spray shrapnel into my back.

A hot, hard wind blows past me. The air turns dark gray. I duck my head and hold onto my helmet.

Hot, burning engine oil sprays my back. I turn to see the impact. The shell has struck an Amtrack parked next to the courtyard wall, about three yards from me. A second later, a huge chunk of metal comes crashing down into the yard, a few feet from us.

Simon and I duck into the nearest building. I'm nervous. We don't know if that round came from the Marines or Iraqis. In either case, another one could be on the way any second. Maybe someone is targeting this building. We have no idea whether we should stay or run. Paralyzed, we wait a half-minute. No more shells.

I look out the window and to the left, I see the charred, smoking wreckage of the Amtrack. Men are shouting. It's chaos. I'm afraid for what I'll find outside.

## THE SCREAMING AND THE DEAD

The blast made a smoking, twisted crater in the top of the Amtrack. It shot fire and bodies out the back end. I walk around to the back side. Blood and oil mix with the dirt. Two crumpled, still bodies lie in the dirt.

Lance Corporal Andrew Aviles and Corporal Jesus Medellin, two Amtrack crewmen, are dead.

"Fuck! Fuck!" some of the Marines are screaming. "Fuck!"

Other Marines lie moaning on the ground. Their buddies huddle around them as the corpsmen try to administer first aid.

Gunnery Sergeant Jean-Paul Courville and 1st Sergeant James Kirkland organize medical help. Then tend to the dead. They get the dead men's sleeping bags, and the bodies are laid into them.

"I was standing just 10 feet away," says one Marine, shaking. Blood streams from his lip.

In fact, everyone is lucky that the shell landed on the Amtrack. If it had landed a couple of feet in any direction, the blast would have surely killed 15 or 20 Marines, maybe more.

What follows is a half-hour of shock and confusion. Corpsmen work on wounded men in the dirt. One Marine is deaf from the sound of the blast. Another is screaming and writhing in pain. In the middle of all this, I see McCoy. His jaw is set and he looks grim.

He says the artillery shell came from the Iraqis, not the Americans. I don't believe him.

By now, the place is lousy with journalists. The unilaterals walked up from their position at the rear of the column, and they're right in the middle of things. Three or four photographers cluster together to take photos of the wounded. I see Marines turn away in disgust. The photographers look like vultures. I understand what their job is, but a lot of Marines do not.

I go back to the courtyard to find Marines huddled there. Men are sitting on the sidewalk, backs to the wall. It's crowded, but I see a small space. I go up to a Marine and ask if I can sit. He says yes. I cop a squat. He reaches into his pocket.

"Mind if I smoke?" he asks.

I had to laugh. The courtyard is filled with smoke and bleary-eyed men. No, Devil Dog, go ahead and light up.

Intelligence reports come in that Iraqis are targeting artillery fire on this position. Apparently, they are prepared to defend the bridge at any cost. Everyone scrambles for cover.

I find a hole and make myself small, waiting for more artillery to come down. Where do you go to hide from artillery? I know now what it must have been like for hundreds of Iraqis, targeted by Marine cannons. You look to the sky, but what good does it do? You won't see it. Even if you could, it would be the last thing you saw on earth.

But nothing comes. After a while, I go back to the courtyard. Kilo Company is gathering for another run at the bridge.

## BLOODLUST

I now understand bloodlust.

Bloodlust starts with anger. Anger at the situation, anger at the heat, anger at the Iraqis, anger at whoever started the war. Then there's pain. Pain from the blisters on your feet, pain from the armored vest that rubs your collarbone raw, pain in your back from sleeping on the ground every night. Then confusion, over what's going on and why and when. And then there's blood. Blood that's been spilled. Your friend's blood. It gets in the air. You breathe it. It hits your brain and some Neanderthal mechanism kicks in.

Fight.

Kill.

Beat.

Destroy.

That combination of fear, pain, confusion, and blood leads you to do things you wouldn't otherwise contemplate.

For Marines, it might be fighting harder, shooting sooner. For a noncombatant, it might simply be taking chances, not caring what happens to you. I had thought I would stay on this side of the bridge when the assault was launched. The Marines plan to run across the bridge totally exposed, with only covering fire. Going to the other side without armor had seemed like a risky venture. But now, I don't care. I'm going across. I'm going to write all about this day.

McCoy knows he has to get a handle on his Marines and prepare them for battle. Bloodlust is a useful tool for a fighting man, but it must be controlled or some really bad things can happen. It isn't easy. Order and discipline and training have to kick in when all seems lost. Guys have seen their buddies blown to bits.

He talks to some men individually. His officers talk to others. Here's where leadership kicks in. There is a sense of urgency. Despite the deaths, the fight has to go on.

A half-hour after the shell hit the Amtrack, Kilo Company masses at the bridge and prepares to cross.

A team of combat engineers goes first, carrying metal scaffolding to place across the blown gap in the span.

McCoy and Shealy stand by the front shack. The colonel is about to run when the sergeant major stops him.

"We can't afford to lose you," he tells McCoy.

McCoy stands back and contemplates the situation. He takes the radio handset from Shealy and starts calling his officers, checking their progress.

Kilo, meanwhile, starts running onto the bridge. They bunch up at the far end and pour fire into everything. The sound is deafening.

But the Iraqi defenders are either dead or gone. There is little, if any, return fire.

I run onto the bridge in the middle of this. Kit Roane, my buddy from *U.S. News and World Report,* is with me. Neither of us is armed, but we feel better working together.

On the other side, heavily armed infantry Marines run into nearby houses, kicking in doors, looking for a fight.

I see two Marines crouch near an alley. One peers around the corner, then goes back into a crouch and readies his weapon. "Ready, Crazy?" he asks his buddy. The other man nods and they leap into the alley. A possible ambush. It reminds me of the final scene in *Butch Cassidy and the Sundance Kid.* The two Marines sprint into the roadway, rifles at the ready. No enemy fire comes.

Along the shore near the bridge you can see fighting holes and bunkers. Large piles of clothing and personal effects—notebooks, pictures, blankets—are strewn about. As are dozens, maybe hundreds, of AK-47s and RPGs. This is where the fire had come from the day before.

*Much has been said about the bravery of our troops, which cannot be reasonably refuted. But after reading Koopman's interviews with these 19–20 year olds, I wonder if any of that bravado is the result of fierce resolve as the Pentagon often suggests. Rather, it seems the Marines are merely kids itching for a fight. I think it's no accident that these Marines are so young—after all, the young are impressionable, easy to excite, and don't worry about consequences. To think that entire villages and neighborhoods are under the protection of trigger happy kids who would never question orders to "light 'em up" should comfort no one.*

## THE LOOK OF DEATH

McCoy says 50 or 60 Iraqis were killed in the two days of fighting.

Many of the bodies are on the road on the Baghdad side of the bridge. Inside a smoking wreck of a car is a clump of charred bones. Farther up, an older man, maybe 55 or 60, is slumped over the steering wheel of a delivery truck.

Across the road, a soldier in the uniform of the Republican Guard lies face down in the dirt, a circle of dried blood next to his head.

In the palm grove are craters made by American artillery shells. Holes in the dirt chest deep and 8 feet wide.

In the aftermath of the deadly fight for the bridge, the ugliness of war gets worse.

I follow a group of Marines north down the road that leads to the heart of Baghdad. They stop about a mile away from the bridge. A burned-up wreck of a car is on the road. A body lies next to it, also burned. The man is in a push-up position and stiff with rigor mortis.

Down the road, a car drives toward the Marine checkpoint. Someone fires a shot, then another. The car screeches to a halt. I see from a distance two men getting out of the vehicle, their hands held high.

"Look at those people," one Marine officer says, "driving around like there wasn't a war going on."

## THE SNIPERS AND THE CIVILIANS

This is how the Marines deal with oncoming vehicles. A sniper is stationed near the checkpoint, atop a roof or on a vehicle. He fires warning shots in front of oncoming vehicles. If a car doesn't stop, the sniper fires a shot into the grill or engine area.

And if that doesn't work, the Marines light the whole thing up. The driver and passengers are often killed.

The Marines are unapologetic. They believe the Iraqis are coming to attack. Better Iraqis die than Marines.

But the situation now seems static. Marines are stopping cars, no fighting is going on. I'm standing with journalists, Simon and Bob, and some of the unilaterals. We're in a doorway to a courtyard next to the palm grove. A dead Iraqi soldier is lying next to us. I keep trying not to look at the blood next to his head.

I decide to return to the bridge. I want information on the artillery shell that hit the Amtrack.

I don't buy McCoy's explanation that it was an Iraqi shell. The timing was too close to the American bombardment. Everyone figures it came from a Marine artillery battery. I want to talk to people, get first-hand accounts of what happened.

So I don't see what occurs on the road after I leave. Some of the other journalists stay.

They tell me later that Iraqi cars keep driving toward the checkpoint only to get shot up by nervous, trigger-happy Marines. They say men fire on cars before the snipers fire warning shots. They say officers and snipers keep shouting at the Marines to hold their fire, but some do not. And civilians die because of it.

But the Marines tell a different story. Crazy, suicidal Iraqis drive cars and trucks straight at the checkpoints, or at Marines, or tanks. They ignore orders to stop and they ignore warning shots. The only thing to do, the Marines say, is to kill them.

The Marines have been warned constantly about suicide attacks. On the way to Baghdad, the 5th Marines lost a tank to a suicide truck bomb. The men of Three-Four saw the M1 Abrams burning fiercely as they drove past it to the city.

The day of the bridge assault, word comes over the radio that Iraqis are using ambulances with explosives to make suicide runs.

The order comes down: You see an ambulance driving fast toward you, shoot it.

Whatever the reason or rationale, a lot of people die on Route 6 that day.

I don't have any answers. But I try to put myself in the shoes of the Iraqis driving down that road. Hell, any road in Iraq at that time. You're driving along and a shot hits in front of you. Or in the hood of your car. What if you don't see the Marines who shot? Do you speed up or stop? Or what? Maybe something could have been done, should have been done, to announce their presence. I don't know.

Questions are easy. Answers are not.

A day later, I'm riding with the sergeant major and we drive to the front of the Marine advance. Tanks and infantry are fanned out near a military compound. Machine guns are firing. But it doesn't seem like a major firefight.

I find Simon standing next to McCoy's Humvee. Robinson says he just witnessed a suicide attack. A small white car drove straight at an American tank. He says the Marines fired warning shots but the car didn't stop. So they lit it up.

"I watched them shoot up this car and they killed the driver and passenger," Simon says, somewhat shaken. "It was an attack, I can tell you that for a fact. But when we looked into the car there were no guns and no bombs. Just two dead bodies. How do you figure?"

Marines and journalists tell other wild tales of that day. A van is shot up and a family inside is killed. The van sits silent all night. In the morning, a man and woman crawl slowly, carefully, out of the wreckage. They had sat in that shot-up van all night, in and among their dead relatives, afraid to come out for fear of getting shot.

The woman had been shot in the toe. A Navy corpsman bandages her, and she and the man leave.

A black Mercedes Benz drives straight at a checkpoint. The Marines shoot it up. They look inside to find a man and woman dead in the front seats. In the backseat is a young girl, maybe 5 years old. Alive and clutching a stuffed bear.

That wrenches hearts. Even tough Marines sympathize with a child, now an orphan. And no one can say why the parents died. Was it a horrible mistake, or was it suicide?

"Imagine that, making a suicide run when you've got your kid in the backseat," says one Marine who witnessed it.

1st Lieutenant Paul Keener, the battalion communications officer, chokes up when he sees the girl. He's got a baby daughter at home.

He puts down his gun and picks up the girl. Holds her close. As close as he could with his body armor and ammo pouches. But close enough to give her some human contact on the worst day of her life. He personally takes her to the battalion aid station. Later, she's gone. Into the system, wherever that is, where war orphans go.

After the Marines sweep the far side of the bridge, the engineers go to work putting in a pontoon bridge over the Dyala Canal. It's a disquieting, shaky ride in a Humvee across that bridge. Must have been even worse in a tank. Slowly, the Marines drive one vehicle at a time across the new bridge.

Someone puts a small American flag on the bridge. A lot of Marines salute as they drive by.

With the pontoon bridge in place, McCoy says the battle for Baghdad will be for real. We've heard reports that the Army has taken the airport and is already attacking from the southwest.

"Now the really dirty work begins," Darkside says.

## THE INQUIRY

When Simon and I return to the rear, to look into the blast that almost killed us, we find Marines who heard explosions from other artillery rounds that landed on the American side. When we say that the official word was that they were Iraqi rounds, the guys just shake their heads and say "no way."

It's not uncommon for howitzers to go off course, or rounds to land short.

A couple of days later, McCoy finds Simon and me and tells us that an official Marine inquiry found that the artillery was Iraqi.

Military intelligence had been monitoring Iraqi radio traffic, he says, and reported hearing Iraqi officers calling for artillery fire on Marine positions near the bridge. And that the request was approved.

The Marines have something they call counter-battery radar. It sees enemy artillery shells mid-flight and can track their trajectory. The inquiry found that counter-battery radar detected Iraqi artillery shells before they hit the Three-Four positions.

Officials also conducted a "crater analysis" of the wrecked AAV. The angles of twisted metal confirm, McCoy says, that the round entered from a forward direction, meaning Iraqi positions.

The official line is that the Marines were hit with a 155 mm shell from an Iraqi GHN-45 artillery piece.

The Marines were also coming to grips, by the end of the day, with the horror of incoming artillery. Kilo Company called it a fire mission that was "danger close," meaning within about 600 meters. The purpose, McCoy said, was to make the infantry Marine comfortable with close-landing artillery again.

"I don't know what the truth is about that round, but I know this," McCoy said. "Artillery has saved a lot of lives. We owe a lot to them."

# CHAPTER 9

# BAGHDAD

After the battle for the bridge, we're officially in Baghdad. The battalion beds down for the night in the same grove the artillery had pounded the previous couple of days. There are craters chest-deep in the dirt, 4 or 5 feet across. Darkness falls, and I can see the stump of a palm tree. An artillery shell must have gone off right next to the trunk, about 15 feet off the ground. It took the top part clean off, leaving only a smoldering, burning stump. It looked like the end of a lit cigarette. A slight breeze caused sparks to fly gently off the top, and waft the smoke through the grove.

The engineers decided to destroy the damaged bridge. They set explosives on the structure, and called by radio to let everyone know it was going to blow.

I was writing a story when the blast went off. It was so loud, and so percussive, I stumbled from my folding stool and dumped the computer in the dirt.

McCoy laughed so hard I thought he would hurt himself.

In the morning, the battalion headed out. Into the heart of Baghdad.

It's different from what I imagined. Relatively nice, relatively new out here in the suburbs. Must have been for rich Iraqis. The buildings are two- and three-story houses. The architecture was vaguely European, like homes I'd seen in the south of Spain and in France. Stonework and squared-off shapes. Most homes have balconies in the rear, along with clotheslines and TV antennas. There is no one here.

It's spooky. We're in Saddam's backyard now. Who knows what will happen? We're still waiting for the Republican Guard to show up. An ambush could be right around the corner.

The Marines find scattered groups of militia fighters. There are sporadic firefights. Nothing of much consequence. No Marines are shot. They say they've shot several Iraqis. I don't doubt it, but I don't see any bodies.

The battalion moves down the main roadblocks at a time, running the Afak drill. They move in and deploy. Grunts knock down doors, snipers get on the rooftops and shoot at anyone with a gun.

The sergeant major is especially good at this.

Howell goes into the buildings while Moreno, Norcross, and I wait in the Humvee. At one stop, we pull into a parking lot next to some three- and four-story buildings. There's a stack of soda bottle crates in the back. Some are only partly full. And they're warm. I'd kill for a sweet drink right now. There are several cases. Who would miss one? But the house is nice. It looks like a nice suburban place. I picture a normal family living there, and somehow it seems wrong to take what belongs to them.

The sergeant major calls for Moreno to come to the roof. I'm bored and hot. I figure I'll go up, too, take a look around. Moreno and I climb a fence and scale a wall to get to a backyard balcony and then take stairs to the rooftop.

I see Marines looking into abandoned backyards down an alley. Closer in, I see a stack of AK-47s found in a house and then piled in the street.

Howell points to a building about 600 yards away. He says he saw someone moving in and out of a window. He thinks the guy had an RPG. Moreno looks through the scope, but sees nothing.

"Well, keep any eye on it. I'm going to take a look around. John's coming with me."

I don't argue; I figure I can use the exercise. Howell jumps a wall to the next building over and I follow. We move up one building and down the next. This is like something out of *Lethal Weapon*. We're going in and out of balconies and rooftops, under clotheslines, and around satellite dishes.

Dave climbs onto the top of a wall and jumps 5 feet onto the next rooftop. I climb onto the same wall and look down. There is a gap between buildings and we're five stories up. It's a long way to the pavement and a short jump to the other roof. I should just turn around and go back.

But I jump.

For another 10 minutes we work our way through buildings, some that had been under construction before the fighting. Howell leads the way, poking his M-16 into everything, ready to shoot. I've got my notebook in one hand and a pen in the other.

No one is here. Not a thing. We get to the ground and climb into the Humvee, and open an MRE. Howell scales another wall. I see him climbing onto a balcony and peering inside, rifle at the ready. But still nothing. He keeps going.

And that's how it goes for another day.

On April 8, there is a small, but furious gunfight on the grounds of a former Iraqi military barracks. There is a long, tall wall made of cinder block that encircles the compound. A team of Marines with a tank is in the entrance firing burst after burst of automatic gunfire. Occasionally, you can hear the popping of an AK-47 answering from inside.

It's hot. The shooting is taking forever. I sit along the wall with Simon and a reporter from the Associated Press who made her way up to our position.

We share an MRE cracker and let the breeze cool us. The shooting stops, and I see people going inside the compound. But we're too tired to move, and it doesn't look like much is going on.

A few minutes later, Norcross approaches. He hands me a cruddy piece of cloth. I unfold it. It's an Iraqi battle flag. Dirty and tattered. On the top part, the red area, he's written "To: John Koopman. From the Eyes Two team. Baghdad. April 8, 2003."

I couldn't believe it. A flag. This is so cool. I go to the Humvee to thank Dave.

"Well, you were too lazy to get your own flag, so we had to do it for you," he says.

That flag is still hanging over my desk.

The battalion sets in on the grounds of a former Iraqi military headquarters. There are barracks and offices and an empty armory. Some Marines have found weapons scattered here and there. Someone set up a brand new tripod mounted machine gun. Never fired. Simon and I wander around, looking for something useful for a story. Maybe documents showing the location of those pesky chemical weapons. We see desks and pictures of Saddam everywhere, but nothing of consequence.

The curious thing about the headquarters is the murals. There are several walls painted with various military-related themes. One has Saddam Hussein pushing a button to fire missiles on Israel. Another shows Saddam in Israel, reviewing Iraqi troops.

The message was clear, and history supports this: Saddam hates Israel and wanted to be seen as the man who liberated the Arab world from its influence.

The really good thing about today is the order that came down from headquarters: Ditch the chemical suits and put on your regular uniforms. Or in my case, civvies. You cannot imagine how great it feels to remove clothing you've worn for a month and put on clean, fresh pants and shirt. My T-shirt is so dirt- and sweat-encrusted, it could stand by itself. I toss it in the dirt.

I want to sing and dance. But don't. In the back of my mind, I'm wondering why the brass told us to get rid of the chemical suits. Someone could still have chemical or biological weapons. Even if they thought Saddam wasn't going to use them, some general or rogue officer could launch an attack. What the hell?

We're so trusting.

The temperature is rising and it's getting more and more uncomfortable. The only excitement comes when the Marines go into the Baghdad Institute of Technology and find some industrial-type chemistry equipment. There are huge glass bottles and glass piping. It looks like a set up for a chemical processing plant. Which wouldn't mean much, but in the next building they find artillery warheads and metalworking machines. The warheads have had holes cut into the top and screw tops attached. It looks like a place where someone would manufacture a chemical agent and pour it into the artillery shell.

But there is no direct evidence, no chemicals lying around. McCoy calls higher up and asks for an inspection team to come take a look, but there aren't enough people to send anyone out. Some of the Marines mutter about it; what's the point in looking for weapons of mass destruction when no one can come out to verify?

We bed down for the night in the main courtyard. There's a circular drive in the front of the institute, with grass and a tree and a small fountain. Gunny Courville is there, his shirt off, showing his body-builder biceps. The show-off. He has an egg. A real egg. I don't know where he got it. He'd already boiled it and he offered it to me. I could have used food other than an MRE, but I did not trust that egg. So he peels it and eats the whites, dumping the yolk. The guy is a health nut, worrying about cholesterol in this place.

Howell has parked the Humvee on the drive, next to the sidewalk surrounding the grass. It's a nice night. I lay out my sleeping bag on the sidewalk to the side and slightly in front of the Humvee.

An hour later, a refueling tanker pulls up 15 feet away. I'm a magnet for refueling tankers. They always seem to set up wherever I'm trying to sleep. They run the generator all night. It's a loud roar, but you put up with it. I fall asleep. Trucks and Humvees come throughout the night to refuel. I wake up to a tank bearing down on me. The driver had maneuvered around the sergeant major's Humvee, heading toward the refueler, and in doing so was driving straight for my legs. I almost soiled myself. At the last second, the tracks pivoted and he turned toward the refueling truck.

"Asshole," I thought, and went back to sleep. Ten minutes later I wake up and see another tank coming at my legs. Enough of this. I'm moving.

The next morning, orders come for more of the same. By this time, I'm worn out. Tired of the war, Iraq, the Marines, everything. The fighting has died down to almost nothing now, and I listen to the radio for reports on what the Army is doing on the other side of town.

I just want to go home.

But we move out, down the road past bombed and burned buildings. At an intersection, we find the remains of a firefight. Shot-up and burned cars and charred Iraqi bodies. Under a highway overpass are Iraqi fighting holes with blankets, canteens, helmets, and weapons.

We go up the road and Dave calls the snipers over to crawl inside a building. Bob Nickelsburg is there and we're just watching and waiting. Dave is sweating and swearing because he can't get the door open. He grabs a fence and tries to climb over it. But the fence bends with his weight, he goes horizontal, and then the whole thing comes apart and he falls. He lands flat on his back from about three feet up. Landed right on his camelback, which sprayed water 15 feet in every direction.

Bob and I fall to the ground laughing. Dave jumps up, gives us a thumbs up, and goes through the opening in the fence. Later he tells me he really hurt his back with that move, but he didn't want anyone to know about it. He's like that, the stubborn bastard.

We move out again and park in front of a tall building that was listing badly. It would have been condemned in the States. Dave goes up to the top and the other Marines sit and wait. And wait some more. I'm sitting in the back of the Humvee, bleary-eyed, nodding off. Too tired to move.

"Hey, John, you better take cover," Gunner Coughlin says. I look behind me and he and his team are hunkered down behind a sandbagged enclosure. I'm directly in front of them, in their line of fire. I go join them.

A car approaches one intersection guarded by a tank and a Humvee with a .50-caliber machine gun. The driver hits the brakes and stops.

"If he drives past that light pole, you can shoot," Coughlin says to a sergeant next to him. "If he keeps coming in the face of all of this, he knows what he's getting into."

The car backs out of the intersection and turns around.

"He doesn't know how lucky he is," Coughlin says.

*I wanted to write you and tell you that I really appreciate you and the media coverage that is being provided for us wives back home. Being able to read your article helps me try to put myself in my husband's shoes for a brief second. I'm sure a brief second is all that I would be able to stand in those conditions. And I admire you and others covering this event for being out there by choice. Things back here in Twentynine Palms are running pretty smoothly. Well of course we all miss our husbands more than words can explain. I pray for \*\*\* daily and almost hourly. My children are too young to know what is going on but old enough to know that Daddy is gone. But by wearing the t-shirts with his picture on it and wearing the buttons of him, we are able to see his face every day. I know you have work to do and report, but I just wanted to take the time to introduce myself and my husband and let you know how much we, as wives back here, appreciate the coverage that you provide for us. It comforts us to know the truth. Thank You!*

The Marines move out again.

Only now, something changes. The Marines were finding a couple of militia or Fedayeen guys to fight here and there, but now there is nothing. Nobody.

We drive down the road faster and go farther. Marines stop and dismount and take the high ground.

And now, something new. People. Civilians on balconies just a few feet above our heads. They're laughing and smiling and waving and clapping.

Our Humvee pulls up beneath a low balcony and the sergeant major gets out to scout the place. Women and girls are smiling shyly at him and waving. A big grin splits his craggy face and he offers a tentative wave back.

He goes up on the roof and the people follow him. Someone hands him a water bottle. He doesn't want to take it but it would be an insult to decline. He takes a swig. Now he's smiling even more. It's the women.

"Remember this place," he tells Norcross when he returns to the vehicle. "We might have to come back."

We mount up and move down to a large traffic circle. Still no shooting. I get down to stretch my legs. On the other side of the circle I see people in blue armored vests with the letters "TV" in white tape. Then it strikes me: We've found the international press corps.

I go over and introduce myself to some British reporters. They'd been in Baghdad during the invasion and "shock and awe" bombing campaign. They were under the control, and protection of, the Iraqi government until the previous day. But the government collapsed and the Iraqis left. Which means the journalists have no protection from looting and angry mobs. They heard a Marine unit was moving up the road and they came to meet it.

I find a reporter from the *Los Angeles Times* and ask about my buddy, Rob Collier. The guy says sure, he's around here somewhere. We find Rob talking to another reporter. "Hey, Collier!" I shout. He turns and sees me, a big grin lights up his face. He and I hug. It's a strong, "I'm-glad-you're-alive" hug.

I can't believe I found him in the middle of all this. Our pact, made months earlier in San Francisco, had come to fruition. It's weird, too, because if I'd been with any other unit in the entire theater, we never would have met that way. We might have linked up eventually, but never under such dramatic circumstances.

Meanwhile, McCoy is on the radio with Ripper 6. He tells the regimental commander about the journalists and their predicament. The military had been monitoring news out of the capitol during the invasion, and knew that the Ministry of Information had folded. They knew the reporters were at risk, and so told McCoy to move down to the Palestine Hotel, where the journalists are staying, and set up security.

It's weird. Baghdad promised to be a bloodbath of urban fighting. But it seems safe. The Marines stay all tense and on alert, but the threat appears greatly diminished after the battles already fought.

*My little brother is in the Marines. He's in the 3rd Battalion, 4th Marine Division out of 29 Palms. I understand you are embedded with that very group. I know that you must be EXTREMELY preoccupied, but if you should somehow, by luck or God's wish or a little of both, happen to run across \*\*\* of Kilo Company, could you tell him his brother, hell, his whole family loves him, and, if at all possible, email me at some point just to let me know how he is? This is a crazy request, and to be perfectly honest, I don't actually expect a response. I'm just a worried big brother who can't take care of his little bro any more and I'm doing all I can to reach out to him. You are my only link to him out on the battlefield, so here I am trying my damndest to do all I can. Now that I think about it, you might not get this until after this is all over . . . crud. Well, like I said, I have to try all I can to find my brother, \*\*\* of Kilo Company. Even if you can just tell him I say hello that would be awesome, I wouldn't know how to repay you. Good luck to all of you out there, stay safe and come home soon.*

## THE STATUE

The Marines move on down the road. Dave left without me, but I caught a ride on an Amtrack. Inside, I find a platoon of Marines, dirty and sweaty and completely full of themselves. Cocky and self-assured, these guys had been in combat and come out in one piece. I hadn't met them before. I told them who I was and that I normally ride with the sergeant major.

"Cool," says one. "The sergeant major is like a god in this outfit."

"Do tell," I say.

"Aw yeah, man, he's always there when the bullets are flying," he says, then turns to his pal. "You remember that firefight we had and the Iraqis were firing on us? How he's standing there, exposed, telling everyone 'Just calm down, gents, they're only bullets.'"

His buddy nods. "Yeah, he's been married about four times, hasn't he? No one gives relationship advice like the sergeant major. It's usually, 'Don't do it. Keep it in your pants.'"

Which starts them all laughing, and sharing Dave Howell stories. Some are funny; some are harsh, but they're all tinged with affection. So it's true, I thought, they did understand the crabby old bastard.

A few minutes later, the Amtrack creaks to a halt and I jump out the back. In front of me is a large traffic circle enclosing a small park. This is Firdous Square. It's dominated by a statue of Saddam Hussein atop a marble pedestal.

The square is next to the Palestine and Sheraton hotels, where the press corps has been staying.

The Marines encircle the square and the Palestine Hotel. Tanks and armored vehicles block side streets. The grunts dismount to set up security on the sidewalks.

Iraqis are everywhere, maybe 300 or 400 of them.

"Saddam NO! Bush YES!" shouts one gleeful Iraqi boy.

A group of men are holding up a sign, about 4 or 5 feet long, like a parade banner. It's aimed at the American "human shields" who had come to Baghdad to try to stop the bombing. The sign says "Human Shields: Go home you U.S. wankers."

The Marines don't know whether to shoot them or hug them. Mustachioed men who look like the enemy are dancing and laughing and shaking their hands. Kids ask for money, which most of us don't have. One kid, about 12 or 13, approaches me and says, "Money." I shrugged and pulled out my pocket to show I had none. He nods and points to my hip. "No, sorry, no money," I repeat. He points to my hip again, and then reaches out and touches my canteen. Oh, shit, water. He wants water. There's been very little electricity or water in the city since the start of the war. The kid just wanted a drink of clean water.

I pulled out my canteen and gave it to him. I only had a couple inches in there, but he downed it. Then gave me a big hug. Someone took our picture together.

The kids put flowers in the pockets of the Marines' armored vest and shake their hands

The war is over.

We don't know this yet. But you feel it in the air. There's too much happiness, too much celebrating. The feel of the liberation of Paris.

"There's still a lot of fighting to be done," McCoy says. "But this is a momentous day."

A couple of Iraqis climb onto the pedestal of Saddam's statue to the cheers of the crowd. They tug on the statue but it must weigh tons. Someone tosses up a rope and they tie it around Saddam's neck. The crowd pulls the rope, but there aren't nearly enough people to do the job. Saddam doesn't budge an inch.

The men get down and a huge Iraqi man walks up carrying a sledgehammer. The guy has a big gut and massive shoulders. He looks like an Olympic weight lifter, and might have been. He starts swinging the hammer against the marble pedestal, but after 10 minutes he chips off about an inch.

I go to McCoy's Humvee. He's on the radio with Ripper 6. Iraqis are standing around his vehicle. Captain Lewis, the tank commander, had just left. McCoy said Lewis had approached him on behalf of dozens of Iraqis who wanted help bringing the statue down. They saw his tanks, and figured one of them would do the job.

"Ripper 6, this is Darkside 6. I got a whole crowd of Iraqis over here who want help bringing the statue down. Request permission to give them a hand, over."

There's some discussion among the higher-ups whether the Marines should get involved in this. Some Iraqis have come over to plead their case. McCoy had the radio in one ear and Iraqis shouting in the other.

"Please, be patient," he tells one man.

"I bloody well will not be patient!" the man yells. "I want that statue down!"

McCoy talks more with regiment and then signs off. He calls Captain Lewis and says simply: "Do it."

Tanks break down and they need maintenance to keep going. They go everywhere with a monstrous tracked vehicle called the M-88 tank retriever. It has a 1,300 horsepower engine, crane, and tools. Everything you need to topple a statue.

The tank crews drive the M-88 over the curb and up the concrete steps, crushing them. They drive up next to the statue. A crowd of Iraqis climbs over the massive vehicle, like ticks on a hunting dog. They jump on and jump off. I'm thinking one of them is going to get run over. That would look great on the evening news.

Simon walks by, sat phone next to his ear. "I'm talking to CNN live right now," he says.

Shit, I forgot about that. I get my satellite phone out and set it up on the ground. I call Metro Networks, a radio outlet I've been calling periodically throughout the war, and describe the scene to them.

At the statue, one of the Marines passes an American flag up to another man, who wraps it around Saddam's head. I'm on the other side of the plaza, so can't see exactly what's happening. Some people say that some of the Iraqis are mad at the appearance of the U.S. flag. Others say they cheered, but then quickly asked to replace the American flag with a pre-Saddam Iraqi flag. I didn't even recognize the controversy of the moment, forgetting about the whole "It's not the United States, it's a coalition" thing.

Whichever the case, the damage is done. The image of the U.S. flag in Iraq is beamed around the world. The American military is mad, because they'd made great efforts not to make the war look like an American invasion. Members of Congress are angry, anti-war protesters are angry. McCoy gets calls from high up the chain of command.

Meanwhile, Marines are trying to keep back the crowd, so the statue won't fall and hit them. It's a mad scene.

Finally, the enormous vehicle belches black smoke. The engine rumbles like a steam locomotive. It moves back and the cable goes taut. The statue rocks an inch. More power. The retriever rolls back a couple of feet and the top of the statue starts to sway. It moves in a slow downward arc.

And then, Saddam is parallel to the ground, about 15 feet off the deck. The retriever gives one more jerk and the whole metal mess comes crashing down.

I'm on the phone with the radio station at that moment. They record it and send it out to their member stations.

Once the statue is down, the crowd is on it instantly. Dozens of people kick and punch the fallen statue. One man takes off his shoe and smacks the metal Saddam in the head. This is a great Iraqi insult.

I go to my backpack and got out my last two Cuban cigars. I find Dave and give one to him. We light up and touch cigar stems in a toast.

"It ain't over yet, you know," he says.

"I know."

As if to punctuate his comment, artillery rumbles in the distance. A moment later, shots ring out on the edge of the plaza. A Marine has spotted an Iraqi with a gun and fires off a couple of rounds. The crowd ducks and scatters. Then comes back.

I've still got my sat phone out. A crowd of Iraqis surrounds me. They ask if they can use my phone to call family members in other countries. I'm not sure I should spend the *Chronicle*'s money that way, but you had to see the look on those people's faces. Fear, worry, happiness, pleading.

I'm so tired, so giddy, so wrung out, I don't have the strength or inclination to argue. I start dialing numbers. To Jordan. To Syria. To Russia. To Flint, Michigan. There are a lot of Iraqi immigrants in Flint.

A lot of the calls wouldn't go through, for some technical reason or another. But some did. And you should have seen the joy on those faces.

A woman would take the phone from my hand and wait for the connection, then yell a name. Sometimes a couple of times. Then shrieks of joy on the other end and a quick, staccato burst of words in Arabic. I'd give them a couple of minutes then ask for the phone back, so someone else could call.

Men hugged me and kissed my cheek. "You are a good man," one said. Yeah, you should thank my boss, Phil Bronstein.

Not everyone is happy in the plaza. A handful of peace activists, who had come over to act as human shields, argue against the war to anyone who will listen. A British woman walks up to a group of Marines and calls them murderers.

Most guys ignore her. Or laugh. But it got to some.

"I didn't bury two of my fellow Marines just so someone like that could call us murderers," says one Marine corporal, choking up. He'd helped remove the bodies of the men killed in the Amtrack. "They died for this country."

The celebration continues until after dark. McCoy works to set up security and coordinate with regiment and talk to the never-ending press corps. Later, as light is just about gone, he and Wetterauer walk back to the plaza. We sit next to each other on a concrete step in the middle of the square. He sighs.

Young kids and their parents stop by to shake his hand and say something in Arabic. One man kisses his cheek and hugs him, saying "U.S. Army, good."

McCoy smiles and corrects the man: "Marines."

A boy approaches. McCoy takes off his helmet and puts it on the kid's head.

A woman asks to use his satellite phone. I'm thinking he'll refuse, but he just stands up and gets the phone out of his pocket.

"What's the number?" he asks.

*"There's too much happiness, too much celebration, what the liberation of Paris must have felt like." My father was one*

*of the soldiers who liberated Paris. Please stop disgracing his memory by using words like this.*

I feel good that the war seems to be over. But I'm dead tired. Irritable. My feet are killing me. I walk around the Palestine Hotel, trying to find Collier. Outside is a grassy courtyard. There are steps leading up to it. I'm walking behind a TV cameraman and he stops on the steps, blocking passage.

"Get the fuck out of the way," I growl and push his shoulder. He turned to look. There must have been something in my eyes, because he said nothing.

I'm not particularly proud of that moment. I'm a nice guy. But I can't explain the irritability. And besides, the dumbass shouldn't have blocked the way.

Collier's on the 11th floor, and there is no electricity to run the elevators. That's a long hump. Finally, though, I find him in his room. It's nice, but there hasn't been maid service for weeks, maybe months. I set up my laptop on his coffee table and started to write.

I feel human again. I'm in a hotel room. It's cruddy, but it's not living in the dirt. Rob has a small refrigerator. It's connected to a generator 11 floors below, that he shares with a couple of other reporters. They turn it on for a couple of hours a day. And he's got beer. It's still lukewarm because the fridge hasn't been on for long. But I don't care. Nothing ever tasted as good.

Rob and I write late into the night, stopping sometimes to talk about our experiences. Sometimes I think how I can't believe we made it through alive. After I get done with my story, I head for his bathroom. He has running water. It's not hot, but I haven't bathed in weeks. So I take a cold-water birdbath in his tub. It's painfully cold, but I have a wonderful fresh feeling when I get done.

While I'm bathing, Rob gets an e-mail from the *Chronicle*. Several news outlets in the States are looking for reporters to interview about the day's events. The O'Reilly show wants one of us at 4:30 a.m. the next morning. I volunteer. I know Rob would be up late, and I was used to getting up at 4:30 because the Marines did it every day.

Then I sack out on his spare bed. And sleep like a dead man. The mattress was perfect and I was perfectly tired. The show's producer calls at 4 a.m. I wake up and have no idea where I am. Or how I got there. After I shake out the sleep, I go sit at the desk, half asleep, and curse myself for agreeing to do the interview. What do I care about Bill O'Reilly?

The silver lining in this is that family and friends saw me on the show. My stepbrother, Jeff Chleboun, was watching the show in Schuyler, Nebraska, and heard the promo, "*Chronicle* reporter John Koopman live in Baghdad" and turned on his VCR.

After the show, I'm awake. The elevators still don't work, so I walk down 11 flights. I meet McCoy in the stairway. He hasn't slept at all. He had been doing TV interviews all night, CNN, Larry King, all the big names. McCoy's a household name.

The lobby of the Palestine is a madhouse. Hundreds of reporters, photographers, and producers come and go, chatting up Marines, trying to set up interviews. Iraqis come in to look for work. Marines set up security outside.

News comes in gulps. The army is roaming western Baghdad. Saddam is nowhere to be found. The Iraqi government has withered. The UN ambassador says "The game is over."

That's good enough for me.

The Marines are still on edge, worried about ambushes and suicide bombers. Not far away, a suicide bomber sets off an explosion that wounds three Marines. The Iraqi's body is cut in half.

About the same time, a squad searching a building finds a suicide bomber central. It looks like a factory. There are leather vests with pockets to hold explosives and detonators. And some empty hangars that, apparently, once held bomb vests. A Marine shows me a note he found inside, with Arabic writing, offering instructions on how to detonate the device. The cards said, essentially, "Press this button and then press the other button and the red light will come on. Then pull the ring attached to the cord to detonate."

I'm thinking, "This note could be the last thing some Iraqi ever reads, or sees."

This is the new reality for troops in Baghdad.

"We can expect small-scale attacks on targets of opportunity," reports Captain Mangan, the intelligence officer. "The strength of the militia is that they know the terrain. Their weakness seems to be that they're poorly trained and they have no command and control."

They will get better later on.

*I'm the wife of one of the marines you have been travel-ing with (***) At 4-11-03 about 2 a.m. my time, my husband called me and told me that you let him use your phone. I just wanted to tell you thank you so much. That was the first time I heard from my husband since the war started. After 2 months of searching and asking my key wife I finally found articles about what his unit is doing. I can't thank you enough for letting him use your phone and giving me a little reassur-ance. [Key "wives" are volunteers who act as liaisons between the Marine unit deployed overseas and their family members back home. Typically they are wives who have been "married" to the corps for a number of years and have experienced mul-tiple deployments. The Marines take care of their own.]*

It's dangerous in Baghdad. The streets are jammed with people, especially around the Palestine Hotel, and the hotel across the street, the former Sheraton. Gunshots can be heard every couple of minutes. Some shots are close; others far away. Shooting is common, so no one really bothers to check it out. You can sit in your hotel room with the window open and hear automatic gunfire. Sometimes it's just a couple of shots; sometimes an exchange of fire.

I'm in a room at the Sheraton with a reporter from *U.S. News and World Report*, Kit Roane. We hear shots coming from outside, near the banks of the Tigris River. We ignore them. More shots. We look out the window. Marines are running, but are they running really fast? With urgency? Not really, so we go back to our conversation. More shots. Now there is sustained automatic gunfire and mortars going off. We can see the splashes landing on the other side of the river.

"You suppose we ought to go down there?" I ask.

Kit rolls his eyes. "I guess we ought to check it out."

By the time we get downstairs, the shooting is over. It's nothing. Someone had set up a machine gun in a building on the other side of the river and taken shots at the Marines on this side. The Marines responded with about a thousand rounds, until there were no more shots from the other side. As usual, we have no idea whether anyone died. Maybe the Marines have killed whoever was shooting. Maybe they just ran away to shoot again another day.

Three-Four is ordered to a new position away from the Palestine. They move into the grounds of an Iraqi ministry about two or three miles away. Kilo Company continues to stand guard along one side of the hotel complex, near the Tigris River. In the evenings, I go over and sit with the guys. Gunny Courville and Jim Kirkland make coffee and we talk about what we're going to do when we get home. I know I'll be gone long before they will.

I set up the sat phone and Kirkland forms a line of Marines to call home for a couple minutes each. Those big, bad killers get choked up when they hear their mom's voice, or wife, or kid. I'd let them keep talking, but Kirkland has to pry the phone out of their hands sometimes.

Some calls are not so friendly. One kid was pissed that he hadn't gotten any letters from his girlfriend. He got her on the phone and said, "Hi honey, I'm sorry to hear about your hand." Pause. "Yeah, I figured you must have hurt your hand OTHERWISE YOU WOULD HAVE WRITTEN TO ME!" Then he steps away and I can't hear the rest of it, but he doesn't seem to calm down much.

Now, with the main threats gone, the guys are loosening up. A couple of Amtrack crewmen are laughing and I ask what's up. A young lance corporal shows me a letter he's written to a third-grader back in the States. The kid had written to the Marines as part of a class project, sending photos of his classmates and talking about their studies and stuff.

The response letter is one the funnies things I've ever read. I wish I had kept a copy of it. I remember the Marine belittling the use of language and grammar. Suggesting that the American educational system is in ruin. Okay, you had to be there. But what really cracked me up was a line at the end, when the Marine wrote: "What's the deal with sending pictures of your friends? If you really wanted to help me out, how about a nudie picture of your teacher? How about some smokes?"

The Marine said he never intended to send the letter. He just wrote it out of boredom. But that's one funny jarhead.


Baghdad has turned into Dodge City. There are shootings every day. Sometimes people get shot for no good reason. One day, a man tries to enter the battalion compound. The Marines at the gate tell the man to get back, but he keeps trying to climb over the fence. The Marines shout and yell and try to physically push him back repeatedly. But he keeps coming.

Finally, a Marine shoots the man dead. There is no weapon on him.

No one knows whether the man was prompted by desperation or fear or hatred.

"It's a tragedy, really, but the Marine did the right thing," the sergeant major says.

Meanwhile, looting has become the national past time. I think the Bush Administration and the military messed that one up. No one seemed to care that the Iraqi people stole from government offices and buildings. The thought was, they'd suffered under Saddam; let them get something for it.

But it really was a mess, and it made it a lot more difficult to put the country together again. They still haven't.

Rob writes stories about the looting. I have nothing to do one day, so I go with him and his driver/interpreter to check it out.

We stop by the German Embassy. Iraqis are running in and out, taking everything. Windows were smashed. Water was running two inches deep on the marble floors. The German flag lay soaked on the floor. But there's nothing to report there, so we move on.

We drive to one of Uday Hussein's homes on the banks of the Tigris River. It's an opulent, three-story home of brick and marble. It's been picked clean. The stairway banister is gone. So are outlet covers. Someone is hauling a toilet down the steps. Iraqis look at us strangely as we come and go. They don't appear threatening. I think they're wondering if we're going to bust them. When we don't, they smile and go about their business.

We drive to a building that once housed offices of the Mukhabarat, the Iraqis secret police. The building is a wreck. Two missiles, or artillery shells, came in through the roof and exploded downstairs. The building is tilted at an angle and the missile holes smolder. Rob is looking for documents. We find out much later that a lot of journalists did this, with pretty good results. But we wonder why the CIA or military intelligence hasn't come before us. Maybe they did. But they left stuff behind.

I'm looking at pictures and equipment. Rob is excited about some documents that show the Russians were helping to train Iraqis in intelligence work right before the war. He ended up writing a front-page story about it. It's great work on his part.

As night falls, we have to get out of there. It's way too dangerous. Not for Rob, though. He'd lived through the bombing. Not much scared him. Personally, I don't want to die for some documents.

So we head back to the Palestine, where I drink warm Belgian beer while Rob goes over his documents and calls the office. I head down to the dining room. Gary Knight and Kit are there with some other reporters. We try to have some dinner, but it's horrible. Hard-boiled eggs and the stringiest chicken in existence. I have a Coke, and break out an MRE. Soon, we're all eating MREs at the ornate hotel dinner table. They suck, but they're better than the Iraqi food at this point.

Three-Four sets up security at a hospital. They send Marines and a couple of tanks. Nothing says "get the hell out of here and don't bother me" more than an M1 Abrams.

That's when the fifth Marine is killed.

Corporal Jesus Gonzalez is a tank crewman. He climbed to the top of the tank when an Iraqi came out from hiding with an AK-47 in his hands. The Iraqi shot the corporal in the back. The corpsman says the bullet entered the Marine under his armored vest in the rear, went upwards through his heart and came out the front, lodging in the Kevlar material.

"That's harsh, man, but that's war," said one Marine.

The Marines are all pretty salty now. They're combat veterans. They've joined an elite group of men and women around the world.

Some have baby faces and some have pimples. They like Game Boy and fast cars. They're just kids, 18 or 19 years old, fresh out of high school. I went looking for some 18-year-olds one day, trying to get at the mystique they carry with their new status.

"I went to war," said Lance Corporal Loc Le, a lanky 18-year-old from San Diego. "Not many 18-year-olds can say that."

So while their buddies from high school were wondering which fraternity to pledge, or whether they would get a job at Wal-Mart, these young Marines were ducking bullets and, in some cases, killing enemy soldiers.

Le still has the gangly, awkward gait of a teenager, and so it is difficult to see him as a combat veteran. Before he joined the Marines, he was into computers and thought about college. But everyone was into computers, he said, and he ended up in the Marines.

Le remembers the first time he pulled the trigger on his M-16 in combat, but he can't remember where it was.

"Where was that town where the RPG almost hit us?" he asks a friend. "You know, the one where Ski jumped on top of the AAV and shot the RPG guy?"

Private First Class Dennis Sardinha fought in the palm grove at Kut, where Evnin got killed. The 19-year-old from Fall River, Massachusetts, watched his fire team leader get hit.

"After it was over, I sat in the AAV and thought, 'I was just in a fire-fight. I could have been shot.' I was glad I was still alive and in one piece."

Lance Corporal Jason Swaim has been a Marine for only nine months, but he's glad to be here. His father was in the military, and other relatives. "We have a tradition of military service," he said. "This war is mine."

In the Marines, there is a mystique about combat. Those who have endured it have an aura; they have tested themselves against death and come out alive. It gives them an edge, or at least bragging rights, over those Marines who might be older and outrank them, but who have never heard shots fired in anger.

"I saw all these older corporals and sergeants who were just seeing combat for the first time," he said. "And I got to do it right away. That made me feel good about myself."

The Marines are given the task of conducting civil affairs in nearby communities. This is a huge departure for them. They're more comfortable smashing and bashing and destroying things. There's no way to sugarcoat it. They fight, they kill. Now they're told to make nice and help the civilians.

Now, instead of kicking in doors and tossing hand grenades, they're knocking on doors and taking tea with Iraqis.

"We will go from hero liberators to despised occupiers," McCoy said. "Whether it takes a year or a week depends on how we conduct ourselves."

It used to be that the Marines shot at any Iraqi holding a weapon. Now they're told to allow some Iraqis to keep their weapons if they're for defensive purposes. They're only supposed to fire if the Iraqi with the AK-47 acts hostile.

For those Iraqis who pose any kind of a threat, McCoy told his men to employ "a continuum of force:" a verbal warning, physical restraint, butt-stroke with a rifle, and then gunfire.

Meanwhile, Iraqis are dropping off wounded family members and friends so they can get adequate medical care. And sometimes they drop off dead bodies, because they may have no other place to put them.

I don't know much about Iraq. I never learned much more Arabic than "Salam Alaikum." I didn't cover the war to write about the Iraqi people, history, culture, or society. That was Collier's job.

Along the march toward Baghdad, I had very little contact with Iraqis. I met a couple of men at the Basra Airport. But that was a small, awkward discussion. They didn't know me or trust me and there was not time to make that work. And the Marines had just gotten done bombing the hell out of their neighborhood.

I saw a few people in Afak and Diwaniyah. Mostly, the Iraqis I saw were dead, or prisoners of war.

Baghdad, though, was a different story. With the fall of the city, and the Marines out doing their thing, I had a few chances to meet some citizens. Every day, I would walk from the Palestine Hotel to the municipal zone where the Marines were headquartered. They all thought I was nuts for walking the two miles down a main road to get there, but I never felt threatened.

The shops were mostly closed because of the war. There was no electricity or running water at the time. But slowly it came back on.

Enterprising men opened shops, or had tea stands on the sidewalk. I stopped a few times to chat, just because I wanted to know a little about them. Look, I'm never going to write a book about Iraqi culture, but you can be civil in times like this.

The people I met had mixed emotions about the war. No one liked Saddam, but having your country invaded is no fun, either. Some Iraqis called Americans murderers. They had hard, angry looks on their faces.

Some were effusively thankful for the removal of Saddam.

One young man in a jogging suit stopped me one day and thanked me for overthrowing the dictator. Like I had something to do with it. I told him I was a journalist, but he simply saw me as an American.

"Only Bush and Allah could stop Saddam Hussein," the man said. "Thank you, Bush."

I asked him about having American troops in his country. His smile faded a bit, and he said it was all right. As long as they didn't stay for long.

How long, I asked, is too long.

"Six months or a year," he said. "If longer, trouble."

I'm out on patrol with 2nd Lieutenant Milan Langella and a squad of young Marines. We load up on an Amtrack and head to a mosque. A Marine patrol took fire from there the night before. The front door, a big metal sheet, is locked. The Marines try bashing it in with their rifle butts. Then stick a wad of C4 plastic explosive on it. Langella covers me with his body, to protect me from the blast.

They blow the door and rush in. They find nothing but an upset groundskeeper, his wife, and daughter.

But now they've attracted a crowd. There are so many journalists in town, a Marine patrol can't drive down the street without a cameraman joining in. They're starting to piss me off. As the Marines go through the building, the groundskeeper invites me into his quarters. I go in reluctantly. I'm alone with them, and we don't speak the same language. But the Iraqis are wonderfully hospitable. I'm a guest, no matter what the circumstances. But I can't stay long, I have to run out with the Marines.

We head over to a financial district, where there have been reports of bank looting. There, an Iraqi man and his young son approach. The man is wearing a brown plaid shirt with blood soaking the sleeve. With the help of an interpreter, he tells the lieutenant that he's been shot, and the shooter is a couple of blocks away.

Langella opens the man's sleeve and looks at the bullet hole, still oozing blood. He tells the squad to move out. The dozen Marines trot down an alley, M-16s pointed toward windows and doors, canteens and ammo pouches swaying, and sweat dripping from beneath their helmets.

"He might be leading us into an ambush," Langella tells his radio operator. "If we don't find anything in a couple of blocks, we'll cut it off."

They twist and turn through the streets and come to a spot on the banks of the Tigris River where buildings have been shot up and bombed out, and ashen wrecks of cars litter the dirt.

There, 100 yards away, are about 25 young Iraqi men. Groups like this make the Marines suspicious. The Iraqi army never really confronted U.S. troops in Baghdad, and most believe they put on civilian clothes to blend in with the rest of the populace.

Langella's men advance with weapons ready and order the men to lie down in the dirt. A Marine searching nearby comes up with an AK-47 assault rifle and two fully loaded banana clips taped end to end.

One by one, the Marines sit astride the Iraqis and go through their pockets.

"Yeah, I know," says one Marine as he rolls an Iraqi over. "This sucks."

During the search, the man and his son scan the men's faces. The boy looks at one Iraqi and gestures to the Marines: That's the one who shot my father.

The man says something to the boy, but he doesn't flinch. A Marine yells at the Iraqi to shut up. A couple of other Iraqis stir restlessly as they lie in the dirt.

"Put your nose in the dirt," one Marine yells at an Iraqi. "This is the last time I'm going to tell you."

"If you need to put your boot on his head to get him to shut up, then do it," Langella tells the Marine.

A Marine starts to sing: "It's a great day to be alive," and an Iraqi, who apparently understands English, laughs.

The wounded man is grimacing in pain and making shooting gestures to indicate how he was shot. A Navy Corpsman, Petty Officer 3rd Class Justin Salinas of Monterey, cuts away the man's sleeve and sterilizes the bullet hole, then wraps a dressing around his arm. The Marines give the boy a bag of Skittles.

As the Marines leave with the suspected shooter and two others in tow, the other Iraqis get up from the dirt and cheer.

"It's weird that they cheer us after we roughed them up like that," Salinas says. "Maybe that guy we got was an asshole with them, too."

We go out again later that day. The neighborhood around the municipal center is pretty nasty. Garbage is left in the streets or set on fire. Black rivulets of raw sewage course down alleyways.

"We have no electric, no water," says one older man. "We have no petrol, no gas for the cooking. Please tell the people we must have water, we must have electric."

It's hard to know what the Iraqis think about all this. When the Marines are out on patrol, most Iraqis smile or wave. A little girl sits in her father's arms and says "bye-bye" to the sweaty, dirty Marines. An old woman looks at a Marine and says, "Good boy, good boy."

Marines respond with the only Arabic they know: "Salam Alaikum." Peace be upon you.

Langella stops to speak with a young Iraqi man wearing a dirty T-shirt with "Internet" on it, who told him there were five bad guys operating out of an abandoned mosque. Langella said he would probably set up an ambush for the men that night.

I plan to go out that night. But I get back to the Palestine after the second patrol and my feet are killing me. I have silver-dollar-sized blisters.

But the patrol goes out. A couple of Marines go up on a roof, trying to spot the bad buys below. Corporal Jason Mileo takes off his helmet. No one knows why. You're not supposed to. For one thing, it protects your gourd. For another, it identifies you as a Marine. The men all wear, more or less, the same outfit, right down to goggles strapped to helmets. But it's hot in Baghdad.

A sniper on a rooftop sees a man with no helmet carrying a weapon and looking down into the street where the Marines are supposed to be. Apparently, he figures it's a bad guy, about to shoot Marines. And he pulls the trigger.

Mileo is the sixth and final fatality the battalion suffers. That is, the last one in this part of the war. There would be others later.

And the patrols go on. The Marines come upon Iraqis who have just finished robbing a bank. They find millions of Iraqi dinars. Later, they come upon some other looters with thousands of American dollars.

McCoy sees himself as protector of the weak. He's especially fond of his "thug patrols." Two burly, beefy tank crewmen go out looking for the meanest, toughest Iraqis and mete out street justice.

The first time is at a gambling den. Locals point out the place and tell the Marines that the men who go there have been robbing and threatening people. So the Thug Patrol pays them a visit. No one will say later exactly what happened, but the Marines apparently beat the hell out of some Iraqis to send a message: Leave these people alone.

"We're out-thugging the thugs," McCoy says. "We want them to know there's a new game in town. We're introducing them to the Marine Corps."

It's time to leave Baghdad.

The war is over. There's more work to do in Iraq, and more stories. But I've had enough; I've been gone for more than two months. I want to go home.

I go to the battalion one more time to say goodbye. It's hard. I've been living with these guys for more than a month. I want to get out, but it bothers me they have to stay. The only consolation is that they have orders to leave Baghdad and head for a staging area in the south. They might still be in danger, but probably not.

I shake hands and exchange e-mails with the guys I know best. Kevin Smith gives me a big hug and then presses something into my palm. It's a rosary. "I carried that with me the whole time over here, for luck," he says. "Now you keep it."

I want to protest. He's in a lot more danger than I. But it's a heartfelt gesture, so I keep the rosary.

I say goodbye to McCoy, and invite him to stop by San Francisco some time. I'll buy him a drink.

Howell and I share an MRE, and I tell him I feel like a slacker for leaving while the Marines are still there.

"Don't be an idiot," the sergeant major says. "If you have a chance to get out of here, take it. I would."

Which is a lie, but I appreciate the thought.

The next day, Macor, the *Chronicle* photographer, and I get on a truck for a ride to division headquarters. We're with a handful of other reporters, including news crews from Fox News and the BBC. Which means we have to help them load about 50 pieces of equipment. Each. At division, we unload the truck and wait for a helicopter. Load that and take a ride to an airfield south of Baghdad. The city is beautiful from the air. The buildings are all caramel and cream color, and the architecture looks like something out of an Arabian fable. A dozen fires fill the sky with smoke.

At the airfield, we climb aboard the first C-130 cargo plane bound for Kuwait City. The plane is so loud, the crew hands out ear protection. I nod off in the jump seat, my helmet gently knocking against the steel beam on the bulkhead.

The entire trip from Baghdad to Kuwait City takes 12 hours. You can drive it in eight. By the time we get to Kuwait City, tempers are short.

A Fox News reporter starts screaming at a Marine gunnery sergeant because no one knows how to get us from the airfield to a highway, or into the city.

I get on my cell phone and call the Hilton. I ask for four taxis to meet us at the front gate. I'm told they'll cost $100 apiece.

The Marines find a driver to take us and all our gear to the front gate. Just before the taxis pull up, a couple of cars arrive for the Fox crew.

Now it's my turn to lose it.

"Hey," I yell. "I called for those cars for all of us. You have to pay like the rest of us."

"I didn't ask for any car," the TV reporter says. "I'm not paying a thing."

"That sucks, man," I say. "You heard me call for those cars. I told everyone I was getting them. Now you want to punk out because you have your own transportation?"

"I didn't ask you to get the cars, so I'm not paying. That's final."

"Oh, fuck you, asshole."

"What did you call me?"

"I called you an asshole."

"You better watch your mouth."

"Or what?"

"What? What is this, you want to fight me? Here?"

I was blind mad. "I will kick your fucking ass right here and now."

With that, the other reporters separated us. The Fox guys grumbled and got into their cars. And left.

I felt like shit. The thing with the taxis wasn't a big deal. It was just the principle of the thing. But I hated losing control and acting like a school kid fighting at recess.

While waiting for the taxis, Macor and I met a Kuwaiti soldier. He invited us to wait inside the tent they had set up at the front gate. It was very nice inside. Carpeted and air-conditioned. I'd never been in an air-conditioned tent before. They gave us tea and cookies. We told them about the war, and joked around. They were good guys.

When the taxis showed up, the Kuwaitis tried to talk them out of charging us full price. There was a lot of yelling and arguing in Arabic. I didn't understand a word. But I thought the one Kuwaiti officer was going to arrest or shoot one of the cabbies. Finally, we'd had enough and thanked the Kuwaitis for their help. We got in the taxis and drove to the city.

We get to the front of the Hilton and Macor, who has the cash, starts arguing with the cab driver about the price. I'm irritable, and I can smell a hot shower. So I say, "Just pay the man, Michael, don't be an idiot." Like I'm one to talk. In any case, it was Macor's turn to lose it. He screamed at me and called me a fucking asshole and said he wasn't going to pay.

A French journalist, the only one who didn't lose his cool, calmed us down. Michael paid for the taxi and we went to our rooms.

The Hilton is air-conditioned, with beautiful stone-cut floors and marble bathrooms.

I order room service: a cheeseburger and Diet Coke with ice. The guy forgets the ice. I give the room-service attendant an extra $6 and ask him to go back for the ice. I need that ice more than air itself.

Then I climb into the marble shower and let hot water wash away the grime of a month in the field.

I fly out on the next available flight.

*The war is over? Not sure how to interpret that sentence. As someone who has treated many veterans for the effects of the type of experience you write about I can assure you it will not be over for a long time if at all for most participants. The current number of suicides and incidences you are not allowed to write about are just the beginning of the long and imminent erosion of mental health that these situations create on a very large scale. Portraying this as some sort of victory is questionable as it does not even appear to be a military victo-*

*ry at this point if one judges by the traditional means of hav-
ing control of areas. War does not produce victors; it produces
different forms of losers. Most of the people now serving over
there will not likely have either happy or long lives. All over
weapons of mass destruction that were never found despite
over a thousand people being paid around the clock to find
them; this was the reason we as a country were given over and
over and over again for the immense sadness that is only now
starting to fall upon us.*

The 3rd Battalion, 4th Marine Regiment, spent the following month
in the desert, near Diwaniyah. They did absolutely nothing for the entire
time. Just sat in the searing sun and waited to go home.

The only incident of note came with a stomach ailment. It might
have been poor hygiene. It might have been the water. In any case, they
were blowing out of both ends for several days.

Major Matt Baker, the executive officer, called it "The Epicenter of
Ass."

McCoy told me later just how bad it got. Everyone puking and shit-
ting.

"I remember being on my hands and knees, spewing into a ditch,
and one of the Marines came over to check on me," he said. "I just
looked up at him and said 'get the hell away from me.' Oh, it was bad."

2nd Lieutenant Oscar Jimenez remembered the heat. Everyone
lying in the heat, in the middle of the day, doing nothing. Didn't have the
energy to move.

But they did put together a memorial for the six dead. They made
the time-honored memorial of a rifle, with bayonet, sticking in the dirt.
With a helmet on top.

They made six of these. Three of them were the helmets of armored
crewmen. The entire battalion comes together in formation.

Every man in the battalion passes by. They touch each helmet. And
say goodbye.

# CHAPTER 10

# GOING HOME

I couldn't wait to get out of Kuwait and back to San Francisco. After more than two months of death and destruction, living in the dirt, and eating shit, I was ready to relax. Two months doesn't sound like a lot. In a way, it's nothing. People went through years of hardship and deprivation in other wars. Even in Vietnam, soldiers and Marines went for a year. But time has an elastic quality. It exists in your mind, as much as reality. If someone says you have to be somewhere for a year, you wrap your mind around that and do your time. If it's a month, you do the same. The real problem is when the time is open-ended. You don't know when it will stop, or how long you have to go. So, for me, nine weeks felt like a lifetime.

I enjoyed every morsel of food, every step in fresh, clean clothes, and every moment of sleep in a soft bed. We all enjoy these things, but they are so much better when you've gone without for a while.

I flew out of Kuwait on September 21 and got back to San Francisco on the 22nd. I took a cab from the airport and went straight home. I wondered whether Isabel would still be there, and if so, for how long. Had the trip permanently destroyed our marriage? And what about Jordi? Would he resent me for leaving? Would he become sullen and moody?

Isabel met me at the door. It was a wonderful, sweet embrace. Made so much more by time and distance. I was glad to be home.

Jordi was still at the after-school center. Isabel showed me a sign she and Jordi had made. A 2x2-foot white paper with the words, "Welcome home, Daddy. We love you." I have that on my office wall next to the Iraqi flag.

Later, we went to pick up our son. I sat on a bench on the sidewalk while Isabel went inside to get him. They came out. Jordi was walking next to Isabel, talking fast about some project or other at school. My little man. As they walked closer, I turned my face toward him and said, "Hi, booger."

Jordi went ballistic. He ran at me. Leapt into my arms and gave me the biggest bear hug ever. He wouldn't let go, even to get into the car. He wouldn't let me go the rest of the day. We stayed glued at the hip. I kept touching him, and kissing him, and he would hug me back. He needed his daddy.

I took him to school the next day. I gave a little presentation to the kids in third, fourth, and fifth grades at Sherman Elementary. I talked about the war and what I had seen. The kids wanted to know if I killed anyone.

As they were leaving the cafeteria, I heard a little girl say to Jordi, "Your dad is so cool." And that helped in the healing process.

The separation was harder for Jordi than I would have thought. I figured he was too young to understand the concept of war, and the dangers of being in Iraq. I also thought the time away wasn't so long, just a little more than two months. I know a lot of parents who have to spend longer times away from their families.

But I sorely misjudged Jordi. He watched the news and read the paper. He saw the bombing and shooting, and heard about death and destruction. His sole focus being on me, he imagined I was a step away from death at all times.

Plus, I had never been away from him for such a long time. So he took it pretty hard. He got moody. He got into some fights at school. Sometimes, he would curl up in bed and cry. Isabel worked with him, and tried to be mother and father for him. She did a great job, but I felt a lot of guilt when I got back and found out how bad it had been.

I had to work hard to re-establish the father-son bond. A couple of days after I got back, Jordi and I made a tent out of blankets in his bedroom. We opened some MREs I'd brought back with me, and we talked about the war.

I showed him how to cook his meal using a little water in the chemical bag, and we shared some Skittles.

"I thought about you every single day," I told him. "I kept a bag of Skittles in my pocket and sometimes I would touch it and it would remind me of you."

"Here ya go," he said, and poured some Skittles into my hand.

"I'm sorry, bud. I won't do that again."

"It's okay, dad. That's your job."

"Well, I don't want to be away from you that long again. Let's not do that."

It took a little longer to work things out with Isabel. although she was glad I made it home alive, and in one piece, resentment lingered. I didn't blame her. I wasn't exactly sorry for what I'd done. Still, I apologized for putting her through such a rough time. She went through hell and it wasn't anything she had asked for. It was thrust upon her. She didn't even get paid for it.

Marriages are funny things. They seem frail, as if any one argument can rip them apart. But you work things out over time. A week after I got back from Iraq, things had changed. The love was back. The affection was back.

"I'm glad you went to Iraq," she said. "I'm glad it worked out for you. Just don't ever put me through that again."

I wouldn't think of it.


Twentynine Palms always looks the same. Sunny. Rocky. Sandy.

It's July and I'm back to cover the battalion's homecoming. I've looked forward to this day for weeks. First, because I'll get to see

McCoy and Dave Howell and Kevin Smith again. And all the others. But also, I get to meet some of the moms, dads, and wives I've met through e-mail all those months.

As I drive down Highway 62, from Palm Springs toward Twentynine Palms, I start to see the signs, sprouting like weeds. Some, from businesses, said "Welcome Home" or "We Support Our Troops."

Closer to the base, and especially along the fence next to the front gate, hundreds of signs and yellow ribbons proclaimed love and support for the Marines and sailors of the battalion.

Some were from wives, expressing love. Many more were from the kids who hadn't seen daddy for four or five months. "It's time to hold me now, daddy," said one big sign with a picture of a young boy on it.

Along the chain-link fences just outside and inside the front gate, thousands of signs are crammed together in one big mosaic of love.

I drive up to the parking lot near the base theater. A huge crowd has already gathered. They've come by the hundreds. Some of them have flown in from Ohio and Indiana, just to stand in a hot, dry parking lot to see their Marines get off the bus. To know, to be certain, he's still alive. Wives, kids, moms, dads, sisters, brothers, and a couple of crazy old uncles.

The amount of raw human emotion is intense.

It's warm and dry in the late afternoon sun. It's a very nice summer evening in the desert.

I walk into the crowd and a woman spots me. "John?" she asks, tentatively. I say yes, I'm John, and she throws a big hug on me. It's Brenda Freeman. "It's great to meet you after all this time," I say. She keeps hugging me.

Finally, she lets go and introduces me to the family. We're talking and someone else walks up. "Did I hear her say you're John Koopman?"

And on it goes. Individuals or whole families would see me and want to shake my hand or give me a hug. A lot of them want to have their picture taken with me. I feel like a rock star. I feel undeserving of all the attention. Honestly. I never felt like I did anything to merit that kind of response. But I understand it. I was their link, their conduit. Just reading my stories kept them close, somehow, to the ones they loved. All the better if I mentioned their loved one's name, but even if I didn't, that was okay. I was there, I was writing, I was communicating.

When their Marines were in danger, far away from home, I gave them a little help. A little relief from the unrelenting fear. They could go online, look for my byline, and see a story saying "Everything is all right."

To me, it was just a job. To them, my job kept them sane.

Eventually, I come upon my original e-mailer, Karen Gentrup. She's there with her husband and other son, waiting for Eric to show up. She and I had spoken on the phone the night before, trying to arrange a meeting here on base.

"There are no words to express how I feel right now," she said, choking up a little.

The buses carrying the Marines are late. They're supposed to get here at 8 p.m., but that time has come and gone. Word is, the buses are stopping at the armory first, so the Marines can put away their weapons before seeing their families.

So, the base band plays the Marine Hymn over and over again. Mothers walk around with buttons or T-shirts with their sons' pictures on them. Wives and girlfriends who had gotten dressed up wait nervously, while children run around in the sand.

Finally, around 10 p.m., a lone figure jogs up the road toward the parking lot. This Marine has broken ranks and chosen not to wait for his transport to pull around to the lot. He spots his wife, or girlfriend, and the two run to each other's arms. They stay lip-locked for what seemed like several hours. The onlooking families cheer. And another Marine runs up to the parking lot. And a third.

Finally, the buses pull up and the Marines start pouring out the door. Families mob the men. Couples cry and hug and kiss. Fathers grab kids and kiss them, tears streaming down their cheeks.

It's just one big quivering mass of joy and love. There's nothing for me to do but stand there and soak it up.

I spot Dave Howell kissing his girlfriend, Suzy. I tap him on the shoulder and say, "ahem." Dave spins around and gives me a bear hug. "You finally made it," I say. "Damn, you made me wait long enough."

"Oh man, you have no idea how long this day has been," he says.

Dave introduces me to Suzy. They hold hands awkwardly as he and I chat. But I don't keep them for long. "Get out of here," I say. "We'll get together later."

The sergeant major smiles. A rare one. And they cross the road to get into his pickup. I wonder if he'll make it out of the parking lot before he jumps her. Probably. He's a disciplined guy.

McCoy is there. He's the star of the night. All the families are greeting him and taking his picture. He never says no, never stops chatting with fathers or mothers who want to thank him for bringing their son home alive. Not even the presence of his own wife, Kerry, who's come from Washington, D.C., to greet her husband.

"It's good to be back," he said. "It was a long haul."

But the crowd doesn't stay long after the buses show up. The husbands and wives have gone home to have sex. The Marines with mothers and/or fathers have gone out to the various hotels to have dinner and talk.

Karen Gentrup stops to say goodbye on her way out. It's a nice looking family, all together, with their uniformed son in the middle. They surround him, as if forming a protective barrier.

Now, for the first time in a year, Eric's mom is breathing easier.

"I'm no longer paralyzed," she said. "I'm thinking that things can get back to normal."

Karen says the family, her husband, Gene, and their other sons Brad and Mark, will stay in the area until the middle of next week, just to spend some time with Eric.

"My husband was in Vietnam, so he kind of knows how these things go," she says. "We'll wait and see what (Eric) wants to do. If he wants to talk about it, fine. We'll take our cues from him."

Finally, there's no more to say. Eric and I shake hands, and the family moves out toward their cars. Karen falls back a half-step and turns toward me. She mouths the words, "Thank you," and I wave, a little embarrassed. I should thank her. Eric took good care of me.

The crowd dwindles. McCoy and his wife are among the last to leave. And then, the parking lot is empty.

Not every Marine has someone waiting at the gate. A lot of young single guys get off the bus and head down to their barracks to drop off their gear.

And then they go to town.

Twentynine Palms is just a wide spot in the road, but there are some good, honky-tonk-style taverns. They have beer, pool tables, and live bands. And women.

I hook up with a couple of the guys and we head out.

One Marine, a good friend of mine, had returned a week before-hand, a member of the advance party in charge of getting stuff ready for the battalion's return. I'd rather not mention his name, because this is a difficult and troubling part of the story. But it needs to be told. Because it's not right.

Anyway, my friend gets off the bus. His wife is waiting for him in the parking lot. She has one of their two kids with her. They hug and kiss and, eventually, go to their house in town. She puts the kid to bed and then hands him divorce papers.

I understand how relationships can go bad. I understand that a Marine wife might decide she can't live with a husband who spends months or years overseas. I understand all of that. But divorce papers on the night he comes home? The guy's been busting his ass for months, enduring heat and cold and bad food and combat. He can't get even a night of peace at home? Or maybe a week?

I heard other stories. One Marine told me his buddy got a "Dear John" letter while he was still in Iraq. His wife said she was leaving him, and that she'd put his stuff in his pickup and park it on base where he could get it. Very nice.

I never confirmed that story, or others. Obviously, there's more to the story but still. That's cold-blooded.

So he and I go to the bar with a group of other Marines from the battalion. We end up at the Rattler, a dive with a live band and several pool tables. We quickly reacquainted ourselves with Mr. Anheuser and Mr. Busch and Mr. Daniel's. Marines who had not been in combat buy drinks for those who have. The guys see old girlfriends and tell war stories.

Some of the women seem to gravitate toward the combat vets. They dance with the Marines and flirt shamelessly. I'm thinking this is a genetic throwback to the time of the caveman. McCoy once told me "Men love war because women love warriors." Here was living proof.

We close down the Rattler. It's 2 a.m. and we're huddled in the parking lot. Mostly drunk. Not wanting to go home yet. The guys are still wired, looking for action after months in the desert. One of the women, a middle-aged brunette who has been dancing and flirting with a 22-year-old corporal, invites everyone to her house.

Sounds good to me.

She lives at the edge of town. In a bungalow with a lawn of sand. Her 18-year-old daughter is inside watching TV. I'm thinking this is a little freaky, but it could be interesting. The daughter talks about her boyfriend, who is a tank crewman who served in Iraq.

The woman calls a couple of friends. I'm slightly more sober than everyone else, so I volunteer to drive over with the woman and my soon-to-be-divorced friend to pick them up. We can't find the apartment right away. It's dark and late. We stop and my friend gets out with the woman to scout around. He's still in protective mode.

"If you hear me shout, you drive to the end of the street and run an Afak drill," he says. Roger that. But there is no trouble. We find the friends. Two women, sisters in their late 30s, and their boyfriends, a couple of Marines in their 20s.

Marines will screw anything.

My friend tells one of the women that he has a Harley. "Ooh, I love Harleys!" she says. "They make me wet. Will you give me a ride?"

Her boyfriend is sitting next to her. This should be an interesting evening.

We drive back to the house and the party goes on. My friend asks the young Marines if the women are their girlfriends. It's a little murky, but it appears that the women are free agents. We're drunk. I'm talking to one of the sisters—the one missing several teeth—about her teenage kids. My friend disappears into the desert night with the other sister. He comes back about 15 minutes later. He said they'd gone to one of the cars parked out front and had sex. Afterward, she asked him for $30 to help pay her rent.

Inside, the woman who owns the house disappears into the bathroom with the young corporal she'd been flirting with. They stay in there for nearly an hour. Her daughter laughs and says, "That's Twentynine Palms. The week before you all got back, the bars were full of women looking for a good time."

I stay until close to 6 a.m. I don't want to leave my friend alone. I'm a little worried about him. He's drunk, there's tension in the air between the women and their boyfriends. This is the kind of setting you usually hear described in court documents. "And then, your honor, I saw the defendant stick a knife in the other young man who was swinging a baseball bat in the kitchen." But there are other Marines at the party, buddies of his. And by now we're all about wiped out from booze and lack of sleep.

Finally, he tells me to go back to my hotel. He says he's leaving the party, too. Everything is cool. We've all had a good time. I take off. Later, I find out he stayed for another hour, but nothing bad happened.

I leave the next day. My skull is splitting from the world's worst hangover. I wish I were dead.

Driving down Highway 62, I connect with Highway 10 and turn west. It's a canyon at that juncture and looking in the distance I see a dark cloud. It's a sandstorm headed my way.

• • •

I got a new friend out of the war. Mindy Evnin, Mark's mother.

About a week after I got back to the States, she left me a voice message, asking me to call her sometime. She wanted to talk about Mark's death.

I was a little fearful. I'm not good with grief. I don't know how she'll be on the phone. What do I say? How do you console a mother who's lost her only son?

But I called anyway. I owed her that.

We talked about Kut, the ambush, the little things I saw that maybe hadn't made it into the paper. She wanted to know everything about the day he died. The weather, the time, who was parked where. And more importantly, was he in pain? Did he suffer? It was as if she needed to put together a complete picture of Mark's last moments, so she could take this three-dimensional picture in her hand, turn it over and around, and try to understand that which cannot be understood.

She wanted to know more about Mark himself. She wanted my impressions of him. I told her what I could, but the truth was, I didn't know Mark all that well. I just think he was a funny, friendly kid who was trying to figure out what to do with his life. He should have been organizing a panty raid for his fraternity.

It was a good talk, though. We must have been on the phone for an hour.

Mindy came to California later in the summer. She made two trips. Once, to meet her son's friends after they got back from Iraq. And again, when she attended a memorial service for all the Marines from Twentynine Palms who died in the war.

I drove nine hours from San Francisco to Twentynine Palms just to meet her. She stayed on base, in housing set up for visiting families. She got to meet McCoy and Howell and Mark's buddies. I spent a while with her, looking at photos of Mark as a young boy, in high school, in his lacrosse uniform. And as a young Marine.

Mindy held up well. Better than I would have.

A couple weeks later, Mindy stopped in San Francisco on her way back to Twentynine Palms for the memorial. She was with her sister, Shira. We went out to dinner and I showed them around the city.

We had a good time. So good, I forgot sometimes that her son had died. I would find myself making a joke and then realizing that maybe it wasn't funny to someone who's only child had died very far away.

But Mindy was okay. She was a normal, middle-aged woman with a great sense of humor and a curiosity about the world.

Every once in a while, she would tear up and think about Mark. Think about her life with him, and how it would be without him. The loss of a future for both of them.

After the politicians talk, and generals wage war, after all the debate over whether the war was right or wrong, there are the families of the dead who have to live with the consequences. And that never goes away.

Mindy is 59. A psychotherapist. Her voice sounds tired, or sad, when she talks about Mark. She doesn't cry much. Only when she talks about the really bad times, the time she got the news, and when she contemplates her future without him.

Her journey started 21 years ago, when she and her husband adopted a 5-day-old baby boy.

Just before Mark was 6, Mindy and her husband divorced. Mindy pretty much raised Mark by herself.

Mark was a fun and funny child. He played lacrosse and football in high school, and had a huge interest in technology. He loved all things military and liked talking to his grandfather, a prominent rabbi in Vermont who had been a chaplain during World War II.

Mark loved airplanes and flying, and for a while wanted to become an Air Force pilot.

But school bored him. He did well in the classes where he was challenged and the teachers disciplined. But for the most part, his mother said, he just never worked hard. As a result, in his senior year, without much direction or a clear idea of what he wanted to do with his life, Mark chose the Marines instead of college.

Later, after Mark had finished boot camp and infantry school, Mindy was chatting with her sisters about where their children were going to school.

"I had to tell them, Mark wants to go to sniper school," she said.

Mark got the discipline he needed in the Marine Corps. He seemed to relish the punishment pushups, and he liked the hard physical climate. He talked to the intelligence guys about a career there, and was interested in working for the FBI or CIA when he got out.

Mark was assigned to the sniper platoon of the 3rd Battalion, 4th Marine Regiment based in Twentynine Palms (San Bernardino County), as part of the 1st Marine Division.

Mindy never visited Mark on the West Coast. She felt he needed his space, and time to grow and be independent.

Late last year, he called to say his unit would be going to Kuwait. They would go to Iraq if there was to be a war.

Mindy didn't worry too much about it. She figured he was well-trained and well-armed.

After she heard of Mark's death, Mindy went to her parents' home and told them their grandson was dead. She remembers her father shaking his head and saying "my heart." Not as in having a heart attack. As in, his heart was broken.

Hundreds of people came for Mark's funeral, many of whom had never known him. The governor was there, and other politicians. The local TV stations covered it extensively, as did the newspaper.

Mindy has a picture of her touching Mark's casket inside the hearse.

"I couldn't let go," she said.

Media from around the world started calling. Mindy spoke about Mark to everyone. But she refused to go on camera. She found the role of "grieving mother" to be undignified.

Some of the calls came from reporters who wanted her to blame the president for the war, and the death of her son.

She wouldn't do it.

"I didn't like Bush from day one," she said. "I thought he was probably finishing his father's war and he was trying to move attention away from the economy.

"But what would it help me to hate Bush? I don't know that this war didn't need to be fought. I hope it does some good for the Middle East. I hope it helps Israel. Was it a just war? I don't have a clue."

Mostly what she felt was, Why did it have to be Mark? Why did he have to be in a high position, so that the bullets hit his abdomen and not his body armor?

"I finally decided that it sucks and I hate it but it happened. It just happened," she said.

We e-mail each other often these days. Every week or so. Mindy sends little care packages. Vermont maple syrup, candies, toys for my son. I like that. I like the connection we have, even though it came from a pain that very few people can understand. I like hearing about her work and family, how she's trying to cope. How tough it was when the anniversary of Mark's death came around. And Memorial Day. How little by little she's getting better, but every once in a while she just breaks down and cries.

Recently, she sent me an article written by a Christian philosopher, Nicholas Wolterstorff, on the subject of sorrow. She highlighted two sentences:

"All I can do is *remember* him. I can't *experience* him."

She wrote in the margin, "I frequently feel this way."

# CHAPTER 11

# BACK TO IRAQ

In the fall of 2003, I worked on a long series of stories for the *Chronicle*. All about the war. As I was writing it, I kept reading about the situation in Iraq. For many months, it seemed stable. That is, stable for the U.S. military. Looked like life sucked for the Iraqis. But there wasn't much fighting. Mostly an occasional roadside bomb or some sniping.

The *Chronicle* asked me if I'd like to go back. I wanted to, sort of. But Isabel was against it. So was Jordi. Christmas was coming up, and I wanted to go see my family in Nebraska. So I said no. And figured my days in Iraq were over.

That should have been the end of it.

I kept hearing, though, that Three-Four might go back to Iraq. The thought made me a little itchy. What if they went and I wasn't there? It would be all right if they just sat around doing security work. But if they went into battle? I don't know, I can't explain it. They were my guys. Wouldn't be right for them to kill and die without me being there to tell their stories.

In October of 2003, the battalion got orders to go to Okinawa. The Okinawa experience has changed a lot since I was a young Marine. They used to keep units there full-time, and rotate people in and out. That was the model they used in Vietnam, too, and everyone thought it sucked. Because you have no unit cohesion, and it's every man for himself. Or woman for herself, as the case may be.

Since then, the Marines changed the policy. Now, entire units go over for shorter tours, usually six months instead of the full year we used to serve over there.

So it was Three-Four's turn on the rotation. Even as the 1st Marine Division was making plans to go back to Iraq, McCoy's Marines were told they would go to Okinawa no matter what. The Okinawa rotation is considered important for national defense, because it's the main military base for operations in case anything happens anywhere in Asia. So they take that rotation pretty seriously.

So the battalion flew to Okinawa. And I kept on working at the *Chronicle.*

I stayed in touch with McCoy and Dave Howell. We'd e-mail occasionally. Life on the Rock was the same as always. Lot of training and boring after hours. Okinawa used to be all about drinking and whoring. But it's a new Corps now. You have to play nice.

Meanwhile, back at Camp Pendleton, the division planners were looking at their upcoming mission to Iraq. They would be stretched thin as it was, and one of their best, most combat-experienced battalions was sitting on an island several thousand miles away.

That wasn't satisfactory. The division came up with a compromise: Three-Four would stay in Okinawa until the division was ready to redeploy, and then the battalion would join up in the flight to Iraq. Best of both worlds for the Corps, but worst for the men of the battalion.

In early 2004, the fighting in Iraq picked up. The division, along with Three-Four, returned to Iraq in February 2004.

I watched all of this intently. I had one eye on the news, and my e-mail, and the other on Isabel and Jordi. Could I go back? Could I put them through all that again?

For a while, everything was good. The regiment was sent out to western Iraq, stretching from Ramadi out to the Syrian border. They worked on interdicting weapons and fighters coming into Iraq from

Syria. They worked with the local sheiks and mayors on all sorts of civil affairs projects, building schools and power plants. That sort of thing.

It wasn't the combat they'd prepared for. But it was a mission.

Three-Four was sent to the city of Haditha, about halfway between Baghdad and the Syrian border. There is a dam there on the Euphrates River. The Haditha Dam, built by the Soviet bloc back in the '70s, stretched for a mile or so along the very flat, desert plain of western Iraq.

The dam had fallen into disrepair over time. Saddam's regime had paid to have it built, but not to keep it working and well maintained. So it was only pumping out a fraction of its electrical capacity. The United States brought in contractors to refurbish the dam. Soldiers from Azerbaijan guarded it.

I got all this in e-mails and letters from the Marines and their parents.

Even as the fighting in Iraq picked up, I didn't feel left out. Because McCoy's Marines were out of the fight. If I were to go back, I'd have to go find another unit to embed with, and I didn't really want to do that.

So I sat in San Francisco. Sipping lattes and enjoying the weather. And watching the news.

I didn't like what I was seeing. Chaos seemed to reign. Soldiers were getting picked off one or two at a time by a new weapon: the roadside bomb.

I had wondered how Iraqi insurgents would eventually fight back against U.S. forces. Everyone knew they would do something. Insurgents, rebels, guerrillas, always find a way to fight back against a heavily armed and professional fighting force. It goes back to the Romans. Earlier, even. In Vietnam, the guerrillas dug pits and placed in them pointed sticks covered in shit. When U.S. troops fell into them, they were killed or severely injured. They made other booby traps using the jungle as cover.

Iraq is completely different. Flat and sandy. How do you set traps for the occupiers? There were two ways. Plant a bomb along the side of the road. Some were in the middle of the road, but they were too easily detected. So now, they're all on the side. Where they can be buried in the sand, or in a pile of trash, or in the body of a dead dog.

An American Humvee drives past, and the bomb is detonated by remote control. There were millions of bombs in Iraq, even before the invasion. A very dedicated bunch of insurgents has collected them, and distributed them with instructions on how to arm them.

The other weapon was the car bomb. Easy. Low tech. Put a pile of explosives in a car. Find a dedicated jihadi to drive it. You don't need any fancy electronics to aim or arm your weapon, as do the cruise missiles and U.S. "smart bombs." The driver knows where to go and how to find the most vulnerable place. He drives into a crowd and hits the switch. He is incinerated along with everyone in the blast zone.

It's been a very deadly and effective tool.

Whenever insurgents have fought toe-to-toe with U.S. troops, they've been slaughtered.

They also developed another tool: kidnapping and murder. But I'm getting ahead of myself.

The thing was, I couldn't get a real handle on what was going on over there. I remembered how the Iraqis I met seemed genuinely happy to see U.S. troops, and the elimination of the Saddam regime. Now they were mad at America. There was little or no electricity or clean water. The reconstruction of Iraq seemed off track, but what did it mean?

Meanwhile, the words of one Iraqi I'd met in Baghdad kept going through my head: The Americans are welcome here, but they should not stay longer than six months or a year.

In April 2004, it was one year.

And that, curiously enough, marked the beginning of the serious resistance.

It started in Fallujah. Four American security officers got caught in a traffic jam, and were then ambushed by insurgents. Their car was hit by an RPG, and those still alive after the initial blast were executed. To the horror of the American public, TV cameras showed Iraqis beating and mangling the bodies. They were dragged behind a car and their body parts hung from the overhead railing of a bridge.

Fallujah has always been a hotbed. Even Saddam didn't mess with the Fallujans. But after the American security guards were killed, the Marines went in and tried to pacify the city. It was messy and harsh. There were a lot more guerrillas than the American military commanders expected.

The situation was bad, and the 1st Marine Division needed help. Three-Four had combat experience, and was not in the middle of any significant operation. So McCoy's Marines drove down from Haditha and joined the fight.

I read this in the news. The feeling in the pit of my stomach said I should be there.

And then, they killed Oscar.

I first met Oscar Jimenez at Camp Ripper, in the Kuwaiti desert, prior to the invasion. He was funny and smart. We spent a lot of time joking in the crappy mess tents. Oscar was a second lieutenant, the most junior of the officer ranks. But he had been an enlisted man, a sergeant. He had gone to college, gotten an education and an officer's commission, and was back at it.

Now, outside Fallujah, he was a first lieutenant. He was leading a small convoy that got ambushed. Fire came in from both sides of his Humvee. Oscar took a bullet in the leg, then got on the radio and said, "We've got to get out of here!"

The next shot hit him in the head, killing him.

The next day, I submitted a proposal to go back to Iraq. The paper said yes.


And that began another round of talks with Jordi and Isabel. The difference this time was that I could not, and would not, lie. They knew what the score was, and they also knew that I had some experience with war reporting.

Jordi didn't get too emotional. But he did ask me why I had to go.

"Aren't there other reporters, dad?"

Yeah, I said, but there aren't very many in Iraq anymore. And this is my job, I said.

"Will you promise to be careful?"

"You know I will, bud."

Isabel wasn't too happy. But she was more resigned to the prospect than she had been the year before. I told her that I would not leave the safety of Marine lines.

"I'll be careful," I said. "I know what I'm doing."

She had to point out that I survived the invasion of Iraq only by pure luck. That there were several specific instances in which I could have been killed, and it didn't matter how careful I was. In a combat zone, death and destruction strike at will.

But we also had a personal issue going on. Isabel's parents were having health problems. We'd decided that she and Jordi should spend the summer in Barcelona, taking care of her mom and dad. I would try to join them for a short vacation, but we wouldn't see much of each other for the summer anyway.

So I got a very grudging green light to go to Iraq.


It took a while to set things up. I had to contact the 1st Marine Division public affairs office, as well as the military command in Kuwait and the Pentagon. I had to buy some new gear and make arrangements for our apartment in San Francisco and such. Our neighbor, Eddie, took care of the apartment and bills. He was a lifesaver.

Time slipped by. At first, the fighting remained fierce in Fallujah. I figured I would go straight to Haditha and see McCoy and Dave Howell and the other guys. From there, I planned to go to Fallujah and see what happened.

But Fallujah petered out. The U.S. military command decided it would be too bloody—too many dead civilians—to launch a full-scale assault on the city. They could have done it. The military power of the United States is out of this world. But too many deaths would be a public relations nightmare.

So they created something called "The Fallujah Brigade," of Iraqi soldiers, and created a very tenuous peace. The Marines controlled the outskirts Fallujah, but would not go into the city itself. Marine snipers would occasionally kill Iraqis they deemed to be hostile. The Iraqis would launch mortars and rockets at the Marines, and sometimes score a hit.

Meanwhile, the Coalition Provisional Authority, which was trying to run Iraq, had announced that control of the country would be returned to Iraqis on July 1. That seemed like a likely time for a major uprising. I was thinking it could be something like the Tet Offensive in Vietnam.

But maybe not. How big was the resistance? How well organized, and armed?

I went to see Andrew Ross, the foreign/national editor who I would work for on this trip again.

"Not that I want to get shot at or anything, but what if I get over there and nothing happens?" I asked.

"So you'll write a couple of stories about that and come home."

Oh. Okay. I can live with that.

The thing is, trips like this cost a ton of money, especially for a regional paper like the *Chronicle*. So you want to get as much out of the trip as you can. We just figured it wouldn't be terribly expensive for me because I would be living and eating with U.S. troops again. So no need for hotels and drivers and translators.

By late May I was ready to go. Isabel and Jordi left for Barcelona the first of June. I had a few loose ends to tie up, and eventually left San Francisco on June 17. On my way back to Kuwait.

• • •

I flew into Kuwait City on June 18. We landed about 11:30 at night. The pilot said it was 105 degrees.

Oh lord.

I had a real fear of the heat. See, I live in San Francisco, which has the mildest, coolest climate in, like, the world. It's cool and foggy here year-round. Even in the middle of summer, the fog can cool the temperature down in to the low 60s. A real hot day here is 90.

And here I was in Kuwait, 105 degrees near midnight. Well, can't do anything about it. Just jump in and sweat.

Of course, I knew it would be hot. And I sort of wanted to be in Iraq at the height of the summer season, so I would know what the troops were going through. You can read a news story about how hot it is over there. But you don't really know until you feel it. Plus, summer is always a tough time in a war zone. People act crazy in the heat. Bad shit can happen. And that's news.

In the summer of 2004, Americans didn't need to have a visa to fly to Kuwait. The Kuwaitis would give you one at the airport. I was still a little hesitant about this—I can never shake the fear of jail—but I'd been assured by everyone that it would be no problem. It wasn't. I got off the plane, waited in line for an hour, and a friendly, smiling Iraqi police officer stamped my passport. No problem.

I went back to the Crowne Plaza Hotel, checked in, and went to sleep.

God, it's hot. Kuwait is one of the hottest places on earth. Midday, it got well past 130 degrees. How do I describe 130 degrees to you? It was so hot, when I walked outside, I got goose bumps. I guess my body temperature was so radically below the outside air temperature, my skin thought I was cold.

Preheat your oven, shove your head and shoulders inside, and sit for a moment. That's kind of like what you feel. Only it's hotter, and it affects your whole body and there is no relief.

I started going for walks around the hotel to try to acclimatize myself. It was little use. I could barely see. My eyes hurt. The heat sucked the tears from them. This was going to be rough.

I contacted the Army command in Kuwait. A young woman lieutenant came to my hotel, took my passport, and got a new, upgraded visa for me. One that would allow me to go to Iraq and stay as long as I wanted.

I was ready to go north again.

But the atmosphere was completely different from the first time around. For one thing, there were no other journalists in Kuwait. And not that many in Iraq, either. The hotel was filled with Americans, some military, but mostly civilian contractors in their khaki shirts and tennis shoes. I felt more isolated. There was no one to talk to, or share experiences or ask for advice.

A couple of days later, the Army lieutenant picked me up and we drove north. Into the desert.

The camps were still there. They didn't bustle with thousands of soldiers and Marines getting ready for war. Now, it was all about logistics and supply. The tent cities now stored material. Or they were used as transit barracks.

The lieutenant and I had some time to kill, so we went to the PX and chow hall. Outside, I saw a row of trailers turned into fast-food outlets. Pizza Hut and Burger King did good business.

She took me to a holding area, from which I would be bused to a flight line. Once there, it occurred to me that she hadn't given me any press credentials. So I asked her about it.

"We don't do that anymore," she replied. "People were abusing them, or trying to use them after they expired. You're going to be embedded, so you don't need a credential."

That sounded odd to me. When I was in Baghdad, I had to go through military lines all the time. The press pass gave me access. I figured it must be the same now, but I had no other recourse. I had to go without an ID card. That would prove to be a major problem later.

I lugged my gear into the transit tent. The Marines took my name and social security number, so in case the plane crashed they could notify my family. And I waited.

I really hate the military sometimes. You just wait and wait. It's frustrating, especially for a civilian.

Late in the evening, maybe 10:30 or 11, I got on a bus with a bunch of Marines headed for Iraq. We drove to a nearby airfield. Got out. Waited some more. More troops showed up. There were about 60 of us gathered together, when a soldier came by and called our names. Then led us to a long tent.

"Make yourselves comfortable," he said. "Your flight tonight has been canceled. You're scheduled to leave in the morning. Assuming that flight hasn't been canceled. Good luck."

Excellent. I grabbed an MRE and made small talk with a major while we ate. It was cold in that tent. The air conditioning blasted, and dropped the temperature to near freezing. I slept on the wooden floor for a couple of hours, and woke up to the sound of my teeth chattering. Went outside and the heat hit me like a bat.

What the hell am I doing here?

Dawn comes and we climb into a C-130 cargo plane. It's loaded with gear in the back, and dozens of heavily armed Marines in front. I'm wedged between them. It's a three-hour flight and I've got to pee.

We landed at Al Asad Air Base in western Iraq. On the tarmac, the temperature was easily 115 degrees. The base bustled with activity, but no shots or fighting. It was quiet, except for the sound of generators and air conditioners humming.

Al Asad used to be an Iraqi air force base. It's got a huge runway that can land just about any kind of aircraft. It's flat and dry and dusty. The American military brought in hundreds of prefabricated buildings, for living quarters, chow halls, post offices, supply and maintenance areas. It's a bustling little city out in the desert.

The Marines put me in a truck with a bunch of Marines going to the other end of the base. There, we found a convoy parked near the chow hall. The convoy was headed to the Haditha Dam. Where McCoy's Marines were stationed.

"John? John Koopman?" I heard a voice behind me. I turned to look. It was the battalion chaplain, Lieutenant Bob Grove. I hadn't seen him since the beginning of the war.

Bob had come to Al-Asad because the regiment was based there. It is the hub, around which all the Marine units work in the area. So all mail, supply, information, and comings and goings go through there.

Everyone moved in convoys in Iraq. If you were from Three-Four out at the Haditha Dam and you had business at regiment, you waited until a convoy headed in that direction. There was no jumping in a Humvee and driving to where you wanted to go. Not ever.

Bob and I had a nice chat there in the heat. With sweat dripping down my back, I leaned against his Humvee door and burned my arm. We talked about Mark Evnin. Bob had known Mark before he got killed, and Mindy Evnin had shown me the letter Bob sent her after Mark was killed.

"That meant a lot to her," I said. "You did a good job, Bob. You'll be head chaplain for the division some day."

"Well, I very seriously doubt that, but I'm glad I could offer Mrs. Evnin some comfort."

Bob saw a Marine major approaching and he introduced me to him: Andrew Roberto, a reservist from Arizona who headed up the civil affairs program for McCoy.

Roberto was a good guy, normally a police officer in Phoenix. Short and wiry, he was trained as a Recon Marine, and led a Recon company during the invasion. Now he was back to help rebuild the country.

He invited me to drive out the to dam in his Humvee. Late in the afternoon, the convoy left the protection of the front gate, and headed down a two-lane paved highway.

"I don't want to scare you, but roadside bombs are usually direct-ed at the second vehicle in a convoy," he said, turning in his seat to smile at me.

We were the second vehicle in the convoy.

It's about an hour's drive out to the dam. As we drove, I saw a crater about a foot deep on the side of the road. "We had a couple guys wounded there," Roberto said.

A couple of miles down the road, I saw two craters, about 15 yards apart. That was the latest development in roadside bombs. The daisy chain. Link two roadside bombs, so that the second one hits the vehicles that stop because of the first one.

Damn, hot, miserable, dangerous place.

But I was excited to get to the Haditha Dam. I hadn't had much contact with McCoy or Dave since they'd been back in-country. I figured the division must have told them I was coming.

We got to the dam about 5 p.m. It's an impressive piece of work. It lies long and flat there in the dusty plain. A huge lake has formed on the upriver side, but it's polluted and not good for drinking or swimming, tempting as that was in the severe heat.

On the back side, the dam stretches a couple of hundred yards across. On either side, built into the hillside, are two triangular structures. It's like a huge, ten-story office. Each floor is shorter than the next as it rises to the top floor. And balconies line each floor, as well.

On the one side, the dam offices housed the civilian contractors who were refurbishing the electrical components of the dam. The other side housed Three-Four, McCoy's Marines. Platoons and companies occupied different office spaces, turning them into barracks.

It was a pretty nice setup for the Marines. The dam always had electricity, so there was plenty of power. Not like other parts of Iraq. The men had double-decker bunks with mattresses, air conditioning, fans, TVs, DVDs, radios, movies, junk food.

Plumbing was a problem, though. There were some indoor toilets, but they were good only as urinals, and even then they often broke down. The top and bottom levels of the dam had rows of portable toilets and small prefabricated shower buildings.

Chow was just so-so. The Marines brought in T-Rats, short for Tray Rations, twice a day. T-Rats are basically foods that can be cooked elsewhere and brought in containers to a distant location. And then served on cardboard trays. The food all tasted the same, as if it were canned. The meat and mashed potatoes were brown, and the fruit was in heavy syrup. One meal a day was an MRE.

A road ran along the top of the dam, and that's where the Marines parked their Humvees and tactical vehicles. That's where the command center was located, too.

You could come into the dam on the road along the top, or at the bottom. And then you would go up or down the stairs, depending on where you slept.

We pulled in, and Roberto offered me a bunk with the civil affairs unit. I didn't want to have to bug anyone else in the battalion, so took him up on the offer. I dropped off my stuff, and Roberto said I could find McCoy and the sergeant major at the afternoon briefing, which had already started. We walked to the other side of the dam, to the briefing room. The room was built like a small theater, or classroom, with a sloped floor and padded seating.

The room was packed with Marines in desert camouflage. Three-Four only had another 10 days at this site, and then were headed back to the States. Their replacements, the 1st Battalion, 8th Marines, had begun to arrive. Most of the men I flew in with were from One-Eight. Now, many of them were in the briefing room, listening to intelligence reports on insurgent activity. Or hearing about how many cases of dysentery the medics had treated that day.

Finally, it came time for the sergeant major's report. He stood and turned toward the audience. Saw me standing in the back.

"Okay, first thing, there's a reporter on deck," he said, "so be careful what you say around him. He's bad news." Then he smiled and added, "No, he's solid. Welcome back, John."

McCoy greeted me, too, when he got up to give his report. That was useful, because it put the new Marines at ease around me. It meant

I didn't have to work so hard to gain people's trust. Which I was just going to abuse, anyway.

It was great to see McCoy and Dave. Walking through the hallways and stairwells of the dam, I ran into a lot of Marines I'd know the year before. Most didn't know I was back, and would give a double take upon seeing me, like "what the hell are you doing here?"

After the briefing, I followed Bryan to his quarters. He shared a small space with the executive officer and operations officer. Next-door to him, Dave Howell shared a space with the other senior NCOs in the unit.

They had their laptops and Internet hookups. Around the corner from their quarters, the division had set up an Internet café. A dozen or so computers were hooked up to a satellite dish that brought the Internet to them. Everyone had e-mail and a lot of guys used Instant Messenger. Live, from Iraq, it's your husband on Webcam!

I gave Bryan a cigar, a big old Dunhill. He took it, but didn't need it. Like everyone over there, he had all he needed. I brought cigarettes and cigars and chewing tobacco, but you could get all you wanted at the PX in Al-Asad, or in the little store they put up at the dam.

"So what are you doing here?" Bryan asked. "I thought you had enough of this shit."

"I couldn't let you have all the fun," I said. "But it looks like you all have it pretty cushy here."

"Yeah, it's not bad," he said, plugging in his coffee pot. "But it's nothing like Fallujah."

I got out my notebook. "I heard about Oscar," I said.

"Yeah, that was tough," he said. "He was a hell of a guy."

McCoy was quiet, and busied himself making coffee. I looked into his eyes, trying to detect what was going on there. He'd lost three more Marines on this trip. How was it affecting him?

I didn't ask him that outright. It seemed a little too, I don't know, either obvious or personal. How are you supposed to feel when men have died under your command? Bad? Yes, of course. But how bad?

"I can't let myself think about it," he said, finally. "I don't. That's not a luxury I can afford. I have a thousand other Marines to think about, and a mission."

It was the same for him as it was losing six Marines during the invasion. I'm not sure if Bryan ever let himself think about those deaths for the entire time he was commanding officer. He must have, especially in the States between the invasion and the second tour in Iraq. But he's the commanding officer. It's a god-like status in the Corps. And you have to bear the burdens yourself, deep inside you. In McCoy's world, death was unfortunate, but dwelling on it put other people at risk. And that was unacceptable.

We had a chat, got caught up on families and work and mutual friends. I told him I wanted to do a real sit-down interview, so he could tell me about Fallujah, and everything that had happened in his second tour there. We agreed to meet the next day.

You could see the gleam in McCoy's eyes when he talked about Fallujah. That was a fight. That was war. And for better or worse, McCoy is a warrior. He's the sheepdog, and he's good at chasing the wolves. It sounds bad, but if there's shooting and fighting and killing to be done, he wants to be there.

"If there's a fight going on, I want to be there for it with my fellow Marines," he said.

When Three-Four returned to Iraq, the country was relatively peaceful, with small pockets of violence here and there. McCoy said he didn't really care where his battalion was sent. He just wanted to get into the thick of things.

So Haditha was as good a place as any. It was relatively quiet when McCoy's Marines moved in. They replaced an Army unit.

"But there hadn't been a big coalition presence out here," he said. "We were the new guys on the block. Once everyone in the area found out we were here, they wanted to bloody our nose and see how we would respond."

The local insurgents stepped up the use of roadside bombs. In Iraq, they're called "Improvised Explosive Devices" or IED. It's improvised in the sense that the insurgents use any and all kinds of bombs or weapons. Often it's an old artillery shell or a rocket. It's "improvised" to explode and kill. Most commonly in Iraq, guerrillas would connect a Nokia cell phone to a detonating cord, and attach that to the bomb. Then, from a safe distance, the guerrilla would wait until a U.S. convoy drove past and dial the phone. The ring would detonate the bomb.

"That's a cowardly attack you can't punch back at," McCoy said, disgusted. "These guys are mostly cowards. They definitely plan to run away, and fight another day."

Three-Four began to run patrols in Haditha and the surrounding towns. Getting to know people, letting them know who they were. In Iraq, everything is about clans. People identify more with their clan than they do their city, province or nation.

In Haditha, the Marines became another clan. Sure, one with heavy weapons and armor. But a clan nonetheless.

McCoy was the leader of the clan. He met with the local sheiks and other tribal leaders. He learned some local customs. He had to greet important men with a kiss on each cheek, and sometimes had to hold hands with them as they negotiated some problem.

"Yeah, that got a lot of chuckles out of my staff," he said.

McCoy is an aggressive guy, and had his Marines out looking for bomb-making materials and insurgents. It's always a carrot-and-stick approach. Towns that cooperated, and kept attacks to a minimum, got money for schools or to build civic centers and mosques. The ones who didn't got nothing.

McCoy earned a nickname: "The Lion of Haditha."

*Thank you for keeping us informed on our marines. I think I speak for many wives when I say how much it helps to receive information on what they're doing and how they are living. My husband is \*\*\*. I have already read and reread*

*the article several times and have forwarded it on to our fam-*
*ily. I know they will appreciate it as much as I do. Again,*
*Thank You!*

*P.S. If you see him—I Love Him, Miss Him and am very*
*Proud of him!*

Meanwhile, Fallujah was turning into shit. The contractors were killed and the Marines were in a fight for their lives. They needed reinforcements.

The 7th Marine Regiment was spread out in the west. McCoy's colleagues were protecting the border with Syria, or otherwise engaged in important work. So was Three-Four, but the division felt they were the most expendable, and they had a lot of combat experience.

"We got the call on the 8th of April," McCoy recalled. "We loaded up and took off. We spent the night driving down there."

McCoy left behind a security force to protect the dam. He took his best infantry companies with him on the nighttime drive southeast toward Fallujah. It was a hairy, scary convoy roaring along the blacktop, on their way to help out their brothers.

Intelligence reports indicated there were 100 insurgents planting roadside bombs in their path. But the Marines made it to Fallujah without incident. By noon the next day, April 9, 2004, they were at the highway cloverleaf outside Fallujah, waiting for orders.

It was exactly one year after McCoy had stood and watched the statue of Saddam fall.

"In many ways, this was the fight that we expected last year," he said. "House to house, urban warfare."

The next day, the battalion was sent to the northeast corner of Fallujah and told to clear the area east to west. The mission: kill Mujahideen.

Specifically, the Marines were part of a cordon that tried to keep Fallujah secure. No one goes in or out of the city. No reinforcements.

The Marines were under attack regularly, by mortars, AK-47s, and

RPGs. They fought back with everything they had.

"We were killing people like it was going out of style," he said. "The Iraqis called this section, the northeast corner 'The Plague.' You didn't want to go there."

The fire died down after three or four days, McCoy said.

The battalion was ordered to go clear the town of Karma. The division had been taking a lot of rocket and mortar fire from there, earning it the nickname "Bad Karma." Three-Four was to go in, knock down anyone with a weapon, and give their fellow Marines a breather from the constant harassing fire.

During a cease-fire in Fallujah, McCoy pulled Kilo Company out and the Marines moved in Humvees toward Karma.

"No one had been there for several weeks," McCoy said. "The Muj were thick in there."

There's only one road in and out of Karma. Kilo Company moved toward the town. The road was filled with obstacles, making driving difficult and the possibility of an ambush very real. McCoy didn't have any heavy equipment, so couldn't push the stuff out of the way. He called in fire support from an AC-130 gunship flying overhead. The crew of the aircraft used infrared scopes to check for insurgents' movements in the vicinity, and to look for alternate paths into the town.

From 10,000 feet in the air, the ship shined a spotlight onto the ground, showing the Marines a way past the obstacles.

McCoy had on his night-vision goggles and could see contact with insurgents up ahead.

"This was tactical decision-making on the fly," he said. "I was just thinking, 'what can I get away with?' I hoped we could get away with winding our way into town this way once. If we got caught in the middle of all these obstacles, we couldn't get turned around. We could have been in a very tough fight out there."

At a point near where the road opened into the town, a pickup truck drove into view. The AC-130 gunship lit it up with machine-gun fire. Gasoline on the truck exploded into a fireball. Which is normally a good thing, except at night, the bright flames made the Marines' night-vision goggles useless. Too much light.

The driver of a 7-ton truck couldn't see, and drove his vehicle into a water-filled ditch. A bunch of Marines were injured in the crash, some severely. At that point, Iraqi insurgents opened up with small arms and RPG fire.

The situation looked dire.

But the Marines drove in, and took up positions in the town. And there started a continuous firefight with a very large, very determined force of guerrilla fighters.

"Karma was just full of bad guys," McCoy said. "You know how it was at Al Kut, in the grove? That was just a couple of hours. We had a full day of that at Karma."

At first contact, McCoy said, he thought the Marines would kill a few insurgents and the others would fade away, as is normally the case in Iraq. But these fighters kept coming and coming. Night turned to day, and the fighting became more intense. The Marines were taking a lot of fire from a nearby building. They called in air support and blasted the structure with two 500-pound bombs.

"There had to be 25 guys in there," McCoy said. "It was about 50–100 meters away. That was pretty close. But we couldn't fire back at that particular building because we had other buildings in the way."

So far, the Marines had suffered no casualties other than those from the truck accident. But the guerrillas were attacking from three directions. The Marines set up a 360-degree perimeter and stood their ground.

"We had a good defensive posture," McCoy said. "For the next six hours, they just kept coming at us, and we kept killing them."

The fighting got fierce, and McCoy had to call in artillery. He brought in 70 rounds of 155 mm cannon fire. It landed "danger close," which is less than 400 meters. That's not much room for error, in case one of those rounds lands short. But they all landed where they were supposed to, in a tree line across an open field.

"Those things were like freight trains coming in, obliterating everything," he said. "You could see torsos flying through the air amid the blasts."

Then it was a building under construction. Concentrated fire came out of it, and the Marines couldn't get out to clear it. Once again, air support was called in. An Air Force F-16 dropped a laser-guided 500-pound bomb on it. The bomb hit, and the building erupted like a beehive, Darkside said, with insurgents leaping out and blazing away with small arms.

The Marines fired from cover, blazing away with M-16s, squad automatic weapons, heavy machine guns and an MK-19 automatic grenade launcher.

Ammunition was running low, and the guerrillas spotted a gap in the Marines' defensive line. McCoy spotted it, too, but he had no men to throw into the breech. Other than his own Humvee crew and the guys who were wounded in the truck accident. Some of those Marines had broken bones, others were banged up and bandaged. But they could move.

"I went over and said, 'Hey, who's still in the fight? We need you,'" McCoy said. "All but one responded, and that one was pretty bad off. There they were, bandages and all, picking up their weapons, and filling that gap."

The line held. The guerrillas couldn't break through.

"It was like a game of Whack a Mole," McCoy said. "A guy would pop up and we'd kill him."

Meanwhile, Darkside began to wonder how he would get his men out of Karma. The road in was still obstructed. "A well-trained Boy Scout could have pinned us down in there," he said.

Tanks and engineers came in and started clearing a path. The timing was good, as the Marines had fired off all their mortar rounds and were now running dangerously low on ammo for every weapon. Every Marine in Karma fought, he said. Medics, officers, drivers, everybody. They all did a good job, he said, and he wrote up several

Marines for citations of valor. No one died, although there were six ambulatory wounded.

McCoy could have stayed if he'd been resupplied. But the division needed reinforcements back closer to Fallujah. And the mission had been accomplished. McCoy's Marines had flushed out hundreds of insurgents, and fought them to a standstill. They killed dozens of fighters, maybe hundreds.

"At that point, most of them were either killed or left. There was no way to keep the pressure on them, so we pulled back."

They couldn't get the wrecked 7-ton out of the ditch, so they destroyed it in place on their way out. They drove back to Fallujah and were ordered to the town of Numaniyah for a similar kind of mission. Violent supremacy. Death and destruction. That's what it was all about.

> *Please, enough propaganda. I'm not interested in an "in-bed-with" reporter glorifying a shameful war no one wanted. How about a series on the soldiers in Iraq losing life and limb right now? Or perhaps printing an article on one of the thousands of wounded (many of which are amputees) coming home now?*
>
> *How about one on the fact that President Bush has yet to attend the funeral of dead soldier.*
>
> *Enough Already.*

There were small skirmishes in Numaniyah, but nothing like the time the Marines had in Karma. McCoy's Marines stayed in the area for several more days. Fighting and waiting to see how the battle would go. Preparing for an all-out assault on the city.

Throughout this time, the Marines used psychological warfare against the guerrillas. They set up a loudspeaker and shouted insults.

"You fight like women!" they would have an interpreter say. "You are a disgrace to your religion! Come out from behind your women's skirts and fight like men!"

Other times, they would blare music at the guerrillas. Wagner's "Ride of the Valkyries" (like in the movie, "Apocalypse Now") and the heavy metal song, "Let the Bodies Hit the Floor" by Dead Pool.

And sure enough, every once in a while an enraged fighter would leap from behind cover to charge the offending Americans. Only to be cut down by ruthless and highly accurate rifle and machine-gun fire.

The Marines called the fight "Lollafallujah."

"We kept waiting for the big push into Fallujah," McCoy said. "But the higher-ups went with the Fallujah Brigade to keep the peace. So we pulled out of the city."

Intelligence reports indicated that the insurgents planned to cut off the battalion and kill as many Marines as possible. The convoy pulled out. Not a shot was fired. No one wanted to mess with Three-Four at that point.

They made their way back to Haditha to resume their previous mission: keeping the peace and hunting insurgents.

When it was all over, McCoy had lost three dead: 1st Lieutenant Oscar Jimenez, 34, from San Diego, Corporal Daniel Amaya, 22, from Ector, Texas, Lance Corporal Torrey Grey, 19, from Marion, Illinois. All died on Easter, April 11, during the fighting that occurred during a cease-fire with the Fallujah insurgents.

McCoy talked for hours about the fight in Fallujah, and what his Marines had been doing in Iraq. When he talked about the deaths, he got a little quiet. We talked about Oscar some more. He said Oscar had acted heroically. That the ambush on Oscar's convoy had been similar to the one that involved the famous Jessica Lynch during the invasion.

"Oscar trained his men well," McCoy said. "They killed ten people in that fight. The convoy got stopped in the middle of that fight, and there were guys killing at point- blank range. They got unstuck and pulled out."

McCoy said he couldn't afford to lose Oscar. "He was a good man. I felt bad, but I can't afford to talk about it. I didn't want the men to obsess about it, either. It's an emotionally draining time, and things like that lead to everything from despair to thoughts of vengeance. You just have to get over it and get back to the fight."

We sat in McCoy's room for a time, sipping coffee and reflecting on the war, and where it was headed. I told McCoy that a lot of the men griped about Fallujah. There was talk that Iraq was turning into another Vietnam, with politicians holding back the men who are paid to fight and kill.

"We accomplished our task. As eventually satisfactory as it would have been to go in there and kill every last Muj, that was not the solution. War is an extension of the political process. It's not up to Marines to question that. We would have won a tactical victory, but at what cost?

"You know Marines just like to fight. I'll tell you this, though, if we would have gone into Fallujah, and really taken it to them, the Marines would have covered themselves in glory."

# CHAPTER 12

# HEARTS AND MINDS

L ife at the dam is deceptively peaceful. Haditha is way out in the sticks. There are not a lot of attacks out there.

All right, it's boring.

A couple of days after my talk with McCoy, I went out on a raid with the Marines of Three-Four. It was like old times.

I wake up before dawn to get dressed and ready, and take my gear up eight flights of stairs to the top of the dam. Humvees were idling and Marines performing equipment checks. Dave Howell was talking to his driver. The sun wasn't even up yet and it was already hot.

The Humvees got in line and started to pull out. Just before they got to the gate, they did what every soldier and Marine does before going out: lock and load. Machine guns in the turrets, M-16s, pistols. Everything is loaded and put on safe. It's standard operating procedure, ordered by the generals, and everyone must comply.

It's dangerous out there.

The vehicles lumber down the road. That's another big change from the previous year: every Humvee is loaded down with armor. When the IEDs started going off, they ripped through the flimsy Humvee doors, and the soft flesh huddled inside. Even the Humvees that had armor plating didn't have enough. Now, everything is 3/4-inch metal with double-paned bullet-proof glass. The feel is much more like being in a truck or tank, and the Humvees lose a lot of speed with all that extra weight.

We drove into a neighborhood before dawn. Helicopters clattered overhead and dogs barked in the distance. Overnight, a team of Special Forces operatives had come through and spray-painted marks on the homes where suspected insurgents were staying.

The Marines went in heavy. That's their way. Nothing subtle about them. Walk in with a gun in your hand and start asking questions.

The neighborhood is dirty and ragged. The homes are built of mud or brick, and not very well built. Teams go into homes and, using interpreters, look for insurgents and weapons. In a lot of cases, the men they're looking for identify themselves. It's weird: They could just say they don't know who so-and-so is. But they don't.

A team has captured a man who was on a list of suspected insurgents. They put him in the back of a truck. Someone took a strip of cloth and blindfolded him.

"We used to put a sandbag over their heads, but Abu Ghraib put a stop to that," Dave tells me.

Howell walks over to the truck and hands the prisoner a bottle of water. The man says something to him and Howell responds, "Shut the hell up!"

In the courtyard of a house nearby, a family has gathered. Mostly women and children. They're speaking in Arabic, and two women are wailing uncontrollably. Apparently, the prisoner was staying there. Dave said the interpreter told him the guy was from Ramadi and was here visiting cousins. The man appears to be in his 20s, and he's got a nice haircut.

"That's usually a sign that he's Muj," Dave said. "They're the only ones who can afford that kind of thing these days."

This was my first raid of the "occupation," or OIF-II, and it seemed to describe perfectly the situation of U.S. troops in Iraq. Heavily armed troops roll into a neighborhood and start throwing their weight around. The locals, whether they have something to hide or not, hate the treatment. There is a huge cultural and language gap and you have to wonder if this kind of thing won't erode goodwill over time.

I don't mean to say the Marines and soldiers are wrong in their approach. They're getting shot at and killed, and their response is to go after the bad guys. A lot of times, they find insurgents and weapons that can be used to kill U.S. troops. But it's a bad deal all the way around. No one comes out of those experiences with any sort of goodwill.

The Marines called in a small bulldozer to dig a hole in a yard. They've been told there might be weapons buried there.

"You might want to take cover, just in case he hits something," a Marine told me.

"What about the guy running the bulldozer?" I asked. "He hasn't got much protection up there."

The Marine didn't respond, just looked away. Damn, I thought, who do they get to do that work? It feels vaguely suicidal.

But they find no weapons. And that's typical, too. They roust someone from bed to interrogate and the guy tells them anything to buy some time. Or, in a lot of cases, people rat out the neighbors they don't like, or had some feud with. Figuring out who hates whom and why is impossible, and so a lot of the intelligence is worthless.

The Marines moved on down the road, sweeping through semi-rural villages along the Euphrates River. They know they have to tread lightly, so they don't barge into people's homes and start digging around for weapons. It's usually more of a polite knock and a respect-ful request to take a look around.

Not always, though. By this time, the Marines have done this too many times. They're tired of getting shot at, or hit by roadside bombs. So the searches can be brusque, or worse.

Iraq is littered with munitions, some of which go back decades. No one throws anything away, so the men find old artillery and mor-tar shells that are rusted and caked with dirt.

Iraq is a lawless place, too, and its citizens have always had to protect themselves. The AK-47 is a household staple, like a broom or cook pot. The U.S. command authorized every adult male to have one rifle in his possession.

We stopped on a barren, dusty hillside and Dave went with the Marines through some farm houses. McCoy came by as Howell brought out a brand-new AK-47 and some mortar shells.

"I thought we went through that place already," McCoy said.

"We did," Dave answered.

"So how did you find this stuff?"

"I have a sixth sense. I can always find something."

McCoy told me another team had found spools of detonating cord, used for setting off high-explosive devices. The adult men in the house were being questioned, he said.

But that was about it. A couple of guns and shells. No shooting, no looting. Nothing.

"Bryan, you're boring the hell out of me," I said.

"Good," he said. "That's the way I like it."

The Marines spent another couple of hours out there and then headed back to the dam.

Later, after the sun went down and Dave had done all his sergeant-major duties, I brought a couple of cigars to his room. We went out on the balcony and lit up. It was beautiful out there. The moon was full and blood-red. The Euphrates shimmered.

"So, how are you doing?" I asked.

"Fine. Why?"

"You seem a little off, a little distant."

"Nah, nothing. Just the same old shit."

"Sergeant-major shit?"

"Yeah, there's a lot of that crap. But also, just this place."

"It's not like last year, is it?"

"Nothing like last year. Last year, you knew who the bad guys were. It's a lot easier to go on the attack than to sit here and wonder when someone is going to set off a bomb."

The Marines don't like occupation duty. Attack or don't attack, but don't ask them to sit and wait.

On my way out, I stopped by McCoy's room to talk to him about a story I wanted to do about civil affairs. He told me I ought to meet Captain Matt.

Captain Matt was not really a captain. Not then, anyway. He was a first lieutenant and former weapons platoon commander named Matt Danner. His job now was to act as the liaison between the Marines and the Haditha police force. Which meant he lived at the police station with a squad of Marines. They trained the Iraqis and helped them with things like getting weapons and radios. He was also McCoy's representative in the town. If the police chief, or anyone, needed something from the Americans, they talked to Captain Matt. He could make decisions for himself in some cases, or get on the radio to Darkside for important decisions.

The Marines started calling Danner "Captain Matt" because a captain in the police force has power and authority. And the Iraqis needed to see that in the Marine officer among them.

"Matt's gone native," McCoy said. "He eats their food and lives with them. He even started smoking just because that's the thing to do with the Iraqis. We call him 'Lawrence of Haditha.'"

I packed up my gear and caught a ride into Haditha.

This was a good place to be at the end of June. The United States was set to turn over authority of the country to the Iraqis on July 1. Everyone was on edge, waiting to see if the transfer of power translated into violence. It sure seemed likely.

On my way to the police station, McCoy stopped me and said the Coalition Provisional Authority had just made the transfer of power 15 minutes earlier. It was a couple of days before the scheduled date. The thinking was to disrupt anyone's plans to launch a widespread wave of violence.

No one knew what it meant, though. Would the attacks come now? Would they come on the first? Would they come at all?

I headed into town thinking the police station was a good place to be if violence broke out. It would also be a very large target, and I would be there. Could be another Alamo if things really got hairy.

The police station was a two-story building in the heart of Haditha. It had that squared-off, bunker kind of construction. The lower level held a jail, offices for the chief and his captains, and rooms for the officers to sleep.

Upstairs, the Marines occupied several rooms. There was also a room containing a family who were technically under arrest. It was some kind of complex issue requiring them to be incarcerated, but they were more like trustees. They had the run of the place as long as they didn't leave the grounds.

I went in with a couple of Marines to drop off my gear in the office. Corporal Richard Amador led the way and came upon the youngest of the trustees, Achmed, a teenage boy.

"Salaam," Amador said to Achmed.

The young Iraqi responded with one of the few phrases he knew, taught by U.S. Marines: "Wassup, bitch?"

The Marines had a good relationship with the Iraqis. It felt good to watch it. These young Devil Dogs would share cigarettes with Iraqi police officers, laugh and joke with them.

Iraqis kiss each other, hug, hold hands. Marines, typically, do none of those things. At least, not with each other. But they became culturally sensitive over time. And these tough Devil Dogs kissed and hugged their Iraqi counterparts all the time. You'd see an Iraqi cop come upstairs, and greet a young lance corporal. They'd do the cheek and shoulder kissing thing. Share a pack of smokes and talk about women or soccer or whatever.

Danner is a tall, blond, blue-eyed Marine of German heritage. His radio call sign was "Viking," and he looked the part.

He used to be an enlisted man, and so he was pretty loose with his men. He slept in the same room on the bare floor, ate the same food, and lived the same way.

Danner was busy when I arrived. Everyone had heard about the transfer of power. The Iraqi police had gone into town, trying to take the pulse of the people, and see if there was going to be any trouble. Marines and Iraqis checked the perimeter, made sure security was tight. And waited.

Nothing happened. No shooting, no looting. No problems.

In the middle of the afternoon, an Iraqi police captain went to the roof of the building and fired off several bursts from a big 12.5 mm anti-aircraft gun in celebration.

Iraqi police came back from a visit to the market. They said some people thought the early transfer was a trick, a ploy by the Americans. They said attacks would still come. But later.

That night, the Iraqis brought in food. Grilled chicken and lamb, with vegetables on flat bread. That was good stuff, even though I worried about catching something. There are a lot of bugs, and hygiene isn't the best. But anything was better than an MRE.

The next day, Danner held court in the chief's office

Two men came to see the police station inquiring as to the whereabouts of a relative arrested in a raid the day before. Captain Matt said a few words in Arabic, in greeting, then turned to his interpreter.

"Tell them it's out of my hands," he said. "They will be questioned by coalition authorities and treated well. They'll have medicine and they can pray. After that, it's up to the Iraqi authorities. Insha Allah."

The interpreter spoke, and the men nodded, stood, and shook hands. Then left.

They didn't get what they wanted. Some Iraqis who came to talk to the big blond Marine officer didn't get much help. Others did. Sometimes it was a small thing: a new identification card. Sometimes it was much bigger: springing a relative from jail.

This was all about hearts and minds.

What made it work was the relationship he developed with his Iraqi counterpart, Captain Samir.

Samir was a tough, no-nonsense former secret police officer. He spoke some English, and Danner taught himself a little bit of Arabic. Samir worked on behalf of the police chief and Danner worked for McCoy. They became friends and partners.

"I consider Captain Matt to be my brother," Samir told me. "I would do anything for him."

Captain Matt was formally made a member of the Jerafi tribe, the biggest, most powerful in the region.

"They wanted me to marry one of their daughters," he said. "I had to tell them my parents had already found a wife for me."

Danner had an easy-going style that suits the Iraqis. He was not of them, nor did he pretend to be. But he showed them respect and loyalty. And they admired that greatly.

If he wanted to, he could become Colonel Walter Kurtz, from *Heart of Darkness*. McCoy told me that. He also said that if Danner "went upriver" he would go "take him out." I was never sure if he was joking or not.

Danner does most of his work in the chief's office. It's nothing fancy. About 30 by 15 feet. The chief sits at an oak desk at one end, and chairs line the walls. The doorway faces the chief's desk. Captain Matt sits along one wall. His interpreter, an Egyptian-born Marine who was raised in Sacramento, Sergeant Mohamad Akhtar, sits on the opposite side.

Sometimes three or four other officers were in the office. Sometimes it was a crowd of 15 police and local residents, all talking, cajoling, negotiating, and greeting.

An officer with the security force around the nearby hydroelectric dam stopped to say hello to Captain Matt.

"Did you get the new radios?" Danner asked.

The man beamed. Yes. Yes. And hugged the Marine, patting his arm and thanking him. A radio is such a small thing, but can mean a lot to a security guard out on patrol.

Another police officer came to see about getting a badge. Police Chief Hassan wanted to talk about hiring security officers.

Akhtar told the chief that he's got to hire good, brave men. Not just someone he knows, or a family member. The chief nodded. Tribalism is huge in Iraq. And business is all about family. Even in this station, most everyone is related to someone else.

"The chief talks a good game, but we'll see," Danner said.

Danner is the son of a Marine pilot, a retired lieutenant colonel. He grew up all over the place, but generally calls Boston home.

An Iraqi police sergeant, well-known and respected among the Marines for his toughness, walked into the room. A glum look on his face.

"What's up with Sergeant Mohamad?" Captain Matt asked.

"He's unhappy because he hasn't dismantled a roadside bomb lately," Akhtar said. "He wants to blow something up."

Akhtar translated. The sergeant nodded but didn't break a smile. He didn't seem like the kind of guy who joked around much. When he left, he and Danner exchanged goodbyes in the traditional Iraqi way: They kissed cheeks and then bent down to kiss shoulders.

When Danner and his Marines first arrived at the police station, their work was difficult. The Iraqi police were disorganized and dispirited. They had few weapons, no body armor, poor communication, and zero morale.

That's when Danner and Samir started working together, and became friends. When the Iraqi police were reluctant to do what Captain Matt wanted, Captain Samir would kick them into action. When Captain Samir needed something from the Marines, Captain Matt would make it happen.

The day that cemented the relationship came when Captain Samir and Captain Matt went out on a patrol together, looking for some bad guys. They got back and went to the office. Exhausted, they fell into chairs and dropped off to sleep next to each other. That was how the Iraqis found them the next morning.

"It really showed that the lieutenant trusted them," Akhtar said. "He had his weapon out, anyone could have taken it. And he was in a vulnerable position. After that, they would do anything for him."

Corporal Richard Amador said Danner has fixed many problems for the Haditha police force. But none meant as much as their pay. When the unit arrived, the Iraqis had been without pay for two months. Danner went to work, made the calls, harangued those who needed haranguing, and got the money.

"We came back from Al Asad (air base) with a box full of money," he said. "That really opened the door."

Danner worked long days. Everything revolved around him. He had to approve security measures for the Marines, coordinate with the Iraqi police, field countless calls during the day, from Iraqi citizens complaining about damage done during military raids to planning foot patrols.

The next afternoon, a man came in to say a Marine had thrown a water bottle from a Humvee in a convoy. It hit his windshield and destroyed it.

"This is exactly the kind of thing we're trying to avoid," Danner fumed. "I just can't understand this. And it takes so long to get a resolution for this guy, what am I going to do, send him to Mosul without a windshield?

"I gave him two hundred bucks. I ought to strap that Marine onto the car and let him be a wind break."

Danner kept the same hours as Iraqis. Stayed up late. Got up early. Took a break during the midday heat. He ate their food and drank their sugary tea.

By all accounts, Danner's team was a huge success. Unfortunately, the military system of rotating units in and out of Iraq meant that Team Viking had to go when Three-Four returned to the United States. When I met him, he had only one more week in Haditha.

"It's tough," he said. "It's real tough. If the division asked me to stay, I'd have a hard time saying no."

But his family worried about him being in a war zone. And he was engaged to be married. So he had a lot to look forward to when he got home.

He turned over the station to a lieutenant from the battalion replacing McCoy's Marines: 1st Battalion, 8th Marine Regiment out of Camp Lejeune, North Carolina.

I stayed with Danner for a couple of more days, just to see if there would be any violence. I slept on the hard floor of the office, with the air conditioner blasting cold air into the room.

It was a good time, though. For the first time since I'd been covering the conflict, I had a chance to hang out with Iraqis. To talk to them about their lives and their hopes and dreams for the future. I'd met a few in Baghdad the year before, and found them to be warm, funny, and friendly. I liked their hospitality and their warmth.

That was always the problem with the embedding program: you only saw one side of the war.

> *Please inform me how the editors of Chronicle pick the names you use for those who are in Iraq, fighting against foreign occupiers, the most brutal & powerful military force in the history of the world. Let's see, today they are "rebels", and "insurgents", and the all-purpose "enemy". Sounds so colorful but I beg your pardon; they are not MY enemy. Golly, what are you gonna do if some itinerant reporter like Koopman discovers that they are FREEDOM FIGHTERS of the most courageous order, bravely attempting to defend their own goddamn country, since after all THEY haven't fallen for the mega lie that the United States has bombed the living daylights out of their cities not for "freedom & democracy" but, oh maybe, to take over the world's 2nd largest known petroleum reserves for the entertainment of American SUV drivers & the enrichment of Dick Cheney's Big-Oil cronies.*

After it was apparent that the police station would not be attacked, I went back to the dam. McCoy and the rest of the battalion were in the final stages of turning over their area to the Marines of

One-Eight. A couple of days later, the Viking Team came in and got ready to leave, too. That night, Danner was officially promoted to the rank of captain. His brother, Captain Samir, and Samir's father and brother (a police lieutenant) attended the ceremony.

The next day, the Marines held a change-of-command ceremony. McCoy officially turned the dam over to his successor, Lieutenant Colonel Gareth Brandl.

(About three weeks later, a suicide bomber drove a car up to the gate of the Iraqi police station in Haditha and set off a bomb. The blast killed four or five Iraqi officers, and injured dozens of officers and civilians. I tried to call, to find out who died. But communications are damn near impossible in that country. I hope it wasn't Samir. I hope it wasn't any of the Iraqis I met. I wish it wasn't anyone.)

After that, there was nothing left to do. A couple of days later, everyone from Three-Four was back in Al Asad, waiting for a flight out to Kuwait, and from there to home.

There was one more piece of business: a memorial to the Marines who died. In addition to the three who fell in Baghdad, Three-Four lost one more: Lance Corporal Bob Roberts of Portland, Ore. As they did after the first tour in Iraq, the Marines placed rifles muzzle down in the sand and placed the dead men's helmets on top. They passed in review, each touching the helmet and remembering.

I rode with Three-Four's final convoy away from the dam. I had been there only to see McCoy and Howell, and the rest. To see how they were doing the second time around, and how the war was going for them. When they left, I knew I wanted to go someplace else. I was going to be around all summer, and the dam was just too boring for me to stick around.

I said goodbye to McCoy, and to Dave Howell. It was the reverse from the last time we were all in Iraq. This time, they were going home and I was staying.

"You be careful," Dave said. "This is no joke. You could get killed. It's very hairy."

"I know, Dad," I said.

"I know you think you've been around, but don't do anything stupid, okay?"

"I promise," I said. "This place sucks, anyway. I don't think I'm going to stick around too long."

We shook hands and parted. I had a flight out that night, and the battalion was leaving in a day or two.

The saga of McCoy's Marines was all but over.

> *Hi there. If you even read this, which is a big if, because I'm sure you've been receiving hundreds of emails from concerned family members and loved ones, I'm sure you won't have time to be emailing me back. However, I had to take the opportunity to thank you.*
>
> *My younger brother is an 18 year old infantry grunt for the 3/4 Marines. I believe you are embedded somewhere within this same group. Now, I realize there are hundreds of men with you, that you do not know them all. His name is \*\*\*, and you've probably never even laid eyes on him.*
>
> *However, like I said, I want to say thank you. There is a lot of debate over the press and reporters that are involved in this war. I'm a bit conflicted myself. The press coverage is overwhelming, and I often see my parents and find myself chained to the TV, hoping for any little morsel of information on my brothers location. Needless to say, we haven't heard from him since the initial attack, and know that we won't for quite some time.*
>
> *But, as I find myself scouring the information highway, searching hundreds of pictures daily on dozens of different websites, your column for the San Francisco Chronicle is this closest I have come to finding him. And I've realized if it weren't for the reporters attached to these military groups, I wouldn't have any pictures, or articles to look for and read.*

*You risk your lives every day to bring the true story to the American People. The concerned Americans, the ones with family serving their country. Flag waving, Proud Patriotic Americans who support this war. Without you, we, those people, would be without a clue.*

*So, for that, I say thank you, God speed, and please take care. You are with the best of the best, they will certainly take you into the middle of this battle. No one knows how long this will last, how bloody it could get. And I say Thank You for witnessing things that no man or woman should have to witness, in order to keep us in tune with our loved ones.*

*Your writing is blunt, not sugar coated, and you paint a picture with your words on what our "boys" are really going through, and how they are handling it. I read a recent article in which you spoke of MRE's, and living conditions. While it is saddening what our troops are tolerating, it is uplifting to hear how they cope, and the immense brotherhood they survive in. The true meaning of the Marines, Esprit de Corps.*

*Thank you, you are a wonderful journalist, and I look forward to all of your work in the future. Give our love to the troops and, again, please be safe.*

On July 24, 2004, a ceremony was held on the general's parade ground at Twentynine Palms. The 3rd Battalion, 4th Marine Regiment gathered in formation on the well-manicured grass. Sergeant Major Howell called the formation to attention and turned it over to the commanding officer, Lieutenant Colonel Bryan P. McCoy. He surveyed his Marines for one last time.

Then turned them over to his successor, Lieutenant Colonel A. R. Kennedy.

The Darkside era was over.

Battalion commanders usually serve about two years. Staff officers rotate among unit commands and other kinds of assignments like specialized schools, or working with some command staff or another.

"That's the trouble with the Marine Corps," Howell said when I called him after the change of command. "You get a good group of guys together, but it never stays the same. People come and go."

McCoy got orders to the National War College in Washington, D.C. He'll study all manner of warfare with senior officers from all the services. And he'll no doubt get his eagle and become a full colonel soon.

He's already talking to his superiors about his next leadership assignment. He might be in line to take over the 7th Marine Regiment in a couple of years. That's what he wants anyway. Command. Forget the promotions and medals. Just give him Marines to command and let him go.

The assignment in Washington came at an important time, though. It will allow him to be a husband again. Kerry is also stationed there, and they moved into a nice condo. But he wasn't sure, earlier, if he'd get orders to the East Coast. He entertained thoughts of retirement.

"I lost one marriage to the Marine Corps," he said. "I'm not going to lose another. Some things are too important."

With 20 years in the Corps, retirement could come at any time. But now, with the War College assignment, there's a good chance he'll stay in, get promoted, and get promoted again. With his record, his background, and the war behind him, he'll surely become a general one day. He may earn more than one star.

"The Marine Corps is a harsh mistress," he told me in Baghdad. "You love it and you work for it and one day they kick you out. You have to be prepared for that. I think I am."

Yeah, he's capable of fooling himself sometimes, too.

# CHAPTER 13

# A TOTALLY DIFFERENT WAR

What do you call what's happening in Iraq? Is it a war? It looks like one. There's a lot of shooting and fighting and killing. But it's not a war in the classic sense. There are no armies on the move, with offensive operations. It's more static. Soldiers and Marines in place, trying to stay alive and fight insurgents.

What about the initial attack? It seems like an invasion. Most people would think of it that way. But the military considers it a "liberation." Similarly, U.S. forces don't like the term "occupation," even though a lot of people, including President Bush, have used that term. They think of it as keeping the peace.

So they came up with two new terms. The initial phase of the conflict, the invasion, is called Operation Iraqi Freedom 1, or OIF-I, and the current phase is OIF-II.

I hate these semantic games. But the war in Iraq has become much more complex, and it is politically charged.

The first time I went to Iraq, everything seemed so clear-cut. There was a lot of dissent about whether the war was right or wrong. But everyone was sure Saddam Hussein had weapons of mass destruction and so an invasion might be useful. In the year since the initial attack, we found out there were no weapons of mass destruction. Saddam was captured and paraded before the world. U.S. soldiers tortured and humiliated Iraqi prisoners. The insurgents began a campaign of terror, kidnapping civilians and cutting off their heads to make gruesome snuff films.

The American public became increasingly polarized. You were either for the war, or against it. The middle ground, as always, gets lost in the loud debate over the war.

And it's no different in Iraq. The military feels more isolated, and has become more aware of the propaganda war. Journalists are once again viewed with suspicion. If you write a story critical of the military, the public affairs people and top commanders come to you and bug you and try to spin your stories.

*Take your warmongering BS and shove it.*

I'm with the Army now.

After McCoy's Marines left Iraq, I wanted to check out Fallujah. There was a cease-fire, but it was still the hottest spot in Iraq. Something could happen there.

At Al Asad, I caught a helicopter going to Ramadi, which is just outside of Fallujah and home to the 1st Marine Division headquarters.

It was a long, hot ride. I was with a couple of civilian contractors. The helo left about 11 at night. I sat in the darkness with earplugs trying to keep out the roar of the engines, and nodded off as we flew here and there in the darkness. I have no idea where we went. There were no lights on the aircraft, so as not to make it a target for ground fire. We flew and landed and flew and landed. We picked up soldiers and dropped them off.

Finally, well after midnight, we landed at Ramadi. The division public affairs officer met me at the helo pad and brought me into his office.

He told me he'd read my last story about the Marines. He didn't like it, he said. I had mentioned that some of the Marines didn't like

Iraqis and that acting as an occupation force wasn't their favorite kind of work. A bigger sin was mentioning the day the battalion was supposed to return to the United States. I hadn't thought anything of that, figuring a lot of people back home wanted to know.

But in OIF-II, the big keywords were "Operational Security." Everyone hammered on it. It was like World War II, "Loose Lips Sink Ships."

"But don't worry, the general isn't mad at you, he's mad at the guys who told you the date they were going back," he said.

"Are you serious?" I asked. "This is a big deal?"

"Oh yeah."

"Well, I didn't realize that was a problem. Is that why you didn't like my story?"

"Not so much. I just didn't like the tone."

"The tone. Not what was in it? Was there anything inaccurate?"

"No, just the tone."

I was tired and cranky. I wanted to argue with him. What the hell did it matter about the tone of my story, if everything in it was accurate? That's not something a public affairs guy is supposed to tell me. But I was dead tired and cranky and we were going to his room where I was going to bed down for the night. So I kept my mouth shut.

But that conversation was indicative of the way the military-media relationship had gone. The military read our stories within an hour or so of them being posted online. You could write a story in the evening and the next morning someone would call you on it. So all the talk about letting the reporters do their job and just telling the stories of war and what was going on, was just spin. What they really wanted was positive stories, stories that put the troops and the American military in the best possible light.

What bugged me was the unsubtle way they went about it. I expect officers and public affairs people to try to influence me. One way or another. It happens all the time. That's the game. Just don't get in my face and tell me you don't like my story. Especially not in a war zone. Because I'm putting my life in your hands. It's a dangerous place, and if the military decides you're expendable, you can be at risk. I'm not saying they would do that, but the power they have over you in Iraq is much greater than in San Francisco.

Everywhere I went in Iraq, officers would ask, "Are you here to write good stories or bad stories?"

Hell, man, the stories write themselves. Are you a good soldier or a bad soldier? The story is about you. You tell me whether it's going to be good or bad.

Anyway, the next day I got up and went back to the public affairs office. "When can I go to Fallujah?"

"Yeah, about that. We really have too many reporters out there right now. The commanders are begging off getting any more. You'll have to wait."

Hmmm. I couldn't tell if this was for real, or if I was somehow being punished. But there wasn't any major fighting going on anyway, so I figured I'd find some other stories. I asked the officer where else I might go.

"Do you have any objection to being with the Army?" he asked, knowing I had been a Marine.

"I don't discriminate," I said. "What do you have in mind?"

Turns out there was an Army unit, a brigade combat team, attached to the control of the 1st Marine Division. I could go hang out with them for a while, and move over to Fallujah later.

Hey, whatever.

I hopped a convoy over to Camp Junction City, a couple of miles from the Marine headquarters. They called it Camp Junction City because the Army unit that lives there is normally based in Junction City, Kansas. It was the 1st Battalion, 5th Field Artillery.

Yes, this is how the military works in Iraq. Guys trained to fire 155 mm howitzers at an enemy they can't see are patrolling the neighborhoods of Ramadi in Humvees.

They dropped me off at the barracks of Delta Battery. I liked them right away. I don't know what it is about artillery soldiers, but I always had a good time, and felt comfortable around them.

The base used to be an Iraqi army installation, and a lot of the structures still stood. Delta Battery lived in a long, narrow, two-story building that was once an Iraqi barracks. The windows were knocked out, and replaced with plywood and sandbags. The camp took mortar fire now and again. And the occasional RPG was fired into it. Neither was very accurate, but with high explosives flying around, someone could get hurt

I was with the senior sergeants and junior officers of Delta Battery. The other guys had cots, and had created little living areas with TVs, DVDs and other comforts. I had a folding cot, but that was fine. There were two big air conditioning units blowing cold air into the place most of the time. But this camp, like many in Iraq, got its power from diesel generators. And they went down all the time. Sometimes for maintenance; sometimes just because they crapped out.

It was very common to fall asleep with the cool hum of the air conditioner in your ear, and wake up in the morning drenched in sweat because the power was off and the temperature rose to well over 90 degrees indoors.

The Army wanted to know what kinds of stories I was looking for. In this era, reporters came and went with regularity. I kept hearing stories about how this reporter or that one came in for a day, or a couple of hours for a patrol, and then took off. That's not what I was looking for. I liked the embedding thing. I wanted to hang around and really get to know people, and get a feel for what they were doing, so I could write about it.

Delta Battery's main job at that point was to drive up and down the main highway, just outside the gate, and keep it clear of roadside bombs. They called it "IED Denial Patrol."

I called it, "Trolling for bombs." The battalion commander wasn't too happy with that headline.

The same afternoon I got in, the Delta Battery commander, Captain Jason Eddy, offered me a seat in a Humvee that was going out on patrol. That sounded good to me. I figured I could ride around with the IED denial patrol a couple of days, or nights, and put together a little feature story about fear and loathing in Ramadi.

The team that night was led by Sergeant First Class Chuck Gordon. I'd met him earlier, when I dropped my gear in the barracks. Chuck's a tall, lanky guy, who looks a lot like the actor Harry Dean Stanton. He had a plug of chew in his lower lip.

We loaded up the Humvee, and then headed out the front gate with another vehicle.

Chuck sat in the front passenger seat. Sergeant Michael Marchetti stood in the turret hatch and manned the machine gun. Specialist Kevin Neff drove.

I sat in the back, behind Neff.

IED denial is a lot like being a beat cop. This is your stretch of road. You drive up and down, up and down. For hours at a time. You get to know every bump, every bush, every clump of dirt along the side. You know the little roadside stands, called "haji marts." You see the vendors and you know many by name. You buy ice from the ice guy and put it in the cooler with the bottled water.

Up and down the road.

We drove for an hour and then pulled off onto a side road that went up a small hill. There were acres of open land on this side of the highway, and the soldiers had an unimpeded view of the road. They were just killing time, and waiting to see if anyone tried to stop along the side of the road.

By this time, the soldiers had the road pretty well covered day and night, so the insurgents knew they couldn't sneak up and bury a bomb. They took to using a "slow down and drop" method. They'd put a bomb in a bag or something, pull up and quickly drop it. Or fake engine problems. Raise the hood and tinker with the motor while your buddy quickly plants a bomb.

But the soldiers saw nothing down there. Just a steady line of cars.

Chuck and I joked a bit, and talked about our experiences in Iraq. Turns out his father lives in the Bay Area. So he's almost a local boy.

The heat was intense, well above 100. My shirt was soaked under my body armor. I unfastened the Velcro straps and lifted the heavy vest, so I could get some air on my soaked torso. The sweat had dripped down so much that the top of my trousers and crotch were wet. It looked like I had peed myself.

As we stared at the highway, we heard an explosion in the distance. We saw a smoke trail. Someone fired off a rocket. Word came over the radio that the projectile hit, but did not explode.

The soldiers started attracting a crowd of Iraqis, so the Humvees took off again. Down the road. Up and down. We stopped once to check out a pile of garbage. It was nothing.

Back on the road.

Traffic was light now. The road is four-lane, with a median separating the lanes. To the left were some industrial buildings set back from the road by about 100 yards. To the right was an open field, a good 75 to 100 yards across. With houses on the other side.

Chuck tapped Marchetti on the leg. Michael squatted down into the vehicle to talk to Gordon about something. He was on his way back up, but still inside the Humvee, when it hit.

"Boom!" Day turned into night. A thunderous explosion shot dirt and debris into the air, blocking out the sun. The blast hit about 15 feet from the right front section of the Humvee. The sharp, savage burst punched the Humvee like a fist, pushing it to the side like a toy car.

"Goddamn!" Marchetti yelled. "Goddamn! I can't fucking hear." A moment later, "I'm good. I'm good."

Gordon yelled for Neff to stop, then realized the truck was still in the kill zone. So he shouted, "Go, go!"

Neff floored the Humvee, driving through the dirt cloud and coming out to clean sunshine. He drove about 50 yards and stopped.

Everyone checked for shrapnel and blood. There was none. Other than Gordon having a chunk taken out of his Kevlar helmet. He and Marchetti got their bells rung, and their ears hurt. Neff and I were okay.

But I was still nervous. Roadside bombs are scary things, and the guerrillas have found many ways to make them more and more lethal. One way was to plant a second bomb a short distance from the first one, so as to kill the people who stopped after the first blast.

Like, where we were.

I held my breath, and tucked my head down, waiting for the blast. None came.

Behind us, the soldiers in the trailing Humvee saw the explosion and saw our Humvee disappear into the blast area.

The soldiers in the second Humvee stopped and dismounted. They saw a crowd of Iraqis on the far side of the open field, running, and fired warning shots in the air.

We all got out, dazed, and shaken. There was a hole in the dirt about 2 feet deep. Chuck figured that the bomb was detonated by remote control. And that the bomber misjudged the firing by a split second. If he'd pushed the trigger a micro-second later, the bomb would have gone off directly next to us. Probably would have killed Chuck and Marchetti. Neff and I wouldn't have been in very good shape, either.

*Mr. Koopman says he was a former Marine, but he sounds like a pansy most of the time in his articles—always scared of this or that. Sounds more like he was ex-Army to me.*

I imagined a guerrilla sitting in a building—it would have been at least 100 yards from the bomb, or more—and watching as the Humvees approached. It would be hard to hit the switch at the exact perfect moment. The vehicles were moving, and they were far away. It would be like duck hunting, you have to lead your target just perfectly. And our bomber missed the shot.

Moments later, soldiers from the base showed up. Iraqi police shut down the highway. The place was a beehive of activity.

I saw some soldiers checking out the blast crater, so I grabbed my camera and went to look myself. Another soldier came by and said the explosion had fired a piece of shrapnel, or rock, across the open field. It hit a teenage Iraqi boy sitting in a chair in front of his house.

"He didn't look too good," the soldier said.

The battalion commander, Lieutenant Colonel Mike Cabrey, showed up. I could see him arguing with the Iraqi police. Nerves were on edge. Americans started yelling at the Iraqis. "Oh, now you show up. Where the hell were you when one of your buddies was planting that thing?"

In my experience, I found most of the Iraqi police to be honest and professional. But I talked to soldiers who said they were not to be trusted, that they spied on the Americans for the insurgents.

So tensions were running high. Near the bomb crater, I found pieces of aluminum that were riddled with holes. The soldiers compared notes and determined that the bomb had been placed inside a haji mart. The place had sprung up only about a week beforehand, and no one had stopped to talk to the vendor. The supposition was that the vendor was either an insurgent, or he let an insurgent use the cover of the market to plant the bomb right under the noses of the soldiers.

Pieces of the haji mart were blown to tiny bits, and scattered over an acre.

After the dust settled, the soldiers were hyped on a cocktail of adrenaline and near-death anger.

"We should just clear out all these haji marts," one said. "Bring in a bulldozer."

The anger touched a nerve with one of the Iraqi translators. He normally didn't say much, but now he felt obligated to defend his countrymen. "They have to live with this more than you," he said. "And there's a young boy who is very seriously wounded from this bomb."

A minute later, one of the solders comes over and says the kid didn't make it. He was dead when he got to the hospital.

After several soldiers had gathered at the crater, they decided to search the nearby homes for evidence that the bomber had worked from there. Chuck got his team together, then saw me standing there. "You coming, John? We gotta go find these motherfuckers."

Chuck's the chief of firing battery. They're nicknamed "Smoke."

"Sure, Smoke," I said. "Wouldn't miss it."

The soldiers went house to house. Most were empty. Those with families turned up nothing. No one knew anything.

"What a surprise, no one knows a thing," one soldier said, sarcastically.

The battalion commander spoke to a crowd, using an interpreter. People said the man who ran the roadside stand was new to the area, and no one claimed to have spoken with him.

"I find that hard to believe," Cabrey said. "I've never been in an Iraqi city where everyone doesn't know everyone."

After an hour of searching and questioning, the soldiers left. I went with Gordon and Marchetti to the aid station, so they could get checked out by the medics. The ringing, they were told, would go away eventually.

Late in the evening, we made it back to the barracks. I pulled out my computer and tried to write a story. No words came.

I sat there in the heat, my clothes sticking to me, and watched a fly on a footlocker. The place was crawling with flies; they were a constant nuisance. This one looked wounded, or dying. It was on its back, buzzing. Going in circles. I just though, "You're going to die, motherfucker. Die, already."

Chuck walked past and we exchanged glances. He shook his head. "Son of a bitch," he muttered.

"You all right?" I asked.

"I have a headache, but I'll be all right. You?"

"Fucked up, man."

Combat is strange. You make instant and life-long connections. All it takes is a near-death experience. From that moment on, Chuck and I shared a bond. I wasn't around long enough for it to take the way it had with McCoy and Dave Howell. But it was there.

I thought that was the end of this story, but it got better. Around midnight, some of the soldiers came in and said they had received intelligence reports about the bomber. Apparently, an Army special forces unit was working in the area, and an informant had called with a name and address of the man who planted the bomb.

Delta Battery sprang into action. The commanding officer rounded up his staff and senior NCOs, they got maps, ordered an aerial recon of the neighborhood, and started planning a raid.

Sergeant First Class George Parker—Chuck's buddy—coordinated the raid.

"Smoke, you don't get to go," Parker told Gordon. "It wouldn't look right."

Everyone wanted in on the action. They'd all been hit by roadside bombs, or knew someone who had. It was payback time.

Chuck couldn't go, but I could. I went in one of the Humvees, in the wee hours of the morning, to a quiet neighborhood. The soldiers brought their vehicles in a semicircle around the house, illuminating it with their headlights.

Parker got out and scanned the rooftops with his rifle. "There's someone on the roof. You see him?" he called to the machine gunner in the turret of the Humvee.

"I'm on him," the soldier replied.

Other men knocked open the metal gate leading to the courtyard of the home. The men charged the place, waking women and children, and going through rooms. They found an older man in his 50s and two young men in their 20s.

They interrogated the men for the better part of an hour. Their stories didn't match up, but the soldiers found no evidence of bomb-making material. They did find some truck tire inner tubes. A lot of IEDs had been hidden in inner tubes lately.

They cuffed the two younger Iraqis and took them back to base.

"This was a good night," Eddy told his men after the raid. "We got a good tip and executed perfectly."

Back at the barracks, Marchetti and Gordon still had pain in their ears. There was pressure built up inside, like they'd been on an airplane. And the next day, they would be out on the road again. Trolling for bombs.

"Well, the day started out like crap but it ended pretty well," Gordon said.

The next day, Chuck and I talked about the bomb. It was the second time he'd been hit by an IED. I told him about my time in the invasion, the firefights, the RPGs, and the artillery round.

"You need to get out of here," he said. "The next one has your name on it."

At that moment I realized he was right. I had come full circle in the cycle of fear.

Before the war, I worried about getting injured or killed. I worried about booby traps and land mines and ambushes. Then the war started and I saw fighting. First far away and then close up. I had close calls. And then closer calls. The problem with surviving like that is it makes you feel invincible. Those bullets didn't hit me before, why would they now? I'm not going to get hit by a mortar or roadside bomb. Not me. After Baghdad fell, I rode around in the back of Humvees, watching windows for snipers, checking for ambushes around every corner. I felt comfortable. I could do this. I felt like I had handled myself well. I had gone through combat and lived to tell about it.

When I came back the second time, I thought of myself as a relatively seasoned war reporter. I wasn't going to fight, but I could take care of myself. I could stay alive.

But it was all an illusion. Because you can't control anything in a war. Bombs go off wherever. Bullets fly indiscriminately. You can run, but you cannot hide.

"When your number's up, it's up," Chuck said.

That point was driven home twice more in the next couple of weeks. I stayed a few more days with Delta Battery and then moved down to Baghdad. I went to the south side and hooked up with a cavalry unit, Blackhawk Troop of the 1st Squadron, 7th Cavalry.

My first night there, I was scheduled to go out with a patrol after midnight. Around 8 p.m., the squadron commander asked if I wanted to go to the motor pool, to see how the soldiers prepared for a patrol. I was tired and it was hot, so I said I'd just stay and rest before the big night.

An hour later, I saw the commanding officer. He said the motor pool had come under mortar attack. Two soldiers were wounded. Right where I would have been.

And then came news of the car bombing at the Haditha police station.

I would have left right away, but there was more reporting to do about military operations, civil affairs, and training the Iraqi National Guard. In the summer of 2004, there wasn't a lot of combat. There were a bunch of car bombings and more roadside bombs. Fighting flared in Najaf but not until I was already on my way out.

*As a U.S. citizen in America. My son \*\*\* is the first generation in America. After his junior in high school, he wanted to be a Marine. He came home one day and asked if we would sign a consent to let him joined the Marines. I said NO but my husband said OK so my son said if I do not wish to do that after he turn 18 he will joined himself. I come to think about it like my husband said better for him to be a Marine than to be a kid on the street and ran into somebody bad. This way we have somebody to watch after*

*him. Now he is a sergeant. We are so proud of him. \*\*\**
*always have a positive thinking. He never give up since he*
*was in the boot camp. My family and all of our friends are*
*very proud of him, specially us because we are minority that*
*proudly settle in America and raised our family as an*
*American. We believed in his trust and love. I do not*
*believed in WAR, but since my son and my nephew were*
*sent to fight the war for the country we wish Buddah bless*
*both of them and all of the soldiers over there to come back*
*home to their families safe and sound. My family are proud*
*to be American and proud to have members of our family to*
*serve the country. I am writing this from the bottom of my*
*heart and I miss my son very much. My heart is with you.*
*This is my first E-mail. Please do not laugh at my writing or*
*my spelling. With love, MOM*

# IMAGES OF IRAQ

The convoy leaves in the early morning, about 8 a.m., to beat the heat.

A half-dozen Humvees line the road inside the gate at an Army base in Ramadi. The men gather around the convoy commander, listening to his orders. It's standard stuff. The vehicle order, the route, radio frequencies.

"If you get hit with an IED, we'll get the medics to you right quick," he says.

The men nod. They've heard this before. They're immune to the reality of what the commander just said: Some of you might get killed or wounded. Good luck.

"There's nothing you can do," one soldier tells me. "You never know when you're going to get hit. You just do your job and hope you get out of it alive."

The army sweeps through neighborhoods looking for weapons caches. It's a never-ending job. Iraq is littered with guns and bombs.

Inside a half-built brick home, a couple of soldiers walk in with a metal detector and wave it over the sand floor in a back bedroom. The machine goes crazy. Another soldier comes in with a shovel. This is sensitive work. You're digging around explosives that could turn you into a fine red mist. He sticks his shovel into the sand and it hits metal.

"I remember the first time I did that, I was sweating bullets, waiting for it to go off," says one officer.

This one's a mother lode. There are rockets and mortars and grenades and TNT. There are RPG sights and mortar fuses. And then the big ones, two artillery shells. One a 155 mm, the other a 120 mm round.

These shells worry soldiers more than anything. They can tear a Humvee apart. And everyone inside.

No one is at the house. None of the neighbors knows who owns it.

Soldiers and kids. They love each other. A Humvee stops and the kids gather around looking for candy. The U.S. Army never disappoints. While the officers and other important people go about their business, the younger soldiers bring out a box of candy and start passing it out. The kids go from vehicle to vehicle looking for as much as they can get.

"Mistah, mistah. Candy? Money?"

There are smiles all around until the candy runs out. The kids say something in Arabic and then run off.

Apart from candy, the kids love soccer balls. I always thought the United States could win hearts and minds by manufacturing a million soccer balls with the slogan "The U.S. loves you" printed on them. Give those to the Iraqi kids and they'll love you forever.

I'm with a group of soldiers looking for weapons caches. Kids come around looking for candy and soccer balls, but there are none. These soldiers are the bad guys right now, going through people's houses, trampling their stuff. They drive around in armored personnel carriers.

They pass the same group of kids they met before. Some are waving, some making "give me football" motions. I hear a "ping" on the armor. Some of the older kids have picked up rocks. They're throwing stones at the soldiers. There's no love in those faces.

It's moving day at the Dina Institute.

A big, green U.S. Army truck pulls up to the curb. Soldiers in full battle dress—helmets, body armor, automatic weapons—jump out and start loading the truck like college students moving into a new dorm.

They file into a small, cramped concrete-and-tile house. In the rooms, kids of various ages and infirmities sit, stand, or crawl. The children have Down Syndrome, cerebral palsy, and a host of other developmental disabilities.

The Army has adopted the Dina Institute. There are about sixty kids in the place, and most of them have had a rough life. There aren't many places for kids with developmental disabilities to go, even in Baghdad. Some of these kids would be locked in a room for hours a day if they couldn't go to the institute.

Today, the Army is helping the institute move to a bigger, nicer house in a suburban neighborhood.

The local unit commander, Captain Mike Burgoyne, speaks matter-of-factly about his responsibility in helping the institute. But clearly, he and his men do more than is expected.

"You have to do it," he says. "You look at these kids, and it's just the right thing to do."

I'm on patrol with an Iraqi infantry platoon along the Tigris River, just south of Baghdad.

The Iraqis are looking for weapons. That's all anyone does in Iraq, dodge roadside bombs and look for weapons. The Iraqis are working with American troops. That's the U.S. plan for the future: Train the Iraqis to do their own soldiering and then get out. It's a long, laborious process.

The Iraqi soldiers are a good bunch. It's interesting how the military is the same in every country. The unit is led by a big, strong guy who looks like a young Omar Sharif. He's a lieutenant and everyone just calls him L. T.

The young troops are kids, mostly in their early 20s. They joke and goof off, laugh at each other and talk about women.

"Madonna vicky vicky," says one soldier, making a crude sexual reference.

Another chimed in with a play on words, "Michael Jackson, freaky freaky baby."

Most of the Iraqis have desert camouflage uniforms, but their boots are castoffs from Americans or old beat-up leathers from another era. Some have body armor, but it is mismatched and usually old. Most wear steel-pot or hard plastic helmets, unlike the space-age Kevlar the Americans are issued.

They don't make much money. And they're taking a great risk by being in the Iraqi National Guard. The insurgents consider them collaborators, and they can be killed just for that. They're more likely to be killed than an American soldier.

"That does not frighten me," one Iraqi soldier tells me. "I'm here to serve my country."

If death comes, they say, it is the will of Allah.

And that's it.

I've become buddies with one of the Iraqi soldiers. I won't name him because that could be dangerous for him. He's a short, sweet-tempered man with kind eyes. Hamid tells his men what to do, but without the yelling and irritation you see in a lot of sergeants.

He's 35, a father of three boys and two girls. His eyes grow soft when he talks about his wife. He has just one, he says, because he's so in love with her, he doesn't need another. (As in other Arab countries, it's not uncommon in Iraq for a man to have more than one wife.) He was a farmer before the war. But there's no money in farming today. Only in soldiering.

We talk about families. He wants to know about my wife and son. We share pictures and later break open an MRE. He wants to know how much Arabic I speak.

"I'm embarrassed to say I speak no Arabic," I tell him. "I'm embarrassed because I think if I am in your country, I should know how to speak at least a little bit of your language."

"I will teach you," he says. He starts pointing to parts of his head and explaining the Arabic word for eye, nose, mouth. I try to keep up but there's no way.

He asks if I've been out in the cities and towns of Iraq. "Only after battle," I tell him. "I wish I could go out, but it's too dangerous for me. They would kill me."

"You come to my house," he says. "No one will touch you."

I look at this short farmer and wonder how he could keep me safe. But something about his attitude tells me he could. I have no idea where he lives, or how he lives. Some Iraqis play both sides of the war. He could be one. I don't mean that in a bad way; I can't see this sergeant being a member of the guerrillas. But he's a complex man in a twisted, convoluted conflict.

I'm tempted to take him up on his offer. It would be a great experience and make a great story.

But it could get me killed if I've read him wrong.

Many soldiers and Marines are on their second tours. Midlevel officers and noncoms try to calculate how many times they'll have to serve in Iraq. The prevailing wisdom is every two to three years. The lifers calculate how many times they'll have to serve in Iraq before they retire.

"You can have my job," one senior sergeant who operates patrols out of Ramadi tells me one day. "It's easy. You just drive around all day and wait for someone to bomb you.

"The only thing is, you have to hate Arabs."

I'm getting ready to go on a patrol in Baghdad. I go to a group of soldiers eating breakfast from Styrofoam containers out of the back of a Humvee. The convoy commander introduces me to his men.

"You a reporter? I got a message for you to send back to the States," a soldier tells me. "Bring the troops home! Tell the politicians: Bring. The. Troops. HOME!"

•  •  •

Americans get the blame for the car bombings and other attacks—or for not protecting Iraqis from the attacks. A lot of Iraqis are fearful of working with Americans. It can get them killed. Soldiers told me about interpreters who were murdered because they dared to work for U.S. forces. Death stalks Iraq. You can smell the fear.

"Don't put my name in your newspaper," one man tells me. "Bad things can happen."

I flew home after about two months in Iraq. I was glad to be out of there, and happy to be going home. I wasn't worried this time about losing my wife, or making my son miserable. We'd worked through all that. Still, it was good to see them. To be back in San Francisco, with clean sheets and hot showers. And no bombs on the side of the road.

As I write this, the war in Iraq continues. It's not the same war that started on March 19, 2003. That was supposed to be a war of liberation. The American military was supposed to take out a tyrant, take away his weapons of mass destruction, and make the region safe.

It seemed so simple and so realistic at the time. And now it's not. It's dirty and complicated and harsh. People are dying. There are no weapons of mass destruction. Saddam is under arrest. Fallujah has fallen. The kidnappings continue. The blood and gore are never ending.

At home, the war is divisive. Even people who support the president oppose the war. Even those who support the war wonder what it's all about. Maybe it's about fighting terrorism. Maybe it's a big mistake.

People ask me my opinion all the time. They think because I was in Iraq a couple of times that I have some knowledge, some answers. But I know nothing. I know Iraq is a dirty, dangerous place. Death and destruction lurk around every corner. Iraqis are kind and wonderful people, but they don't like the American occupation. And it's true that every time U.S. forces raid a home or fight a battle in a neighborhood, they create more enemies than friends. That's just the way it is.

The U.S. military is trained to fight a shooting war. The kind with tanks and jets and infantry troops pushing forward, taking objectives, moving colored pins around on a map.

They did that job well during the invasion, sweeping across hundreds of miles, destroying Iraqi troops, tanks, and big guns.

Most of those same highly trained soldiers are now playing cop. They drive the major roadways to keep them clear of ambushes and roadside bombs. They sweep through dense brush and river valleys, backyards and drainage ditches, looking for stashes of bombs, mortars, and rockets. Or they work with Iraqis, trying to whip them into a useful fighting force.

Iraq is so dangerous that American troops never leave their bases unless they're on a mission. There is no "off time" spent off base. The only contact Americans have with Iraqis is with interpreters, people who are allowed to work on base, and those they meet in the course of their duties. Their bases are well-stocked and well-maintained. They have fast food and stores and movies and gyms. They are small islands of America right in the heart of the cradle of civilization.

It's not a good situation. Morale is slowly deteriorating. The good will that the troops once had for the Iraqi people is turning into anger and disgust. And vice versa.

In a way, I almost wish I hadn't gone back to Iraq. In the beginning of 2003, everything was clean and simple. I don't like war, but covering this one seemed like a noble cause, a worthwhile endeavor.

I think about the war all the time.

But here's the strange thing: I don't feel anything about it.

I don't have nightmares. I don't wake up with cold sweats. I don't see the faces of the dead. I don't jump when I hear loud noises.

Maybe I should. But I don't. I tell people it's because I've been a reporter for a long time. You go to murder scenes, you take some information from cops over the phone. It's all sterile. You put what you see or hear in a part of your brain that files it away with the story. How many times was the victim shot? Where, in the head? How old was the child who got raped? Is that a body part in the bushes over there?

So I tell myself: That's what I did with the war.

I used to wonder what it all meant. Was there a meaning to all this? Did I cover the war for a reason? I don't usually look for a deeper meaning in life. But the war changed that. It was too big to ignore.

But in the end, I found nothing. I witnessed history, but I didn't do anything special. I wasn't on hand for the discovery of weapons of mass destruction. My stories had no particular impact on the world, the war, anything.

Except the families of the Marines. Finally, that's what struck me. If God had some plan, some reason for putting me in Kuwait, in Iraq, in Baghdad, it wasn't for my edification. I was there to help others. Thousands of families across the nation read my stories and were comforted. Not because I possessed any great talent. Just because I was there.

And you know, that's enough.

More importantly, all the déjà vu I experienced in Iraq did not mean the end of my life, as I had once presumed. Interestingly, the sensations died off after I returned to the United States. It probably does mean something, but I won't know until I'm dead.

McCoy said it on the eve of the invasion. "Friends you make here will be your friends for life."

It's strange how that works. I'd never experienced anything like that before. The only thing that comes close, in my experience, was playing sports in high school. Your buddies on the football team became the kind of friends you could always count on.

But there's a closer bond that connects people who have gone to war together. This is a little controversial as it pertains to reporters and the people they cover. Some will misinterpret what I'm saying, and imagine that I got too close to the Marines I covered.

Because the truth is, I consider Bryan McCoy and Dave Howell to be good friends. I have invited both into my home, and I have had dinner with them and their families. I have had drinks with them.

I don't apologize for that. As a journalist, you want to avoid conflicts of interest. I understand that. But you can't avoid personal interaction. I know a lot of reporters who have friends on the beats they cover. And by "friend," I don't necessarily mean the kind of friendship where you might do anything for the other person. I mean friend as in, I like this person and I'm going to have a good time over drinks with him.

Because the fact is, I know my responsibility as a reporter. If I had seen something that McCoy, Howell, or anyone in Three-Four did wrong, I would have written about it. I didn't have to. And I can't say with certainty that either of them would still have drinks with me if I did write such a thing. But that's not the point. I would do my job, as they do theirs. I want to believe we're all professionals here.

I spent an evening with McCoy and his wife, Kerry, when they came through San Francisco on their way back from a weekend in Tahoe.

They stayed at a hotel near my apartment. I picked them up and showed them around the city. Then my wife and I took them out to eat. I suggested an Afghan restaurant in North Beach. Bryan looked at me a little funny–there was a war going on in Afghanistan–but Kerry laughed and said it would be fine.

That meeting helped Isabel. She never understood why I placed so much faith in McCoy's Marines to keep me safe in the war. Then she met Bryan and understood. He exudes confidence.

They left the next morning.

A couple of months later, Dave Howell came to town.

I owed him. In the middle of Iraq, when everything looked bleak and none of us knew whether we would make it out alive, our talk naturally turned to women. I promised him the best, most expensive lap dance in San Francisco if we made it back to the States in one piece.

By the time Dave got to San Francisco, he was pretty close to his girlfriend, Suzy. They were talking about marriage. So I didn't have to make good on the promise. I paid for his stay at the Marines Memorial hotel instead. We went out drinking, and he explained the finer points of bourbon and scotch to me.

Evnin's death still weighs on him. He wonders if he did the right thing. Dave's bothered by the fact that the last words Evnin had for him was to call him an asshole.

"But you know, it wasn't really traumatic," he says. "It was profound. But it wasn't traumatic. What do you think that means?"

"It means you're an asshole," I told him. And I mean that in the nicest way.

Shortly after I returned from Iraq, someone told me "Well, I guess you got the war you wanted." I was stunned. I never wanted a war. But I will admit this: I'm glad I went. I wanted to see the worst in humanity. I lived through combat.

Darkside understands the pride, almost elation, that comes with survival.

"The greatest euphoria," he says, "comes when you've been shot at and missed."

McCoy and I never spent much time talking about the politics of the war. For him, that was all irrelevant. He is a professional Marine officer. As such, his duty is to carry out the orders of his superior officers and the commander in chief. The mission is primary, followed closely by the welfare of his men.

McCoy is a Methodist. He believes his profession and his religion are not at odds. As a Marine, he kills and orders others to kill. He sees it as a necessary evil.

"War is cruelty," he said. "The crueler it is, the sooner it's over."